EPISTEMOLOGY FUTURES

Epistemology Futures

Edited by
STEPHEN HETHERINGTON

CLARENDON PRESS · OXFORD

OXFORD
UNIVERSITY PRESS

Great Clarendon Street, Oxford OX2 6DP

Oxford University Press is a department of the University of Oxford.
It furthers the University's objective of excellence in research, scholarship,
and education by publishing worldwide in

Oxford New York

Auckland Cape Town Dar es Salaam Hong Kong Karachi
Kuala Lumpur Madrid Melbourne Mexico City Nairobi
New Delhi Shanghai Taipei Toronto

With offices in

Argentina Austria Brazil Chile Czech Republic France Greece
Guatemala Hungary Italy Japan Poland Portugal Singapore
South Korea Switzerland Thailand Turkey Ukraine Vietnam

Oxford is a registered trade mark of Oxford University Press
in the UK and in certain other countries

Published in the United States
by Oxford University Press Inc., New York

British Library Cataloguing in Publication Data

Data available

Library of Congress Cataloging in Publication Data

Epistemology futures / edited by Stephen Hetherington.
p. cm.
Includes bibliographical references and index.
1. Knowledge, Theory of. I. Hetherington, Stephen Cade.
BD161.E623 2006 121—dc22 2005031872

Typeset by Newgen Imaging Systems (P) Ltd., Chennai, India
Printed in Great Britain
on acid-free paper by
Biddles Ltd., King's Lynn, Norfolk

ISBN 0–19–927331–6 978–0–19–927331–7
ISBN 0–19–927332–4 (Pbk.) 978–0–19–927332–4 (Pbk.)

1 3 5 7 9 10 8 6 4 2

For epistemologies past and present,
our teachers

Preface and Acknowledgements

Epistemology is currently in friendly ferment, bubbling away at the heart of everyday philosophical focus. Encouragingly many epistemologists are sampling and analysing new perplexities and fresh theories. And—a welcome sign—there are even probing assessments of epistemological methodology. What will emerge from this activity? What *should* emerge from it? How worthwhile a philosophical legacy will be produced? What, if anything, will be achieved? Will epistemology as a whole be *improved*?

Other things being equal, we increase the likelihood of there being real achievement, rather than mere activity, if we pause to reflect upon—and even to question—some of epistemology's more fundamental questions. Which phenomena should epistemology study? Which methods should it use? This book aims to harness some of contemporary epistemology's vigour, while suggesting possible modifications and issues with which to move into a strengthened epistemological future. The book includes a variety of proposals and speculations from lively epistemological thinkers. The contributors' brief was to be bold and adventurous. Which epistemological theses or projects or issues or methodologies could usefully be discarded? Which ones deserve increased attention? Can we discern any limitations in how epistemology has developed—any 'blind alleys' from which it is yet to escape? And what are the key epistemic concepts with which epistemology is most likely to thrive, even if these are not ones with which it is presently preoccupied?

By highlighting such pivotal yet perhaps neglected questions, the book describes or implies some possible futures for epistemology, including some which would differ significantly from its present. Will any of these epistemology futures prosper? Might we become philosophically richer by investing in them? It is hard to know, while working within epistemology as it is right now; like financial speculation, epistemological speculation is highly fallible (in spite of the confidence which many epistemologists feel about their efforts). So, I urge you to read this book with a sense of epistemological adventure—an openness to investing preemptively in some potentially rewarding epistemological futures.

The idea for this book received initial editorial encouragement and sculpting from Peter Momtchiloff. I am grateful for that, as I am for Rupert Cousens's efficient and friendly editorial assistance (along with the many excellent questions and criticisms by the two anonymous Oxford University Press readers). And, of course, the enthusiasm of the contributors themselves spurred the project onwards. One of the book's essays—Paul Churchland's—is reprinted, with permission, from *Proceedings and Addresses of the American Philosophical Association*, 76 (2002), 25–48.

S.H.

Contents

Notes on the Contributors

Paul M. Churchland: Valtz Chair of Philosophy, University of California, San Diego.

Catherine Z. Elgin: Professor of the Philosophy of Education, Harvard Graduate School of Education.

Richard Feldman: Professor of Philosophy, University of Rochester.

A. C. Grayling: Professor of Philosophy, Birkbeck College, University of London.

Stephen Hetherington: Associate Professor of Philosophy, University of New South Wales.

Christopher Hookway: Professor of Philosophy, University of Sheffield.

Mark Kaplan: Professor of Philosophy, Indiana University, Bloomington.

Hilary Kornblith: Professor of Philosophy, University of Massachusetts, Amherst.

William G. Lycan: William Rand Kenan, Jr., Professor of Philosophy, University of North Carolina, Chapel Hill.

Adam Morton: Canada Research Chair in Epistemology and Decision Theory, University of Alberta.

Jonathan M. Weinberg: Assistant Professor of Philosophy and Cognitive Science, Indiana University, Bloomington.

Linda Zagzebski: Kingfisher College Chair of the Philosophy of Religion and Ethics and Professor of Philosophy, University of Oklahoma.

1

Introduction: Epistemological Progress

Stephen Hetherington

1. A *TELOS*

At any given moment, epistemology's general goal—its *telos*, most broadly construed—is either to be, or to generate, epistemological progress. So long as epistemology has not reached its final moment, it continues; and so long as it continues, it can have no more general a goal than that of making progress. Epistemology proceeds today, in order to be better tomorrow. Of course, any given one of us is unlikely to improve it much, if at all. But can our individual efforts somehow join together to do so? The present custodians of epistemology's heritage must at least try to enrich it, making it fitter and stronger than it was previously.

Yet we might be unable to give those simple thoughts much substance, because we might not know what epistemological progress even *is*. There is a famous Sydney architect who says scornfully, whenever his buildings receive public criticism, that progress is inevitable—as if all architectural developments are architectural improvements, simply *because* they are developments.[1] Manifestly, that is absurd; and analogous epistemological thoughts would be no less absurd. At no time in epistemology's history has there been a guarantee that any epistemological progress had either previously occurred or would subsequently occur, no matter how optimistic epistemologists might have felt about this at the time. Even today, there is no such guarantee. Past epistemologists, we believe, have made many unwittingly false statements, often based on surprisingly optional presumptions. Are *we* exempt from that failing? Surely not: our own habits, even of careful and intellectual thought, both help and hinder us. And partly because of that, we might not *recognize* instances of actual epistemological progress. Will they display distinguishing marks? What are the truth-makers for claims of epistemological achievement? Are there special kinds of evidence we should have if we are to

---

[1] I do not believe that he is saying that a new building counts as a development only if it is recognizably an instance of a new *type* of building. Still, even if that is his meaning, not all new types represent progress.

support such claims? How good must that evidence be? And is there a need for surrounding circumstances to be apt? We talk of various epistemological theories as being good, impressive, insightful, and so forth. Does such vague talk easily give way to precise descriptions of why those theories are likely to be, or to generate, epistemological progress? We can hope so; will we know so? On what grounds should we assess an idea as constituting epistemological progress? What would make our assessment true?

2. CRITERIA AND DOUBTS

The essays in this book contain provocative and thoughtful attempts to improve epistemology, by way of refinements, modifications, solidifications, extensions, or replacements. What would make some—hopefully, *all*—of those ideas instances of epistemological progress? Each essay indicates respects in which—or so it is argued—epistemology might become somewhat better. When reading the essays, we should ask whether epistemology *would* be better (all else being equal) if it were to incorporate those ideas.[2] But how do we test for such improvement? Talented epistemologists argue their cases before us; we pay attention; do we need to be gaining justified beliefs, perhaps true ones, even knowledge, as to how epistemology's future can improve upon its present?

It depends upon whether these criteria—justification, truth, knowledge—are *correct* ones with which to assess any putative epistemological progress that would be made by accepting a given suggestion. Naturally, I mention them because they are among the phenomena most centrally studied *already* within epistemology.[3] They (and kindred ones) strike us as being relevant criteria, precisely because past and present epistemology has attuned us to thinking respectfully about them. When we have wondered about intellectual progress in general, epistemology has enjoined us to reflect upon knowledge, evidence, warrant, truth, belief, acceptance, and the like. And yet . . . and yet . . . *should* we be assessing epistemological ideas by applying concepts of knowledge, evidence, warrant, and so on? Maybe other epistemic concepts—ones of which we might not have thought—would be more penetrating and apt. And perhaps only *some* of those usually discussed are particularly useful (with our not yet realizing—knowing?—which these are).[4]

---

[2] Here, for simplicity, I am letting epistemology as a whole at a given time be constituted by the professional acceptances, at that time, of the people conventionally deemed to be epistemologists. (This is compatible with a particular epistemologist making some epistemological progress which epistemology as a whole does not.)

[3] Some of them—notably, truth and acceptance—are studied not *only* within epistemology, of course.

[4] Thus, e.g., Kaplan (1985) argues that knowledge is not a phenomenon that epistemology needs to study, with justification-as-responsible-believing being a richer and more amenable object of epistemological thought. Hence, I take it, he would not require an epistemological proposal to be providing epistemological knowledge. Nevertheless, he would still apply some criterion of epistemic justification to epistemological claims.

Moreover, it is possible that the concepts for which we reach when assessing the epistemic aspects of thinking in general are not the right ones to use when assessing the epistemic merits of cases of epistemological thinking in particular.[5] Again, present epistemology reassures us in this respect, apparently feeling no discomfort at assessing epistemological proposals in terms of whether they are justified or knowledge, for instance. Nonetheless, how confident *should* we be that, armed with our current epistemological categories (our basic epistemic concepts), we are well-placed to determine when epistemological progress is—and when it is not—being made? For a start, only if there has *been* epistemological progress in our coming to have those categories in mind will further epistemological progress be revealed by our applying them to putative cases of such progress.

Similar questions arise about epistemic *standards*, such as ones concerning kinds and degrees of justification. Sustained philosophical effort has insightfully brought some of these to people's attention; or so we believe. Which ones have we *not* noticed, though? Without being self-contradictory, we cannot say! Still, could we *become* aware of them in a way which constitutes our making epistemological progress? New suggestions might be made and contemplated. But it is all too easy for us to undervalue those, as we assess them in terms that reflect standards with which we are already comfortable. Even apart from that danger, there is the puzzling matter of whether epistemological claims *should* be held to the same epistemic standards as those claims affix to others.[6] What if epistemological beliefs as to the nature of knowledge and justified belief in general, for example, were not themselves to satisfy the standards they describe?[7] Is it possible that we need to think of new epistemic standards, which epistemological theorizing must satisfy if it is to make progress (and hence which it must describe if it is to be complete)?[8]

---

[5] There is also the possibility that not all epistemological progress would be epistemic. Might one epistemological theory be better than another for *non*-epistemic reasons, such as its moral sensitivities or aesthetic form? Other things being equal, I do not see why not. We might well want an account of what knowledge is in itself, say, *and* of how it is thereby morally significant. Right now, though, as I am beginning to explain, there are difficulties enough in isolating the epistemic dimensions along which epistemological improvement can occur. I will not attempt to describe other possible dimensions.

[6] One way of making this question manifest is discussed by Stroud (1989). Must epistemological analyses of knowledge be a full and witting—an epistemically internalist—epistemic achievement? In contrast, maybe the knowledge being analyzed need satisfy only an externalist criterion. For a critical analysis of Stroud's account, see Hetherington (2001: 193–201).

[7] See Hetherington (1992) for some development of this idea.

[8] Even if we do think of some new standards, might the same need then apply afresh, with *further* new epistemic standards having to be satisfied by those claims about the prior new ones? Maybe a vicious infinite regress of epistemic standards would thereby sprout, rank and wild. (It is no coincidence that in practice epistemologists assess their proposals via special cases of the traditional triad: coherence, foundationalism, and pragmatism/contextualism. Many seek coherence with existing epistemological theses or ways of thinking. Often, there are claims to have direct, immediate, non-inferential support, usually through intuitions, for an epistemological proposal. And there is the pragmatic reality of whether or not an idea is receiving approval from many other epistemologists, including eminent ones. How epistemically good are any or all of these criteria?)

And consider the empirical possibility—illuminated by Russell (1959: 155) and McGinn (1993)—of our being constituted so that philosophical problems in general are too difficult for us (even if not for some other possible creatures) to solve. van Inwagen (2002: ch. 13) notes the same possibility about metaphysics, and epistemology is no less subject to it. But the worry runs deeper still. We might not even be capable of *asking questions* that will conduce to our making philosophical progress. There is a skill in asking questions which are good in that way. And although we believe that many philosophers possess this skill, we might be mistaken about that. Perhaps few do. Is it even possible that no one has ever had that skill?

And if the right questions have never been asked, then answering those that *have* been posed is unlikely to amount to philosophical progress. Yet it is with such answers in place that we would be assessing subsequent candidates for such progress. And this could, in turn, render even *less* likely our making future philosophical progress (insofar as whatever would otherwise have been progress could proceed to be rejected by the non-progress already in place). So, we need to ask how well we can assess what is probably our presumption that there has been enough prior epistemological progress to allow us—by using current epistemology—to assess whether a specific proposal would constitute progress. If present epistemology does not constitute epistemological progress anyway, then in using it—as to some extent we must, whenever we try generating an improved epistemological future—we are using something which is inadequate for generating further epistemological progress.

This problem has a structural affinity with the classic epistemic regress puzzle (which arises, briefly, as follows):

Epistemologists have long pondered what is seemingly the need for epistemically prior beliefs to be justified or knowledge if epistemically posterior ones based upon them are to be justified or knowledge themselves. Insofar as this need could be found to be endless, we might be forced to conclude that there is *no* justification or knowledge.

Now we should notice this analogue or instance of that familiar worry:

Must temporally prior epistemology have been epistemological progress if temporally posterior epistemology based upon it—and sufficiently constituted by it to have absorbed presuppositions or concepts or theses or projects from it—is to be epistemological progress itself? Insofar as this need could be found to be endless, we might be forced to conclude that there is *no* epistemological progress.

3. HOPES

The previous section has argued that there are reasons of philosophical principle why epistemological progress might forever elude us. Even when we feel as if we are contributing real insights, fallibility—to say the least—is present. Are we doomed never to make epistemological progress?

Most sincerely, I hope not. And that hope is not blind. Section 2's doubts were developed in terms that borrow markedly from *current* epistemology. They talk of fallibility; they advert to regress; they implicitly point to circularity; they worry about epistemic dependence; and so on. Yes, they claim to uncover epistemic problems of principle for epistemological inquirers. However, the problems are stated and reached via currently favoured epistemological concepts and ways of thinking; and perhaps our current grasp of epistemological possibilities is itself more limited than we realise. If we could move into an improved epistemological future, maybe those doubts would discreetly and aptly disappear. How good are we at judging epistemological proposals without reflecting entrenched yet narrow or misleading central concepts, standards, methods, questions, and so on? How good are we at improving upon those, even at imagining *new* central concepts, standards, methods, questions, and the like?[9]

Such questions prompt some of this book's essays: What *should* be our core epistemological concepts and methods? What, if any, new ones are needed? Of course, doubts such as section 2's—particularly by their own fallibilist lights—might in fact *not* be as accurate or pressing as they take themselves to be. So, we should also assess what are already presumed to be epistemology's properly central ideas, fixing a critical gaze upon what they can accomplish and what they reveal about epistemology's chances of making progress. (Maybe those ideas do *not* need to be supplanted.) And that is what the book's other essays do. In one way or another, then, there is a philosophical need for essays such as you will find in this book, ones that test or examine or question central aspects of the epistemological here-and-now, hoping to contribute to an improved epistemological future. Will such a transition's details be relatively foreseeable or predictable? Or might our describing and considering what could well seem, right now, to be *surprising* possible epistemology futures be a necessary step to there being subsequent epistemological progress? Would some such conceptual or methodological or principled 'fresh starts' be required if worries like those in section 2 are to be evaded?[10] Even this is not apparent in advance. How calm, how unsurprising, should we expect epistemological progress to be? How plausible must an idea look to us when it is first proposed (in advance of its ever becoming widely accepted as

---

[9] This process can stagnate, as we assume that some proposals are irrelevant or mistaken, simply because of how 'implausible' they can currently strike us as being. Bare assessments of implausibility tend to give voice merely to our professional training—which has been, after all, in aspects of past and present epistemology. But what is entrenched need not be true. Nor need it be able fair-mindedly to assess fundamental challenges or alternatives to itself.

[10] This programmatic possibility has something in common with Russell's (1959: 156–7) view that philosophy has value only when it is uncertain, when revealing and realizing its fallibility. But epistemological progress is more fundamental to philosophy than epistemic uncertainty is. There is philosophical *value* in uncertainty only when that uncertainty constitutes real epistemological progress. For uncertainty, even philosophical uncertainty, as such is not an end in itself. And *valuable* philosophical uncertainty is generated only by reasoning that meets an epistemic standard which would be deemed good by epistemological thinking that would itself constitute epistemological progress. (Would that epistemological thinking thereby have philosophical value itself? It should do so, in which case, for

Stephen Hetherington

constituting progress)? How well-placed are epistemologists to agree authoritatively, before the event, on which epistemology futures will repay attention? Should they be *wary* when widespread agreement arises especially easily?

4. CANDIDATES

Still, we must try to develop epistemology as best we can, respecting—even while questioning or testing—where we are already within it. And that is what this book's essays do. We may organize them in terms of how they bear upon this thesis: Epistemological progress is epistemic progress[11] in describing whatever is epistemic.

Some of the essays characterize the range of the epistemic; others identify marks of epistemic progress; there are those that do both; and each engages with, sometimes even proposing, questions with the potential to reorient epistemological practice in what might be beneficial respects.

Well, what *is* the realm of the epistemic? Much contemporary epistemological practice suggests that it is a conceptual realm, as epistemology strives, accordingly, to make epistemic progress in describing our pertinent concepts. Yet Hilary Kornblith begins the book by urging us not to conceive of epistemology in that way. He argues that we should move beyond *conceptual analysis* as a core epistemological methodology. We should not reach so confidently for our *intuitions* either, expecting these to be epistemically revelatory. And in these respects Jonathan Weinberg's essay concurs with Kornblith's: epistemology can, and needs to, do better than that, casting aside its existing emphasis upon conceptual analysis and the consulting of intuitions. But what would be a better methodology? How would epistemology more effectively make progress? Kornblith favours a *naturalism* about knowledge: taking our cue from science (along with some philosophy), we should study knowledge itself—not a concept of knowledge—as a natural phenomenon. In contrast, Weinberg advocates a kind of *pragmatism*. It is one that answers questions about the nature of knowledge and justification, in part by imagining what we need knowledge and justification—our epistemic norms—to be like. (And in reflecting upon this, we should also clarify the nature of whatever knowledge and justification we might expect epistemology to provide *about* knowledge and justification.)

Already, therefore, fundamental choices confront us, concerning the contents of the epistemic realm and how to investigate them. Nonetheless, are there important

---

Russell, it contains uncertainty itself. But in that event it only *uncertainly* generates the uncertainty which Russell deems essential to philosophy's value. And it would therefore leave open the possibility of there being no such value. Still, it would also leave open the possibility that philosophical value is not Russellian: uncertainty might not be essential to philosophical value after all.)

[11] Could it be not-*exclusively*-epistemic progress? See footnote 3. Could it be *other*-than-epistemic progress? See footnote 5.

elements within epistemology about which we face *no* real choice? For example, is there a core conception of knowledge which must be retained? It has become an epistemological commonplace, supposedly receiving ample and direct support from readily available intuitions, to describe knowledge as being a state in which an epistemic subject has a cognitive relationship (usually thought to be belief) to a true proposition. Even so, some of this book's essays dispute that commonplace—its truth and its significance. Like Kornblith, Paul Churchland looks to science rather than intuitions. The result is radical, as he recommends that we do not conceive of knowledge as being *judgemental*, as being a cognitive relation to a proposition in the first place. And my own essay provides systemic reasons to doubt that knowledge is even a *state*, such as belief. By reducing knowledge-that to knowledge-how-to, I classify knowledge as an *ability*, with knowers thereby constitutively being agents, not subjects.

Christopher Hookway pursues the latter theme more fully. He describes how epistemology might focus even more generally upon assessing agency—in particular, modes of inquiry—than upon assessing the resulting beliefs. Is knowing important? Only secondarily (says Hookway), and only insofar as it plays a role in effective *inquiry*. Consequently, delineating the latter should be epistemology's primary aim, with the epistemic realm thereby being conceived somewhat anew, in both content and structure. But wait: should our sense of the epistemic realm be modified even further still? Adam Morton asks how a rational agent would move between beliefs. Would a realistic epistemology explain this in terms of belief-*desire* pairings, and large-scale ones at that? Is epistemic progress strategic and practical, psychologically constrained? Is it an exemplification of a related kind of *virtue* of rationality? Epistemic virtues also receive an extended examination in Linda Zagzebski's essay. Drawing upon normative ethical theory, she seeks to explain, even to begin to resolve, some traditional disputes by way of epistemological versions of the concepts of an Ideal Observer or an Ideal Agent. (And she provides some reason to favour the latter.) How should this be understood? Zagzebski suggests that we do so by studying epistemic *exemplars*, people who are paradigms of epistemic virtues. We should evaluate various epistemological theories in the light of our observations of examplars.

Within epistemology, therefore, maybe more should be in flux than we have realized. Possibly, even some well-entrenched projects need to be re-evaluated; we should gaze back, in order to gaze forward. *Should* all of epistemology's presently central projects be so well-embedded? Consider again attempts to describe knowledge's key aspects. Maybe epistemology's infamous Gettier problem should make us wonder whether we will *ever* know what knowledge is. And so William Lycan asks *why* the Gettier problem has been such a problem (even as he proposes a solution to it). What might, and what should, we have overlooked in reflecting upon knowledge? Have needless complexity and distracting lines of thought hindered us in that endeavour? We might even suspect that the Gettier problem has become a test case for the ability of conceptual analysis, in particular, to function as a core epistemological methodology. More generally, what can we learn about epistemology from the Gettier problem's history?

Consider, similarly, the history of *sceptical* perplexities. Around these, too, debates have circled, surged, and foundered. But in their respective essays Anthony Grayling and Mark Kaplan try to defuse some of that frustrating history. Does the lineage of entanglements with sceptical questions reflect epistemology's having failed to notice, or to make proper use of, some readily available escape-routes? For example, does that burdensome lineage reflect epistemology's having strayed too far from its proper methodological roots? Maybe *ordinary* epistemic practices and *ordinary* language can assist us here. Can these help us to regard our fallibilities as inquirers—even our collective fallibilities—with appropriate equanimity? *Should* epistemology ever have been so worried by sceptical challenges?

Perhaps sceptical questions have seemed especially pressing because of our thinking too much about knowledge, too little about other epistemic phenomena. Is that possible? The book's earlier essays present possible modifications of our conception of the epistemic realm (and thereby of whatever it is of which epistemic progress in thinking about that realm might consist). Catherine Elgin's essay alerts us to a further possible inhabitant of that realm—namely, *understanding*. Elgin distinguishes knowledge from understanding, taking *scientific* understanding as her model. This (she contends) shows us how understanding can be insightful even when not being wholly factive. And will that distinction allow us (although this is not Elgin's own focus) to make epistemological progress by understanding knowledge and other epistemic phenomena, without always having to *know* what knowledge is, say?[12]

Yet is even that form of epistemological progress available? No matter what we try to know or understand, how will epistemology ever make progress as a discipline, so long as it remains a home to so much *disagreement*? Obviously, this problem is a wider one, even within philosophy as a whole: If philosophers in general are known for one thing, it is for their apparent inability to agree on much at all. We dispute; we beg to differ; we reject; we dismiss; we even do this while saying, sometimes, how much we respect the acumen and abilities of those with whom we are jousting. This is an epistemically puzzling phenomenon, as Richard Feldman's essay (talking about reasonable disagreements in general) helps us to appreciate. And (as his analysis also implies) there could be correlative problems for us as inquirers. In particular, maybe there should be more *suspension* of epistemological judgement than there is in practise.

Yet what would this imply, in turn, about the nature of epistemological *progress*? Might such progress itself be partly constituted by increased suspension of epistemological judgement? Will epistemological progress require there to be less epistemology, not more, in the future? Will such progress be, in part,

---

[12] Intriguingly, too, would epistemology be able in this way to become more scientific—hence, more likely to make epistemic progress—even while not always being more factive?

silence—epistemological silence, so to speak, perhaps a knowing silence, an understanding silence?

Now *there* is a thought with which we might pause.[13]

REFERENCES

Hetherington, S. (1992). *Epistemology's Paradox: Is a Theory of Knowledge Possible?* Savage, MD: Rowman & Littlefield.

—— (2001). *Good Knowledge, Bad Knowledge: On Two Dogmas of Epistemology*. Oxford: Clarendon Press.

Huenemann, C. (2004). 'Why Not to Trust Other Philosophers'. *American Philosophical Quarterly*, 41: 249–58.

Kaplan, M. (1985). 'It's Not What You Know That Counts'. *Journal of Philosophy*, 82: 350–63.

McGinn, C. (1993). *Problems in Philosophy: The Limits of Inquiry*. Oxford: Blackwell.

Russell, B. (1959 [1912]). *The Problems of Philosophy*. Oxford: Oxford University Press.

Stroud, B. (1989). 'Understanding Human Knowledge in General', in K. Lehrer and M. Clay (eds.), *Knowledge and Skepticism*. Boulder, Colo.: Westview Press, 31–50.

van Inwagen, P. (2002). *Metaphysics* (2nd edn.). Boulder, Colo.: Westview Press.

---

[13] Relatedly, we might ponder—each one of us—Huenemann's (2004) diagnosis of why philosophy in general struggles to make progress. The problem, he claims, is that philosophers wish (even more than they wish to be correct) to be epistemically *authentic*, this being the 'concern to understand something *for himself or herself*' (257; my emphasis). Is there more individualism and personal exploration within philosophy than is compatible with there being 'decisive progress in philosophy' (ibid.)? I do not profess to know whether Huenemann is correct about this. (But if he is, would even collaborative work within philosophy, insofar as it remains philosophical, be afflicted?)

2

Appeals to Intuition and the Ambitions of Epistemology*

Hilary Kornblith

It is a common feature of epistemology, and philosophy generally, that appeals to intuition play a prominent role. Thus, Laurence BonJour (2002: 48) remarks: '... our commonsense intuitions about cases of knowledge ... are ... our main and indispensable basis for deciding what the concept of knowledge really amounts to.' On BonJour's view, and that of many others as well, it is the job of epistemology to provide us with an account of the content of our epistemic concepts, and our intuitions provide us with the data upon which epistemological theories may be built. David Lewis (1973: 88) endorsed a similar method for the metaphysics of mind in particular, and metaphysics in general:

One comes to philosophy already endowed with a stock of opinions. It is not the business of philosophy either to undermine or to justify these pre-existing opinions, to any great extent, but only to try to discover ways of expanding them into an orderly system. A metaphysician's analysis of mind is an attempt at systematizing our opinions about mind. It succeeds to the extent that (1) it is systematic, and (2) it respects those of our pre-philosophical opinions to which we are firmly attached.[1]

Bertrand Russell (1912: 25) endorsed this same method for all of philosophy:

Philosophy should show us the hierarchy of our instinctive beliefs, beginning with those we hold most strongly, and presenting each as much isolated and as free from irrelevant additions as possible. It should take care to show that, in the form in which they are finally set forth, our instinctive beliefs do not clash, but form a harmonious system. There can never be any reason for rejecting one instinctive belief except that it clashes

---

* Versions of this paper were presented at the University of Fribourg, the Free University of Amsterdam, and the University of Bristol. I am grateful to audiences on each of these occasions for comments. In addition, I have received helpful comments from Stephen Hetherington, René van Woudenberg, Brandt Van der Gaast, and an anonymous referee.

[1] Lewis makes clear that he means to apply this same method to all of metaphysics. In the paragraph immediately following the one from which the quoted material is taken, Lewis comments, 'So it is throughout metaphysics...'

with others; thus, if they are found to harmonize, the whole system becomes worthy of acceptance.[2]

Russell and Lewis disagree about the upshot of this manner of philosophical theory construction. While Lewis insists that, 'It is not the business of philosophy either to undermine or to justify these pre-existing opinions, to any great extent,' on Russell's view, our pre-theoretical views become justified by way of their systematization. But despite their disagreement about the epistemic status of the resulting philosophical theories, Russell and Lewis are in agreement about proper philosophical method: we start with our intuitions, and then we try to systematize them as best we can.

Appeals to intuition, and attempts at their systematization, constitute a familiar and widely practiced philosophical method. Indeed, George Bealer (1993) has referred to this as 'the standard justificatory procedure' in philosophy. My own view, following Stephen Stich (see especially 1990: ch. 4) and Robert Cummins (1998), is that this is a procedure which we should abandon; philosophy cannot live up to its ambitions if it rests content with the systematization of pre-theoretical intuitions. I have argued for this view elsewhere (2002: ch. 1), and I will develop those arguments further here. Arguments against the standard justificatory procedure by themselves, however, leave many philosophers puzzled. What I have found, in presenting such arguments, is that many philosophers find it difficult to see how it would even be so much as possible to do anything other than appeal to one's intuitions as a source of philosophical insight, and then attempt to clarify and systematize them, as Lewis and Russell suggest. Indeed, some have argued that any attempt to abandon the method of appeal to intuition must inevitably be self-undermining.[3]

I will respond directly to some of these arguments here.[4] In addition, I present a positive account of philosophical method quite different from the standard procedure. I hope to show that this method is, beyond doubt, intellectually respectable, and that, unlike the method of appeal to intuitions, it may allow philosophy to fulfill its most important ambitions.

I

Appeals to intuition are designed to allow us to illuminate the contours of our concepts. By examining our intuitions about imaginary or hypothetical cases, we should be able to come to an understanding of our concepts of, for example,

---

[2] It is quite clear that Russell's idea of an instinctive belief is just the same as what philosophers nowadays refer to as 'pre-theoretical'. Here is how Russell introduces the term:

Of course it is not by way of argument that we originally come by our belief in an independent external world. We find this belief in ourselves as soon as we begin to reflect: it is what may be called an *instinctive* belief. (24)

[3] Including Bealer (1993), BonJour (1998), Goldman (forthcoming), Jackson (1998), and Pust (1996).

[4] I have also discussed some of these arguments at length elsewhere. I discuss Bealer, BonJour, Goldman, and Jackson in (2002: ch. 1), and I discuss BonJour's views on a priori intuition in detail in (2000). See also my (forthcoming *b*).

knowledge and justification. The goal of epistemology on this view, or, at a minimum, an essential first step in developing an epistemological theory, is an understanding of our concepts.

My own view is that our concepts of knowledge and justification are of no epistemological interest. The proper objects of epistemological theorizing are knowledge and justification themselves, rather than our concepts of them. Just as chemistry is a study of certain features of the natural world, and not our concepts of those features, epistemology, on my view, is a study of certain real features of the world, namely, knowledge and justification, not our concepts of those features. Similarly, just as early chemists would have been ill-advised to study their concept of an acid or of an atom rather than to look at the natural world, I believe that epistemologists would be ill-advised to study features of our concepts of knowledge and justification rather than to examine the phenomena themselves. In the chemical case, early investigators were ignorant of many of the essential properties of the natural kinds they sought to study; in addition, they held many false beliefs about those kinds. These twin problems, problems of ignorance and error, make a study of one's chemical concepts irrelevant to the advancement of chemistry. But the problems of ignorance and error are not limited to the chemical case. We may misunderstand the true nature of knowledge and justification just as much as we may misunderstand the true nature of acids. And if we are, in any way, ignorant or in error about the true nature of the phenomena, examining our concepts will do nothing to remedy the problem. If we wish to have a genuine understanding of knowledge itself, we need to look at the phenomenon, not our concept of it.

One might think that even if these remarks are correct, some examination of our epistemic concepts is required in order to begin our investigation, if only to fix its subject matter. Frank Jackson (1998: 38) and Alvin Goldman (forthcoming) have defended this view. How am I to explain why it is that I look at people's beliefs, when examining knowledge, rather than, for example, various rocks? Surely the answer must appeal, as Goldman (ibid.) suggests, to some sort of 'semantico-conceptual account', precisely what an examination of our concepts provides. Thus, even if this semantic investigation is only preparatory to an investigation of knowledge itself, it is, nevertheless, an essential preliminary to any such investigation.

Where Goldman and I disagree is on the scope of this semantic investigation. On Goldman's view, the examination of our concept of knowledge is a highly non-trivial affair. Plato was engaged in this semantic project in the *Theaetetus*, and this investigation is continuous with the Gettier-inspired literature, and the discussion, for example, of internalist and externalist accounts of justification. The semantic project here is an extremely subtle one, one which has been going on for more than two thousand years, a project which remains a subject of considerable dispute. This is the semantic project which Goldman sees as a pre-condition for an investigation of the phenomena of knowledge and justification, assuming proper sense can be made of talk of knowledge and justification themselves, apart from our concepts of them.[5]

On my view, however, Goldman, Jackson, et al., may well be right that we need to appeal to some sort of semantic or conceptual truths to explain why it is that we look at cases involving belief, say, rather than cases involving rocks when engaged in an examination of the nature of knowledge. All the same, the semantic investigation needed here is far less extensive than the millennia-long project which Goldman would have us sign on to; indeed, the semantic investigation required is utterly trivial.

Thus, consider the chemist who is interested in investigating the nature of acids. He lines up a number of putative acids—vinegar, *aqua regia*, and the like—and proceeds to investigate what it is that they all have in common. He looks at the phenomena in the world, not at his concept. Now imagine that someone else comes along and claims that he wants to assist in this project, but instead of looking at the sorts of things which the first chemist has lined up, he assembles a random collection of household furniture, claiming that he too is trying to understand the nature of acids. Clearly something has gone very wrong, and it may well be that the way to explain what error is being made must involve a semantic or conceptual point turning on the difference between the concepts of the two investigators. But this investigation will not take millennia. One would not want to tell the chemist that he must engage in a subtle and detailed accounting of the features of his concept of acid before he can begin looking at the substances themselves. By the same token, I believe, the semantic work needed to explain why it is that we look at beliefs rather than rocks when investigating the nature of knowledge and justification will be equally trivial, and all of the real work involved in understanding both knowledge and justification will inevitably require looking at the phenomena themselves rather than our concepts.

If we investigate our concepts of knowledge and justification, rather than knowledge and justification themselves, the ambitions of philosophy are severely curtailed. Since our concepts may be infected by error and ignorance, any investigation of our concepts may simply fail to reveal features of the phenomena we wish to understand, substituting a refined understanding of our misguided concepts for an accurate understanding of their target. This is not, I believe, how philosophy ought to be done.

II

How then should epistemology be practiced if we are to avoid the misdirection involved in looking at our concepts instead of the phenomena they seek to capture? While Bealer is certainly right that conceptual analysis by way of appeals to

---

[5] What I have not mentioned here is that Goldman takes this conceptual investigation to be an a posteriori matter, requiring the investigative techniques of cognitive science. For a full explanation of this approach, see Goldman (1992). The issue of whether conceptual analysis is a priori or a posteriori, however, is orthogonal to the issue discussed in the text.

intuition is the standard justificatory procedure in philosophy, it is not the only philosophical method currently available, nor is it rightly seen, I believe, as typical of philosophy historically. What I want to do is introduce a number of examples of philosophical work which clearly proceed by way of a method other than appeals to intuition, a method different from Bealer's standard justificatory procedure. Not only is this method quite different from the standard procedure; it frequently produces results which are completely at odds with the method of appeal to intuition. This is, I believe, just what one should suspect if my diagnosis of the standard procedure is correct. Since our concepts are often a product of ignorance and error, if I am right, they should often prove to mischaracterize the very phenomena which they are concepts of. Conceptual analysis is not the only game in town for philosophers; there are alternative ways of proceeding currently available which may fulfill the ambitions of philosophy.

Consider, first, the literature in philosophy of mind dealing with the issue which divides dualists from materialists. From the very beginning, this literature involved appeal to empirical evidence, evidence about mental phenomena themselves, and not exclusively to our intuitions. Thus, for example, in Descartes, we see arguments for dualism appealing to features of human language use which, Descartes (1637: Part V) suggests, could not be explained by any physical mechanism, no matter how elaborate. Contemporary discussions are informed, of course, by a wide range of literature from the empirical sciences.

The empirical results of these investigations may, of course, clash with the contours of our concepts. Suppose an analysis of someone's concept of mind should reveal that some sort of substance dualism is simply built in to the concept. Surely this would not be sufficient to show that materialism is false. What we care about, in trying to understand the nature of mind, is not our concept of the mind, but the mind itself. It may well be that some individuals, or entire cultures, build a commitment to substance dualism right in to their very concept of mind, a feature of their concept which appeals to intuition would reveal. But the reason we care about the mind, and the reason questions about the mind have had such a central place in the history of philosophy, is that minds are extremely salient features of human beings, and the question about whether materialism is true is a question about these phenomena in the world, not our concepts. We are able to advance our understanding of our place in nature not by understanding our potentially ill-informed concept of mind, but by an examination of our minds.

Consider Chomsky's work on language acquisition,[6] his discussion of innateness, and the way in which this work has informed the debate between rationalists and empiricists. As Chomsky has consistently argued, the case for his account depends on a very wide range of empirical considerations, and the extraordinary strength of the Chomskian position resides in the way in which these different

---

[6] Beginning with (1957; 1959; 1965), among many others.

empirical considerations converge, lending independent support to a certain view about the large-scale structure of the mind. Chomsky's work has nothing to do with our concept of mind; he is not trying to reveal the contours of our pre-theoretical views. Instead, Chomsky is interested in a certain feature of the natural world, namely, human minds themselves, and his work is illuminating precisely because it corrects our pre-theoretical and uninformed views about the mind.

Consider Jerry Fodor's (1975) argument for the language of thought hypothesis. Fodor argued that a very wide range of theories in cognitive science can only be made sense of if we suppose that there is a language of thought. In effect, what Fodor argued is that cognitive scientists had developed a broad range of theories which shared a common and unrecognized presupposition. The argument for the language of thought hypothesis was thus straightforwardly empirical. It did not appeal to our concept of thought, which would, in any case, be irrelevant. Fodor's claim was a claim about the medium in which thoughts are actually represented, not a claim about our implicit views about such a medium.

There is nothing mysterious about this style of argument, nor does it reduce to, or presuppose, some prior analysis of one's concepts. No more conceptual analysis is involved here than is involved in the chemist's attempt to determine what acids are. There can be little doubt that the method employed in these arguments is quite different from the standard justificatory procedure, nor can there be any doubt that the method, which seeks to discover certain fairly abstract features of the world by detecting common presuppositions in empirical theories of more concrete phenomena, is entirely legitimate. I do not mean to be endorsing the particular conclusions which Fodor, for example, comes to in defending the language of thought hypothesis; rather, I take Fodor's argument, however successful or unsuccessful it may be in its details, to be one application of an obviously legitimate method of empirical theorizing which is familiar in the philosophical literature.

Tyler Burge (1986) makes use of the same strategy. Burge there argues in favor of an anti-individualist account of the content of mental states, not by appealing to our intuitions about imaginary cases and what we might take the content of our mental states to be, but rather by examining the details of a particularly successful empirical explanation by Marr (1982) of the workings of visual perception, and arguing that this explanation does not go through unless the content of the representational states involved is construed anti-individualistically. Intuitions about Twin Earth, Swampman, and so on are simply irrelevant to the project Burge is engaged in here, for at least in this paper Burge is not attempting to make explicit the contours of our concept of mental representation; he is, instead, trying to figure out something about mental representations themselves. Like Fodor, Burge is trying to make explicit some of the commitments of a well-confirmed empirical theory.

The same is true, I believe, of Hilary Putnam's account of the reference of natural kind terms, although I recognize that it is not always understood in this way. Putnam does certainly appeal to a number of imaginary cases, and it is thus perfectly natural to see his argument as an application of the standard justificatory procedure. Frank Jackson, in his defense of conceptual analysis, certainly sees it this way: 'Putnam's theory', he tells us (1998: 39), 'is built precisely on folk intuitions.' But I believe that reading Putnam in this way fails to appreciate the context in which his argument was presented.[7] Putnam's account of the reference of natural kind terms was part of an attempt to offer a realist philosophy of science.[8] As Putnam argued, the traditional descriptions theory of reference made it impossible to understand the possibility of disagreement between individuals committed to different theories. If the referent of Newton's use of the term 'mass' is determined by his theory, and that of Einstein's use of the term is determined by his, then Newton and Einstein are not disagreeing about a common subject matter when one claims, 'Mass is independent of velocity' and the other appears to deny it; instead, they are simply talking about different things.[9] Putnam's argument against a descriptions-based theory of reference for natural kind terms was designed to show that such a theory fails to explain a certain real phenomenon, namely, progress in science; it should not be viewed merely as an attempt to account for intuitions.

Philosophical work of this sort will often deliver results which conflict with the deliverances of intuition, or on which our intuition is silent. Richard Swinburne (1981: ch. 7), for example, has argued, on the basis of the standard justificatory procedure, that space must be three dimensional, and Laurence BonJour (1998: 220 n.5) has endorsed this argument. Just recently, however, at Fermilab in Illinois, Maria Spiropulu, of the University of California at Santa Barbara, has been conducting experiments designed to test the view that space-time has 10 or 11 dimensions.[10] Suppose the outcome of Spiropulu's work were to confirm that space, as she suspects, has 10 dimensions. We now have a conflict between the deliverances of intuition and an empirical investigation of the phenomenon. What should we say in the face of such a conflict?

One could, of course, insist that intuition simply wins out in any such conflict. On such a view, we need not even wait for the results of Spiropulu's research, for we know in advance that space has exactly three dimensions. In this case, a great many researchers at Fermilab, and at CERN in Geneva, are wasting their time. A great deal of money is being wasted on these experiments as well, since the correct answer to questions about the dimensionality of space may be achieved without any equipment at all. I take it that this view is exactly as plausible as the

[7] This point is also made by Stephen Laurence and Eric Margolis (2003).

[8] This was prior to Putnam's move, in 1975, to 'internal' realism. In the language of his post-1975 work, the argument under discussion was part of a *metaphysical* realist account of science.

[9] Indeed, Thomas Kuhn (1970) seems to have embraced this conclusion on the basis of this very argument, concluding, since both Newton and Einstein were each so clearly successful in referring, that they worked 'in different worlds'. The argument which depends on the descriptions theory of reference appears on 101–2; talk of working 'in different worlds' appears on 135. I owe this observation to Richard Boyd.   [10] *New York Times*, 30 September 2003.

view that looking through a telescope is unnecessary to determine the features of celestial objects.

One could, perhaps, hold the view that the results of intuition are relevant here, and ought to be taken into account in addition to the more straightforwardly empirical evidence. In this case, if Spiropulu were to suggest that her data at Fermilab support the theory that space is ten dimensional, we might reasonably respond that she has only taken into account one of the relevant sources of evidence; she needs to consider the results of intuition as well. Somehow, each source of data would need to be given its appropriate weight. But this view, I take it, is not much more plausible than the view that her experimental work is simply irrelevant. Surely the experimental work, in this case, will do all of the work in supporting any reasonable conclusions about the shape of space. Spiropulu would be right simply to brush aside any of the intuitional data.

One might suggest, far more plausibly, I believe, that consulting our intuitions gives us information here, not about space itself, as BonJour and other rationalists suggest, but about our concept of space. What philosophical analysis provides, then, is an account of what space is according to our conception of it. We may then conduct our empirical investigations to determine whether the world contains space as we conceive it to be, or whether, instead, it contains something else. This is just what Frank Jackson (1998: 31) has suggested.

What then are the interesting philosophical questions that we are seeking to address when we debate the existence of free action and its compatibility with determinism, or about eliminativism concerning intentional psychology? What we are seeking to address is whether free action *according to our ordinary conception*, or something suitably close to our ordinary conception, exists and is compatible with determinism, and whether intentional states *according to our ordinary conception*, or something suitably close to it, will survive what cognitive science reveals about the operations of our brains.

This is, as Jackson emphasizes, a modest role for philosophy, but it leaves room for a distinctive philosophical method. Philosophy tells us what our ordinary conceptions are;[11] scientific investigation tells us whether there is anything in the world which answers to them.

In applying this to the case of the dimensionality of space, Jackson would, of course, hold the view that philosophers tell us what our ordinary conception of space is, and the physicists will tell us whether the world answers to that pre-theoretical conception we have of it. This avoids the problem of having to tell the physicists at Fermilab and CERN either that they are simply mistaken, when their

---

[11] Jackson defends the descriptions-based approach to reference by suggesting, at certain points (1998: 40 n.16), that the descriptions which determine reference may be metalinguistic: 'the person called "X",' or 'the kind called "K" '. But if this is the way in which the descriptions theory of reference is to be defended, then the results of conceptual analysis will be singularly unilluminating, revealing none of the non-linguistic characteristics of the referent, or even of our conception of the referent. If this is all that philosophy can reliably reveal—that, for example, right actions are those we call 'right', or knowledge is what we call 'knowledge'—then it is hard to see why philosophy is worth doing at all.

views of space do not answer to our intuitions about it, or that they have failed to take important data into account. But the job it leaves for philosophy is more than just modest; it seems utterly pointless. Why should we spend our entire careers worrying about the details of our ordinary conception of space or time if enough is already known about the physical world to rule out anything in the world remotely like those conceptions? Why in any case should intellectual work be devoted to a detailed articulation of our ordinary conception of things, rather than to examining the things themselves? As we saw in the case of the chemists investigating the nature of acids, virtually no conceptual work is needed to fix one's subject matter. An investigation of our concepts seems irrelevant to the real project of understanding the nature of space, or intentional states, or freedom. And surely it is the proper ambition of philosophy to tell us something about the nature of space, intentional states, and freedom, not just about our ordinary pre-theoretical conceptions of them, even when these are hopelessly inaccurate characterizations of anything which actually exists in the world.

If our intuitions were, as some rationalists such as BonJour have suggested, a reliable route to information about features of the world itself, then philosophy might make progress by examining our intuitions. But too often our intuitions about some subject matter have come into conflict with empirical investigation of that very area, and when such conflicts occur, our intuitions must give way. But this makes the examination of our intuitions look like nothing more than a tem-porizing measure—something we might do until the real data are available. Worse still, it surely suggests that this temporizing measure, while it may help us kill time until we are able productively to address the questions we really care about, is of little intellectual worth. Far better to acknowledge, when no substantive informa-tion is available on a topic we care about, that we really know nothing about it. Data about our intuitions do not tell us about features of the world.

Jackson's empiricist alternative, that our intuitions give us information about our ordinary conceptions, while science tells us whether the world answers to those conceptions, does little to defend the ambitions or integrity of philosophy. There is no need to examine our pre-theoretical conceptions of what the world is like before we investigate the world itself. The picture of philosophy as a precursor to science which serves to fix its subject matter puts philosophy to work on a job which doesn't need doing.

If philosophy is to fulfill its ambitions then, and maintain its integrity, we need to stop examining our intuitions and look at the phenomena themselves.

III

Attempts to understand the nature of human minds, or mental representation, or space, clearly require empirical investigation of the world around us, and so, perhaps, a good deal of philosophy of mind and philosophy of science will require that we abandon our armchairs and give up the standard justificatory procedure.[12] But not all philosophical subjects lend themselves so obviously to empirical investigation, and much of epistemology, in particular, might seem to be in this category. Indeed, it is interesting that BonJour, who sees intuition as a source of insight into the nature of *an sich* reality—it tells us about space itself and not just our concept of space, on his view—speaks of intuition as providing us with information about the *concept* of knowledge, rather than knowledge itself.[13] In seeing why a rationalist might talk this way about epistemology, I believe we may better understand not only the rationalist position, but also the views of many other epistemologists who see the subject matter of epistemology as closely tied to our concepts of knowledge and justification.

There is an obvious gap between our concept of what an acid is and the facts of the matter about what makes something an acid. Historians of science have shown us in some detail just how large that gap may be with careful studies of the early history of chemistry.[14] The property of being an acid is a natural kind, and what makes something an acid is thus in no way a product of human convention or choice. Our concept of what an acid is may be accurate or inaccurate, because what an acid is is something independent of how people think about it. One of the goals of scientific theorizing is to develop concepts which accurately characterize the nature of kinds like this, kinds whose boundaries are determined not by our thinking about the world, but by the world itself.[15] And what is true of the nature of acids is arguably true of the nature of minds, and mental representation and space.

Not everyone is sympathetic with this view of natural kinds, of course, but even many of those who are will want to stop short of suggesting that things like knowledge and justified belief are natural kinds. There are certain standards for justified

[12] Timothy Williamson (2004) has taken an interesting position on this issue. Intuitions about imaginary cases, he argues, 'simply involve particular applications of general cognitive capacities—most notably, the capacity to process counterfactuals—that are widely used throughout our cognitive engagement with the spatio-temporal world'. It is therefore, he argues, a mistake to think of appeals to intuition as involving some distinct faculty, or *sui generis* processes, or as justified a priori. All of this seems to me to be entirely correct. But Williamson wishes to defend the view that, 'If anything can be pursued in an armchair, philosophy can', and this, I believe, is difficult to square with his other remarks. If the deliverances of so-called intuition merely involve the use of our ordinary empirically-driven cognitive faculties, then the armchair method in philosophy would involve an arbitrary and unmotivated restriction of the data to be considered in theorizing. While rationalists may easily explain, on their view, why intuitions alone are relevant to philosophical theories, and those, such as Frank Jackson, who believe that philosophy is interested in the contours of our concepts, may also readily explain why intuitions are all the data philosophy needs, Williamson's view seems no more motivated than the idea of a physics, for example, which restricts itself to data collected on Mondays, Wednesdays, and Fridays. If the data of so-called intuition are just the product of our usual empirically-driven cognitive capacities, then surely we should use those same empirically-driven cognitive capacities outside the armchair to produce better informed theories.   [13] See the passage quoted at the very beginning of this paper.
[14] See, e.g., Maurice Crossland (1978).
[15] I develop and defend this view of natural kinds in my (1993).

belief, and for knowledge, and these standards are not ones which we discover, it seems, existing in the world apart from human choice or convention, like rocks or acids; instead, these standards seem to be ones which we impose upon the world, ones which are a reflection of our own decisions. On a view such as this, there can be no gap between the concept of knowledge and what knowledge actually is because knowledge is, as it were, something which we have created, not something we have discovered. In a word, the very category of knowledge itself is socially constructed.

Now this is a view which I do not accept, for I myself believe that knowledge is a natural kind,[16] but the view that knowledge is a socially constructed kind has an undeniable attractiveness, and it is one worth examining. It makes some sense of why rationalists such as BonJour would see epistemology as an investigation of our concepts when they themselves think of intuition as providing insight into the nature of the world itself; and it makes some sense of why more empirically-minded philosophers would think an examination of our concept of knowledge should be of real interest to epistemology, when an examination of natural kind concepts, such as our concept of space or of mind, is not of interest to the disciplines which make use of these concepts, such as physics or psychology.

Let us consider a clear case of a socially constructed kind: an artifactual kind. Consider, therefore, the case of sport utility vehicles. SUVs are a certain kind of motorized vehicle, different from sedans, station wagons, and pick-up trucks. The fact that our culture divides the vehicular world into a number of different kinds does not reflect our intellectual acuity in the same way that our recognition of the existence of acids and bases reflects our understanding of the chemical world. A culture with the very same vehicles we have—molecule for molecule duplicates of our vehicles—but which did not conceive of them as divided into station wagons, SUVs, and so on, would not thereby show a lack of understanding. Instead, a culture which divided those molecular duplicates of our vehicles into kinds by way of a different system of categories would merely show that their interests and concerns are different from our own. There is no pre-existing fact of the matter about how to divide these vehicles into kinds, some ways of doing it accurately or inaccurately. These systems of categorization do not attempt to describe real pre-existing kinds in nature, to cut the vehicular world at its joints, as it were; they merely reflect our parochial concerns and interests. Once such a system of categorization is in place, it is possible, of course, to miscategorize an object; but the system of categorization itself is neither accurate nor inaccurate.

Now in these circumstances, it makes no sense, of course, to wonder whether our culture's concept of an SUV properly answers to the true nature of SUVs themselves, as if we somehow might have missed the real essence of the kind. While we may have a concept of acid which is inaccurate, since what makes something an acid has nothing to do with our concept of it, artifactual kinds are

---

[16] I defend this view in my (2002).

different in this respect. What it is to be an SUV just is to answer to our culture's concept of one. The concept, in this case, is the source of the very existence of the kind; unlike natural kinds, our concepts here do not attempt to characterize some pre-existing kind in nature.

Might our categories of knowledge and justified belief, the objects of epistemological theorizing, be relevantly similar to artifactual kinds? Might our desire to divide the world of beliefs into those which are justified and those which are not, or those which constitute cases of knowledge and those which do not, reflect standards which we impose on the world, arbitrary divisions which simply reflect our parochial concerns, rather than real distinctions in the world, independent of our interests? If knowledge and justification were categories of this sort, then my earlier remarks about the possibility of a gap between our concept of knowledge and knowledge itself would seem to be based on a misunderstanding. And thus if epistemic concepts correspond to socially constructed kinds, the project of conceptual elucidation in epistemology would, it seems, inevitably get at the phenomena themselves, for what it is to be a case of knowledge would be nothing more than to answer to our concept. The method of conceptual analysis, the standard justificatory procedure, would thus, it seems, be redeemed.

I don't believe that matters are as simple as this picture presents them to be, and so what I wish to argue is that even if our epistemic categories correspond to socially constructed kinds, the role of intuitions in epistemology would still be extremely limited, at best; the standard justificatory procedure would still be of no use in explaining the nature of knowledge and justification.

There can be little doubt that the metaphysics of natural kinds and the metaphysics of artifactual or socially constructed kinds is quite different. What makes a natural kind the kind of thing it is has nothing to do with human purposes, intentions, interests, or decisions; artifacts and other socially constructed kinds, however, are what they are by virtue of their relationship to human intentional states. It would be a mistake, however, to draw any quick epistemological conclusions from these metaphysical differences because the relationship between human intentions and the nature of artifacts is complex and indirect.[17] In particular, artifactual kind terms are subject to the very same division of linguistic labor which Hilary Putnam made so vivid in the case of natural kind terms.[18] What this means, in practice, is that my own concept of any given artifact may be no more accurate in capturing features of the kind than my own concept of an acid. Just as in the case of natural kinds, individuals may be subject to the problems of ignorance and error. So the fact that my own private concept of a given artifactual kind includes certain features in no way guarantees that the artifactual kind itself must have those features. When each of us therefore turns to an elucidation of his or her own private concept, we are each, as in the case of natural kinds, revealing

---

[17] For more on this theme, see my (forthcoming *a*).
[18] See, among other works by Putnam on this topic, his (1975).

our own conception of the kind, a conception which may or may not answer to the kind itself. The fact that SUVs are socially constructed kinds and acids are not does not mean that each individual's conception of an SUV accurately characterizes the kind.

A number of writers who seek to defend the role of intuitions in philosophy show some sensitivity to this point, for it is widely recognized that one's intuitions cannot play a foundational role in philosophical analysis unless they are widely shared. Thus, Frank Jackson (1998: 36–7) remarks,

> I am sometimes asked—in a tone that suggests that the question is a major objection—why, if conceptual analysis is concerned to elucidate what governs our classificatory practice, don't I advocate doing serious public opinion polls on people's responses to various cases? My answer is that I do—when it is necessary. Everyone who presents the Gettier case to a class of students is doing their own bit of fieldwork, and we all know the answer they get in the vast majority of cases.

As Stich and Weinberg (2001) have pointed out, this makes it sound as if philosophers who are engaged in conceptual analysis are really just performing some sort of social scientific research, but doing it very casually, without any of the attention to sample bias, priming effects, and so on, which are required for achieving meaningful results. Even if this research were done carefully, however, and even if there were some widely shared concept which was thereby detected, and even if the object of philosophical analysis were some socially constructed kind, this would still be a poor way to determine the features of the kind under study.

On all of the available accounts of the metaphysics of artifacts,[19] the connections between the intentions of the users and makers of artifacts and the features which define artifactual kinds are extremely complex and indirect. Any account of the nature of artifactual kinds must allow for the possibility that most of the individuals who use an artifactual kind term may be largely ignorant or in error about the kind. This applies not only to individuals who use the term to refer to the kind and yet have little direct contact with it; it applies as well to those who actually make the artifacts, and those who use them. Any account of the nature of artifactual kinds which does not allow for widespread error is, in virtue of that very fact, mistaken. It is for this reason that an accurate account of the metaphysics of artifactual kinds is so difficult to give. Much as it is obvious that artifactual kinds are what they are, at least in part, by virtue of some connection to human intentions, the precise connection required is extremely difficult to determine. The same is true, of course, in the case of any socially constructed kind. The mere fact that a given kind is the sort of thing it is in virtue of some relation to human intention does not make the nature of the kind transparent to reflection.

What this means, of course, is that the project of conceptual analysis is no more bound to succeed in the case of socially constructed kinds than it is in the case of

---

[19] For recent work on this, see Margolis and Laurence (forthcoming). For work on the nature of socially constructed kinds generally, see the essays in Schmitt (2003).

natural kinds. If it were, sociologists could abandon their empirical researches and endorse the standard justificatory procedure as a means of understanding the nature of social institutions. But as empirical work in sociology often shows, the very nature of our social institutions is often an object of common misconceptions. Social constitution does not make our concepts an accurate guide to the natures of socially constructed kinds.

As I've said, I myself believe that knowledge is properly viewed as a natural kind. But my objections to conceptual analysis, and my reasons for thinking that we must look at the phenomenon of knowledge, rather than our concept of it, do not depend on that view. Even if epistemic kinds are socially constructed, the standard justificatory procedure would lend no insight into the nature of those kinds.

IV

I have been arguing that the standard justificatory procedure does not do justice to the ambitions of philosophy, but it should be acknowledged that my own view of proper philosophical method requires some cutting back on the ambitions of philosophy as well. At least traditionally, philosophy has been viewed as having a subject matter which transcends the merely local and contingent truths about the actual world. From this perspective, scientific investigation may seem 'parochial', as William Talbott (forthcoming) so nicely puts it, and my own conception of philosophy will seem similarly narrow. Philosophy which proceeds by appealing to our intuitions, either as a means to conceptual analysis or, as rationalists would have it, to direct insight into modal reality, has no such limitations.

I believe this objection overdraws the contrast between philosophy, even on the traditional conception, and the results of scientific investigation. While it is certainly true that many scientific results are utterly contingent, this is not true of all scientific discovery. That water is H_2O is not a contingent truth; it is necessary. But this was a matter of scientific discovery nonetheless. It is through scientific discovery that we are able to determine the essential properties of natural kinds, and if knowledge, for example, is properly viewed as a natural kind, then there is reason to think that the sort of empirical investigation of knowledge which I advocate may also serve to discover its essential properties. If philosophy is conducted by way of empirical investigation, this does not entail that all of its results will be contingent.

Nevertheless, I would not want to argue that all of philosophy, on the conception I advocate, would inevitably deliver nothing but necessary truths. The heart of the objection, that my conception of philosophy makes it quite a different sort of inquiry than tradition would have it, should not be denied.[20] On traditional rationalist views, we have a special faculty that allows us direct insight into the

---

[20] This would be so even if, on my conception, philosophy were to yield nothing but necessary truths.

necessary features of the world. On traditional empiricist views, philosophy yields knowledge of necessities by way of conceptual analysis. I do not believe that we have the kind of faculty which rationalists would have us employ in philosophical inquiry, and, as I have been arguing, truths about our concepts, and the necessities which flow from them, are a poor substitute for truths about the very features of the world which our concepts are concepts of.

Only rationalists promise to deliver everything which philosophy has long aspired to: truths about features of the world, rather than just about our concepts, arrived at by way of our intuitions.[21] Anyone who would reject rationalism will need to cut back on philosophical ambitions in one place or another. Traditional empiricists would hold on to appeals to intuition at the cost of giving up truths about the world. I propose instead that we should pursue the opposite course: giving up appeals to intuition so as to retain the philosophical ambition of better understanding the world. We should hold on to the traditional ambitions of philosophy, while at the same time recognizing the limits of traditional methods.

REFERENCES

Bealer, G. (1993). 'The Incoherence of Empiricism', in S. Wagner and R. Warner (eds.), *Naturalism: A Critical Appraisal*. Notre Dame, IN: University of Notre Dame Press, 163–96.

BonJour, L. (1998). *In Defense of Pure Reason: A Rationalist Account of A Priori Justification*. Cambridge: Cambridge University Press.

—— (2002). *Epistemology: Classic Problems and Contemporary Responses*. Lanham, MD: Rowman & Littlefield.

Burge, T. (1986). 'Individualism and Psychology'. *Philosophical Review*, 95: 3–45.

Crossland, M. (1978). *Historical Studies in the Language of Chemistry*. New York: Dover.

Chomsky, N. (1957). *Syntactic Structures*. The Hague: Mouton.

—— (1959). 'Review of B. F. Skinner's *Verbal Behavior*'. *Language*, 35: 26–58.

—— (1965). *Aspects of the Theory of Syntax*. Cambridge, Mass.: MIT Press.

Cummins, R. (1998). 'Reflection on Reflective Equilibrium', in M. DePaul and W. Ramsey (eds.), *Rethinking Intuition: The Psychology of Intuition and its Role in Philosophical Inquiry*. Lanham, MD: Rowman & Littlefield, 113–27.

Descartes, R. (1637). *Discourse on Method*.

Fodor, J. (1975). *The Language of Thought*. New York: Crowell.

Goldman, A. (1992). 'Psychology and Philosophical Analysis', in *Liaisons: Philosophy Meets the Cognitive and Social Sciences*. Cambridge, Mass.: MIT Press, 143–53.

—— (forthcoming). 'Kornblith's Naturalistic Epistemology'. *Philosophy and Phenomenological Research*.

Jackson, F. (1998). *From Metaphysics to Ethics: A Defence of Conceptual Analysis*. Oxford: Clarendon Press.

Kornblith, H. (1993). *Inductive Inference and Its Natural Ground*. Cambridge, Mass.: MIT Press.

---

[21] My reasons for rejecting the rationalist position are presented in my (2000).

—— (2000). 'The Impurity of Reason'. *Pacific Philosophical Quarterly*, 81: 67–89.

—— (2002). *Knowledge and Its Place in Nature*. Oxford: Clarendon Press.

—— (forthcoming *a*). 'How to Refer to Artifacts', in Margolis and Laurence (forthcoming).

—— (forthcoming *b*). 'Replies to Alvin Goldman, Martin Kusch and William Talbott'. *Philosophy and Phenomenological Research*.

Kuhn, T. (1970). *The Structure of Scientific Revolutions* (2nd edn.). Chicago: University of Chicago Press.

Laurence, S., and Margolis, E. (2003). 'Concepts and Conceptual Analysis'. *Philosophy and Phenomenological Research*, 67: 253–82.

Lewis, D. (1973). *Counterfactuals*. Cambridge, Mass.: Harvard University Press.

Margolis, E., and Laurence, S. (eds.) (forthcoming). *Creations of the Mind: Essays on Artifacts and their Representation*. Oxford: Oxford University Press.

Marr, D. (1982). *Vision: A Computational Investigation into the Human Representation and Processing of Visual Information*. New York: Freeman & Co.

Pust, J. (1996). 'Against Explanationist Skepticism Regarding Philosophical Intuitions'. *Philosophical Studies*, 81: 151–62.

Putnam, H. (1975). 'The Meaning of "Meaning"', in *Mind, Language and Reality: Philosophical Papers*, vol. 2. Cambridge: Cambridge University Press, 215–71.

Russell, B. (1912). *The Problems of Philosophy*. London: Oxford University Press.

Schmitt, F. (ed.) (2003). *Socializing Metaphysics: The Nature of Social Reality*. Lanham, MD: Rowman & Littlefield.

Stich, S. (1990). *The Fragmentation of Reason: Preface to a Pragmatic Theory of Cognitive Evaluation*. Cambridge, Mass.: MIT Press.

—— and Weinberg, J. (2001). 'Jackson's Empirical Assumptions'. *Philosophy and Phenomenological Research*, 62: 637–43.

Swinburne, R. (1981). *Space and Time*. London: Macmillan.

Talbott, W. (forthcoming). 'Universal Knowledge'. *Philosophy and Phenomenological Research*.

Williamson, T. (2004). 'Armchair Philosophy, Metaphysical Modality and Counterfactual Thinking', *Proceedings of the Aristotelian Society*, 105: 1–23.

3

What's Epistemology for? The Case for Neopragmatism in Normative Metaepistemology[*]

Jonathan M. Weinberg

How ought we to go about forming and revising our beliefs, arguing and debating our reasons, and investigating our world? If those questions constitute normative epistemology, then I am interested here in normative *meta*epistemology: the investigation into how we ought to go about forming and revising our beliefs about how we ought to go about forming and revising our beliefs—how we ought to argue about how we ought to argue. Such investigations have become urgent of late, for the methodology of epistemology has reached something of a crisis. For analytic epistemology of the last half-century has relied overwhelmingly on intuitions,[1] and a growing set of arguments and data has begun to call this reliance on intuition seriously into question (for example, Weinberg, Nichols, and Stich 2001; Nichols, Stich, and Weinberg 2003; Cummins 1998). Although that method has not been entirely without defenders (BonJour 1998; Bealer 1996; Jackson 1998; Sosa forthcoming; Weatherson 2003), these defenses have not generally risen to the specific challenges leveled by the anti-intuitionist critics. In particular, the critics have attacked specific ways of deploying intuitions, and the defenders have overwhelmingly responded with in-principle defenses of the cogency of appealing to intuition. An analogy here would be someone's responding to arguments alleging systematic misuse of a particular scientific instrument, with accounts of how such an instrument could in principle be a reliable source of data.

But perhaps the best, or most psychologically persuasive, anyway, case for intuitions is a sort of 'what else?' argument. In the absence of a rival method to

[*] I would like to thank Steve Crowley, Stephen Hetherington, Henry Jackman, Mark Kaplan, Peter Klein, Adam Leite, Peter Markie, Mark McCullagh, Aaron Meskin, Ram Neta, Baron Reed, Ernie Sosa, and the faculty and students at Auburn University, the University of Memphis, and Texas Tech University for their many useful comments and suggestions.

[1] Joel Pust (2000: ch. 1) documents the central evidential role of intuitions in contemporary philosophy.

take its place, it is surely more rational to keep the problematic epistemology we know, than to abandon epistemology completely. My intention is not only to strengthen the case against traditional intuition-centered methods, but to articulate a better metaepistemology, too. First, I present a framework for debating these questions (a meta-metaepistemology?), based on articulating our desiderata for our normative epistemology. I then apply that framework to compare three basic methodological ideologies: intuitionism, naturalism, and pragmatism. I hope to suggest that pragmatism (or my version of it, anyhow) is an under-explored option on the table, and to that end, I further demonstrate applications of its method to some extant philosophical problems.

I. METAEPISTEMOLOGICAL DESIDERATA

The mode of argumentation here is a normative parallel to inference to the best explanation. In inference to the best explanation, we consider some phenomena, and then evaluate competitor theories by how well they explain them. The winner need not perfectly explain all the phenomena, and indeed it may fail miserably on some, if only those failures are compensated with greater overall explanatory success. For our purposes here, we do not have phenomena so much as desiderata, characteristics that we'd ideally like our methodology to have. In comparing different methods, we see how well each would promote each desideratum. The winner will be the method that performs best overall, though it may not perform perfectly on all, and indeed may be outscored by competitors on some.

I shall put forward a list of seven desiderata. There is nothing sacrosanct about this list. Each item is hopefully attractive as an empirical generalization as to what we really would want from a philosophical method here. The list is also not necessarily a closed list, and I welcome the articulation of further desiderata that ought be addressed. But these should be plenty to get my argument rolling:

1. truth-conduciveness
2. normativity
3. dialectical robustness
4. progressivism without radicalism
5. interdisciplinary comportment
6. minimal naturalism
7. plausible relativism/universalism

I will briefly discuss each in turn.

The two most central desiderata are *truth-conduciveness* and *normativity*. We require that the method tend to produce true results, and the greater the ratio of true deliverances to false, the better. I won't try to use this desideratum as a consideration between intuitionism, naturalism, and pragmatism, though I hope it justifies so abbreviated a list of candidates, e.g., astrological metaepistemology is right out. Moreover, we are looking for a method for normative epistemology, and as such, it had best give us results that are themselves normative in nature. Note that these desiderata receive a greater weighting than the others—unlike the other five, failures here may not be compensatable with success elsewhere.

Perhaps in service of truth-conduciveness is the desideratum of *dialectical robustness*: we want our method to be one that supports, encourages, and enables successful conversation and debate between epistemologists. It should foment the discovery of both points of agreement and disagreement, and in cases of the latter, it should help us to resolve such disagreements fruitfully. (See section II.B below.) *Progressivism without radicalism* suggests that we want a method that can take us beyond mere common sense, and give us new norms as our overall epistemic and cognitive circumstances change. We want our normative epistemology to change its deliverances as our circumstances change; the norms appropriate today may not be those that were appropriate in Plato's day or even Descartes's, and we want our methods to be able to register those changes. However, our proposed norms cannot fall so extremely remote from common sense that we cannot find them intelligible as epistemic norms for creatures like us to follow. Hence, we want progressivism without radicalism. Moreover, a method is better to the extent that it can learn from, or at least remain consistent with, the deliverances of other fields. An epistemology isolated from such sciences as psychology and such humanities as history is, *ceteris paribus*, less desirable than an epistemology with rich *interdisciplinary comportment*.

The last two considerations are more metaphysical in nature. First, our methods should be consistent with the kind of naturalism that I take to be part of the contemporary philosophical *Zeitgeist*. I'm only insisting on a *minimal naturalism* here, however, which I take to be the requirement that all causally efficacious entities be materialistically respectable. It is less a strident reductivist sort of physicalism and more a loose anti-supernaturalism. There may be numbers, sets, or fictional objects in our ontology, but if there are any such, then we cannot have them causally interacting with the chairs and electrons and organisms of the world. Thus, for example, various sorts of Platonic epistemologies are ruled out. Finally, we ask that our method's picture of the epistemic norms take a sensible stance on epistemic relativism. If it is a universalist method, we should be able to see why it licenses that universalism; if it allows a certain degree of epistemic relativity, then we should be able to see why that much relativism makes sense.

Let us see how the two main current metaepistemologies score.

I.A Intuition-driven romanticism

The main paradigm methodology in epistemology of the last few decades has been recently termed *intuition-driven romanticism* (Weinberg, Nichols, and Stich 2001). The proper epistemological norms are somehow already inside of us, and the job of the epistemologist is to get them out and set them out clearly; and the best way to do so is to pump our spontaneous judgments about applying or withholding terms of epistemic praise or blame to various hypothetical cases. 'Gettierological' projects are paradigm instances of IDR methodology.

In terms of our desiderata, clearly the results of an IDR analysis are normative: they purport to tell us the structure of *the* concepts or terms that govern our epistemic lives. And the most basic Reidian self-trust in our own capacity for judgment requires that we take IDR to be at least moderately truth-tracking.

On other desiderata, however, IDR fares less well. For starters, IDR has not proven itself able to interact fruitfully with other disciplines. Perhaps it meshes well with some elements of logic and mathematics, though not all. (For example, withholding attributions of knowledge in standard lottery cases reveals a decided resistance on the part of our intuitions to be neatly mathematicized—there is no probability p less than 1 that is sufficiently large such that a true belief with degree p of both objective and subjective probability automatically thereby counts as knowledge.) Despite the best efforts of the likes of Alvin Goldman, IDR has not learned anything from or taught anything to cognitive psychology.

Moreover, IDR runs the risk of being insufficiently progressive. One might worry that our folk epistemology reflects the last few centuries of development in the norms of reasoning and believing, but won't have had a chance to incorporate any lessons learned more recently. For example, it seems that the epistemic intuitions of educated Westerners tend to be very sensitive to even the mere possibility of a belief's turning out false. But, given that modern science's results are so thoroughly lacking in claims to infallibility, those more absolutist intuitions may simply not be up to the job of guiding us in today's epistemic world.

IDR doesn't obviously have to reject minimal naturalism, though at least some practitioners have felt compelled to do so. In BonJour's (1998) defense of rationalism, for example, he is clearly tempted towards a version of non-naturalism in which our minds are somehow in direct contact with such abstract entities as triangularity itself. One can see why there might be a natural supernatural tendency here: it is natural to ask of IDR what explains the truth-conducivity of our intuitive judgments, but it may be hard to give a naturalistically acceptable answer without the consequence that our intuitions can tell us only about our own minds, and not about the norms themselves (Goldman and Pust 1998). So some IDR-practitioners may attempt to opt out of naturalism.

So far, IDR seems to score reasonably well on two desiderata, and somewhat poorly on three others. On the two remaining ones, however, it performs disastrously. Dialectical robustness requires that the evidence we cite to each other be evidence that we can each recognize the force of. But intuitions are damnably subjective. If I have a putative intuition that p, and you have a putative intuition that not-p, there's very little for us to appeal to other than mutual accusations of being captives of our respective theories. (I develop this worry about intuitions and dialectical robustness more thoroughly below, in II.C.)

The problem of varying intuitions also challenges IDR with regard to relativism. IDR practitioners typically invoke 'our' intuitions about a case, yet it is unclear just who 'we' are. For Shaun Nichols, Stephen Stich, and I argue in our (2001) that the intuitions about various cases in the epistemological literature, including Gettier cases and cases central to debates about reliabilism, may vary significantly with ethnicity and socio-economic status. IDR practitioners would have to either find a way of contending that one such group's intuitions are to be privileged over the others, or surrender to some form of epistemic or linguistic relativism. The former of these options remains untaken, and the latter reduces IDR's score on this desideratum. At a minimum, we need an account of why it makes sense for epistemic norms to vary along *these* dimensions, since one would not have expected beforehand that, for example, two native-English-speaking undergraduates from New Jersey *ought* to follow different norms, just because one student's grandparents are from Germany and another's from China. (We do not now have a practice of grading papers with different standards according to ethnicity, for example.)

In sum, IDR scores two hits, three so-so's, and two bad misses. We shall now see whether its chief contemporary rival—metaepistemic naturalism—fares any better.

I.B Metaepistemic naturalism

There are many positions that one could have in mind by the phrase 'naturalized epistemology', but only one of them has been put forward explicitly as a rival methodology to IDR: Hilary Kornblith's theory of knowledge as a natural kind. As he argues in his (2002), we should treat knowledge as a natural kind akin to how we treat water. It has a hidden essence, and we find that essence by seeing what it is that good science makes of it. The best science involving water picks out a substance whose chemical structure is H_2O. Similarly, he argues, the best science involving knowledge—cognitive ethology—picks out beliefs that have been produced by reliable processes. Now, one might accept Kornblith's framework but read the ethological literature differently; or perhaps plump for a different field to defer to, such as psychology or informatics, and thereby potentially get a different analysis of knowledge. Nonetheless, since our concerns here are at the meta-level, we should distinguish the methodological proposal from his intended results of that method.

It is of course unsurprising that *metaepistemic naturalism* (MN) scores highly on minimal naturalism and interdisciplinary comportment. We should grant it a default high rating on truth-conducivity as well, unless we are skeptics about science. MN is probably strong on dialectical robustness, though some recent worries about the objectivity of ethological observation have been raised.[2]

We might raise a concern about the implications MN has for relativism, in that perhaps it is *too* universalistic. Namely, we might worry that it has mistakenly

---

[2] See Allen (forthcoming), for a discussion both of those worries and some responses to them.

conflated our proper epistemic norms with those that might govern chimps or plovers, when our greater cognitive and linguistic capacities, and more sophisticated social organization, might merit a distinct set of norms.

Finally, MN fails miserably on the last two remaining desiderata. MN has the potential for progressivism, but at the risk of extreme radicalism. Juan Comesaña recently proposed to me in conversation, only half in jest, that this kind of naturalism seems to allow that knowledge could turn out to be fried potatoes, but one need not allow for a hypothesis that radical to see that MN might permit our epistemic norms to fall unrecognizably far from the tree of common sense. Steve Crowley (manuscript) has suggested that the notion of knowledge operative in cognitive ethology is one that does not even require truth, in that the notion includes representational states that are too purely action-guiding or too widely distributed across a group of conspecifics to be propositional.

Worst of all, however, is that MN falls down on one of the two most key desiderata: normativity. (This is of course an old complaint against naturalism in epistemology, going back at least to Kim 1988.) Once we've learned what knowledge 'really is' according to science, the question still presents itself as to whether knowledge is something worthy of our pursuit. Kornblith argues for such a value, but his argument is, notably, not itself a matter of scientific inference. Rather, he tries to suggest that knowledge, as revealed to us by ethology, is something that in fact we might find of instrumental value. But there is no guarantee that MN's deliverances will have such a normative dimension. Indeed, MN might not apply at all to more explicitly normative terms in our epistemic repertoire, such as 'justified' or 'rational'.

So MN does not appear to score any better than IDR, and in fact does somewhat worse: three hits, two so-so's, and two bad misses, one of them in the central desideratum of normativity. The poor performance of both of these methods should lead us to pursue other options.

I.C The case for reconstructive neopragmatism

The metaepistemology I am lobbying for is a variety of pragmatism, but it should not be confused with such brute versions of pragmatism that simply flat-out define the epistemic good in some other terms, such as the agreement of our peers (Rorty 1989) or the attainment of whatever we find intrinsically valuable (Stich 1990). I take such views to have been successfully harpooned by Haack (1993), and can be faulted as having given up on the epistemic altogether. My neopragmatism takes a subtler, two-stage approach.

Analytic philosophers typically focus on the conditions for the correct application of a concept, organizing their investigations along the axis of the question, 'What does it take for something to count as an X?' But of course we do not use concepts merely to categorize the world: we deploy those categories to help us make further judgments and generalizations. It is one thing to know that to be neon, it is necessary and sufficient to be a sample of an element with 10 protons. But then the cash value of knowing that something is a sample of neon comes from knowing what having 10 protons further entails about the substance, for example, that it will be a noble gas. If there were no further entailments, we simply would not care to use the concept. (Philosophy is more than lepidoptery of the intellect.) Our interest in philosophical concepts like PERSON or VOLUNTARY is not just to parse the world in such-and-such a way. Rather, we think that persons should be treated differently than non-persons (only they get rights, perhaps), and voluntary actions should be treated differently than involuntary behaviors (only they are morally evaluable, perhaps). We carve up the world for certain descriptive or explanatory or evaluative purposes, and if we wish to understand the role of a certain concept in our lives, we might well ask the question, to what end do we deploy this concept?

Thus, my neopragmatism's method is to ask: *for what purposes* might we reasonably prefer to have beliefs formed in accord with a given epistemic term? For example, why might we choose to evaluate beliefs in terms of the presence or lack of justification, or knowledge, or certainty? Such questions are asked in a normative tone. We are not seeking simply an explanation for our happening to have such preferences: there are probably many such explanations, of a psychological or evolutionary or cultural sort. We want to know why we should on reflection endorse these preferences (and not, say, decide to try to give them up as some distracting cognitive habit, a tic of the mind). Our question is: why ought we include such dimensions in our epistemic appraisals? To ask such questions is an attempt (in James's terms) to 'pump free air' around a given concept, and try to get a sense of how it fits into our epistemic lives on the whole. Should we be able to harmonize such a teleological view of a concept with the traditional attributional view, we would thereby attain a deeper understanding.

This teleological maneuver is also not unprecedented in epistemology itself. Here's a lovely and compact statement of it, with a bit of analysis:

If the epistemic concepts can earn an honest living they must form a natural intellectual kind. Even if some multi-part analysis accurately matched our judgments in difficult cases, it would still need asking why we are interested in just *that* set of conditions.... But how can it be important to organize our lives around one complex of conditions rather than another? We need a role for the epistemic concepts, and the role which seems most natural is that of ranking and selecting titles to respect. We have to pick up our beliefs about the world from our senses and from each other. So we need a vocabulary to settle whether our sources are ones which themselves properly indicate the truth. This is a natural need, and it gives us the natural intellectual kind in which to place our epistemic verdicts. (Blackburn 1984: 169–70)

Blackburn is clearly dissatisfied with IDR here, when he questions our interest in having a successful descriptive account of our attributions. He wants to defend a concern for truth in our epistemic attributions, and he appeals to our desire to be able to categorize our doxastic sources with respect to their reliability. The passage also brings out the sense in which we can ask the question, 'Why do we care about knowledge?' in a manner that is not merely a psychological inquiry. The question is not, 'What underlies our mental pro-attitude towards knowledge?' but, more importantly, 'What role does the concept of knowledge play in organizing our lives?' (The question generalizes to other terms of epistemic appraisal.)

But we want to provide a more thorough analysis than can be supported in the one-paragraph form just quoted. We require not just a maneuver, but a method. We need a tool for organizing an investigation into the purposes of our epistemic norms, something to play the role for a teleological analysis that analysis-by-cases plays for attributional analysis. Fortunately, Edward Craig has recently given us a full-scale attempt at just such a methodology. In his *Knowledge and the State of Nature*, he expresses a similar dissatisfaction with the attribution-prediction type of project. Even were we to produce a successful version of such an analysis, he argues (1990: 2),

> I should like [that analysis] to be seen as a prolegomenon to a further inquiry: why has a concept demarcated by those conditions enjoyed such widespread use? There seems to be no known language in which sentences using 'know' do not find a comfortable and colloquial equivalent. The implication is that it answers to some very general needs of human life and thought, and it would surely be interesting to know which and how. . . .
>
> Instead of beginning with ordinary usage, we begin with an ordinary situation. We take some prima facie plausible hypothesis about what the concept of knowledge does for us, what its role in our life might be, and then ask what a concept having that role would be like, what conditions would govern its application.

Craig invokes the 'state of nature' framework in social contractarian political philosophy (hence his title). Where Locke et al. concerned themselves with our basic social needs of cooperation and security, Craig concerns himself with the basic epistemic need of telling whose testimony can be trusted and whose discounted. If we are to understand how our political and epistemic institutions ought to be structured, we should consider for what human purposes these institutions might have been founded in the first place.

I am extremely sympathetic to this framework, and am greatly indebted to Craig in what will follow.[3] But I have one significant difference in my choice of methodology here. For the 'state of nature' metaphor is fundamentally history-oriented. For example, it seems somewhat hostage to arguments about the actual past origins of the relevant institutions and practices. Moreover, the 'state of nature' approach assumes that our relevant human needs today are basically the same as they were back at the time of the mythological founding of our political or epistemic institutions and practices. Our more basic and biological needs probably are more or less unchanged; however, the epochal shifts in our social structures

---

[3] Ram Neta (forthcoming) makes a similar metaepistemological appeal, though towards different epistemological results, to Craig's work.

and base of knowledge over the last few centuries have changed what we want from the political and the epistemic. It could be argued that in the political realm, citizens have begun to require that the state become something stronger than just a guarantor of personal safety and property rights, and transform into a proactive agent for positive change and social justice. And clearly our demands in the epistemic realm have changed, becoming more tolerant of probability and less obsessed with certainty, less suspicious of testimony, and more suited towards socially cooperative investigations. Given such historical and ongoing developments, it could be unwise to attend too closely to the past conditions imagined in any analysis-by-state-of-nature.

In order to retain the teleological viewpoint forwarded by Craig, while avoiding the potentially historical biases of a state-of-nature approach, let me invoke instead a framework of analysis-by-imagined-reconstruction.[4] My operative question will be: were we to consider a radical re-constitution of our epistemic norms, what would we include, what might we strengthen, and what might we abandon as outmoded?

An analogy may help. Many modern societies' political norms are to an important extent encoded in their constitutions. And by and large questions of political acceptability can be simply referred to that document, with perhaps some consideration of the 'original intent' of its composers. But, significantly, a society also retains the capacity to amend that constitution, or, if necessary, to call a new constitutional convention. Such foundational changes are sometimes necessary, because changing conditions render the original document less well-suited to performing its function. A society can consider altering existing structures (for example, expanding the franchise to include African-Americans or women or 18-year-olds); introducing new norms (prohibiting the sale of alcohol; permitting a national income tax); or eliminating existing norms (repealing such a prohibition).

The epistemic world has changed continually as well. Early modern thinkers had scientific models and mathematical tools available to them unknown to the ancients. Since the early days of science, as Ian Hacking has documented in his (1990), it has been a slow path by which statistical reasoning came to be accepted as a source of knowledge. And our growing (if still nascent) science of the inner workings of human cognition, and the chunky realism about mental mechanisms underlying our behavior that it requires, raises the question of the epistemic status of those faculties.

The objection might be offered at this point that, to perform an analysis-by-imagined-reconstruction on our epistemic norms, we would have to imagine ourselves in some sort of Archimedean point outside of the norms themselves. And how could a rational outcome arrive from beyond our norms? Bealer argues in his (1998) that we cannot construe as rational any radical rejection of our 'standard

---

⁴ I intend this as more a friendly variant on, than a rival to, Craig's framework.

justificatory practices', since to reject those practices wholesale would be to reject the epistemic itself. One cannot step outside the realm of justification altogether and have a justified theory of that domain. I will grant the argument, because the sorts of critical revision of our epistemic institutions I am proposing do not require us to stand utterly outside of our standard justificatory practices. For those practices themselves include the means for reflection upon them. It is part of our standard practices to evaluate and re-evaluate our norms and procedures. (That is what philosophy is for, one might say.) It is for that reason that we no longer use trial by ordeal in our legal system, and we do now allow for the legitimacy of some probabilistic forms of inference while relying far less on appeal to Church authority in scientific matters.

So, how does this form of neopragmatism—I will call it *reconstructive neopragmatism* (RN)—score according to our desiderata? It is comparable to IDR and MN with regard to truth-conduciveness, in that only a skeptic would deny our ability to examine our goals and evaluate what rules would promote them. Normativity is also obviously satisfied, and there is no obvious conflict with minimal naturalism. The reconstructive element accommodates progressivism, in that it allows for the possibility that the norms developed in the past may not be the best for our future; at the same time, radicalism is only possible if we are currently deeply wrong about our goals and what would promote them. And interdisciplinary comportment is guaranteed as well, since we will recruit psychological and social science to aid in our norm engineering.

RN's status on dialectical robustness and relativism is a bit trickier, because of the question of what our epistemic goals are. Once some set of epistemic goals is fixed, there is no worry about the robustness of our discussions about how best to satisfy those goals, for we have ample experience with such means–ends reasoning. And we may reasonably expect significant agreement about those goals—the acquisition of true beliefs, for example. Yet there may be irresolvable disagreement about other of the basic goals themselves.[5] Under such circumstances, RN would admit of a degree of relativism as well, as different epistemic goals will generate different norms. But I hope that this limited relativism will seem plausible: if two groups truly wanted fundamentally distinct things for and from their beliefs, then perhaps it is appropriate for them to be governed by divergent rules. Moreover, that relativism about ultimate epistemic goals mitigates the worry about stubborn disputes concerning those goals. Where fruitful discourse cannot solve disputes about goals, relativization can dissolve them.

So, at worst, RN gets a solid rating on five of the desiderata, with a mixed rating on the last two. Compared to the poorer-scoring IDR and MN, RN promises hope for the future of epistemology. The rest of this chapter will aim at showing how we might begin to fulfill that promise.

---

[5] There are other possible moves—one could perhaps argue that only one set of goals is truly epistemic—but I will not canvass them here.

II. RECONSTRUCTIVE NEOPRAGMATISM,
INTERNALISM, AND THE A PRIORI

The best argument for the viability of RN, and the only way to show that our hopes for it are not in vain, is to demonstrate it in action. I will do so here by applying this method to a connected pair of central epistemological topics: the internalism/externalism debate about epistemic justification, and the question of the existence and extent of a priori justification.

II.A What is justification for?

Since we are applying the RN methodology here, we shall address the issue of internalism/externalism not through intuition-mongering, but rather by asking: why should we care about our beliefs' having justification, instead of only caring about whether a belief is simply true or false? One can find in the literature at least two basic reasons we might want our beliefs to be justified in addition to being merely true. In a nutshell, they are *diachronic reliability* and *dialectical robustness*. (One may feel a bit of déjà vu from Part I; but it should not be surprising that two metaepistemological desiderata should also resemble two desiderata for justification itself.) I will call these the 'DR desiderata'. Let me articulate them here, and then discuss how they relate to this issue.

First, suppose that you were about to make a momentous, life-changing, potentially life-ending decision. You have no time for reflection or research, but must instead decide immediately. Which would you prefer to have guiding your actions at that moment: a belief-set that is mostly true but generally unjustified, or a belief-set that is mostly justified but generally false? Prudence prefers the former—all the justification in the world comes to naught if you make the wrong decision, and without further reflection it is the current actual truth or falsity of your beliefs that will determine the outcome of your action.

Thankfully, we are rarely in such circumstances (except, perhaps, whenever we cross the street). Rather, when confronted by a decision of any importance, we can seek out further relevant evidence for our choice. But then we want to be sure that we make any and all appropriate revisions to our belief-set as a result of this information-harvesting. At this point justification becomes key. If we are able to trace the rational relations amongst our original beliefs, and between those beliefs and the new evidence, then we can adjust our doxastic condition, re-apportioning our epistemic resources as needed. This is not doxastic voluntarism, but just our ability to refocus our concentration and redirect our investigations. As our awareness of the facts changes, or when the facts themselves change, we want our beliefs to change with them, and the justificatory links between our beliefs are the channels along which such changes can rationally propagate. This desire for our beliefs to have this kind of across-time accuracy is one good reason to desire justification for our beliefs.

We also desire that we be able to integrate our beliefs with those of others. Polonius tells Laertes neither a borrower nor a lender be; but *pace* such epistemic Polonii as Descartes, we borrow and lend each other's cognitive abilities, expertise, and information all the time. Our intellectual lives would be hopelessly impoverished otherwise, to our personal and collective detriment.[6] In seeking out others' testimony we require that we interweave their beliefs with our own. If two heads are truly better than one, then the outputs of each pair of eyes and ears had better be able to find their way into the other pair's cranium, and vice versa. And this process of informational exchange needs to be harmonious. By establishing such processes, you and I can form a community of cognizers, and can avail ourselves of an epistemic division of labor and investigate together, as a 'we', the nature of our world. To do so requires something more than just being willing to take others' testimony at its face, for we need also a way to resolve conflicting testimonies between co-investigators.

Here, I would argue, justification plays an important role. Each of the various contestants must put forward her justifications for her claims, which can then be interrogated by the other contestants. We can use the overall quality of their various justifications as a criterion for making our choice between contrary theories, each of us deciding which theory is the most justified so that each can believe it herself. To the extent that we all opt for the same theory, we can be said to have come to believe it, ideally. But even if none of us are able to change each other's minds, the next generation of graduate students will be able to make those judgments, and vote with their feet. Norms of justification are also required to distinguish between legitimate and unwarranted challenges to a theory, and sufficient and insufficient responses to the legitimate challenges. Our justificatory practices should provide an infrastructure for our investigative communities. We thus further desire, in addition to general reliability, that our epistemic practices be *dialectically robust*.

So our justificatory norms ought to promote diachronic reliability and dialectical robustness: the DR desiderata. There may be other key desiderata for justification, and I would welcome anyone's making the case for such. But I trust that they are sufficiently central that we will not acquire too distorted a picture of our justificatory norms, if we view them through the lens of only those two values.

Having articulated two of our purposes in having norms of justification, we can next attend to what epistemic principles do, or do not, follow from them. It might very reasonably be asked first, though, whether these two values exhaust our epistemic desiderata. I grant that we will probably have other values that should be expressed in our justificatory norms. Indeed, I in no way intend these arguments to be considered the final stage of a pragmatist analysis of justification, but very much a first step. This method can work only by engaging in serious discussion about what our ultimate epistemic desiderata really are, and one can accept

---

[6] See various essays in Schmitt (1994*a*), including Solomon (1994), Gilbert (1994), and Schmitt (1994*b*); it is also a theme sounded in Alston (1989), Craig (1990), and Sosa (1991).

everything I have said up to this point and still get different results, if different epistemic goals are put forward. Nonetheless, diachronic reliability and dialectical robustness are clearly very central desiderata for our norms of justification, so I do not believe that we will acquire too distorted a picture of our justificatory norms if we view them through the lens of only those two values.

With the DR desiderata for justification in sight, the appeal of a version of internalism becomes clear. It will generally serve the DR desiderata for agents to be able to tell, by means of reflection or introspection, what the sources of justification for their various beliefs are. If we wish to maximize diachronic reliability, it will often be useful for us to be aware of possible evidential grounds of our beliefs (for example, BonJour 1985; Moser 1985). Holding beliefs on the basis of conscious reasons, or at least being able to provide such reasons upon reflection, allows an agent to direct her own investigations on relevant sources of evidence she does not yet have. She can take conscious control of her doxastic life, and apportion her resources as she sees fit.

Moreover, the agent will be able to take better advantage of information that crosses her path unexpectedly. Suppose that she believes on her brother's say-so that Microsoft stock is doomed to crash, but later learns to her surprise that her otherwise well-informed brother has been radically misled about matters of economics and computers. She can attempt to adjust her doxastic state accordingly, by reading *Fortune* and listening to 'Marketplace', and changing the topic whenever her brother brings up Bill Gates. Hopefully by doing so, she can ultimately replace any significantly false beliefs about that company with more accurate ones. Or, should she in the end concur with her Apple-loving sibling, she will do so in a way that keeps her in touch with the facts: if her justification is internally accessible, then, should she learn that Microsoft's situation has altered in ways relevant to the justificatory anchors of her belief, she can commence a new investigatory cycle.

Furthermore, it is in general the case that only epistemically available reasons for beliefs can be put into public discourse. As Gilbert writes in her (1994), our ability to investigate and to know as a community depends on our capacity for a 'joint commitment' (246) to the terms of the investigation: each member must acknowledge an obligation to each other member to uphold those terms, and further expects that each other member is similarly obligated to her. The group can accept some proposition as a group only if each member can be explicitly committed to that acceptance, and recognize others' acceptance. So such commitments must be a public affair, that each member can see that they are being upheld by the others, and can indicate that she herself is upholding them. Of course, we can more easily make others aware of such acceptances and commitments when we ourselves are aware of them. Therefore, internalistically-accessible justifications will best subserve this role of maintaining joint investigative commitments.

Our success as an epistemic community will also depend on our mutually co-adjusting our beliefs. If I will not change my mind no matter what you say, and you are equally cognitively stubborn, then we can merely co-exist as cognizers, not truly cooperating. As individual organisms we each possess unconscious mechanisms for belief adjustment, but the deliberations of the investigative community require a more public medium. We must be able to make our justifications visible to each other, but if you are not aware of the grounds of your belief, then you cannot cite them to me. And, when we can put our reasons out into public discourse, they can be confronted by the good reasons of others, and themselves confront the bad reasons of others, thus increasing our ability to achieve a harmonious set of community beliefs.

So the DR desiderata motivate some internalism in our neopragmatist analysis of epistemic justification. We should place great value on an agent's capacity to have, within her reflective and introspective grasp, awareness of her bases of justification, and to be able to express that grasp to her fellow agents.[7] But much of the internalism/externalism debate in epistemology revolves around whether our norms require that an agent have this accessibility to what makes her beliefs justified. Paradigm 'externalist' authors have usually been willing to grant, at least, that there is some value to consciously-held justification,[8] but have insisted that we can also have justification beyond the scope of our introspective capacities. So we should next ask whether the DR desiderata can also motivate an *absolutely* internalist constraint on justification, or only something more limited. Ought we impose an exceptionless internal-accessibility clause as a necessary condition on justification?

Our neopragmatism suggests that we should ask whether instituting the norm of such a necessary condition would create favorable circumstances for achieving the DR desiderata. Any proposed strict constraint must satisfy two criteria: (i) it must not place so onerous a burden on our cognition that too little of our epistemic lives can be sustained, and (ii) whatever beliefs and inferences do pass through must be appropriately DR-promoting. If a proposed constraint fails either condition, then it is inconsistent with our DR interests and should thus be weakened.

II.B Why strict internalism won't get us what we want

If a strict internalism is to be observed, then the source of epistemic justification must be available to introspection and/or reflection. We can divide the set of candidate internally-available sources in three: (a) the processes by which the belief was formed, or inference performed; (b) the belief or inference itself; and (c) some internally-available mental entity distinct from the target belief or inference. We must now consider whether our minds in fact have enough internally-available

---

[7] The exact forms of acceptable reasons may be much broader than asserted propositions. Under many circumstances, simply pointing in the right direction may constitute a sufficient public reason.

[8] Cf. Goldman's willingness in his (1979) to accommodate the intuition that improper use of consciously-held evidence can disable the justification he thinks a reliable process can otherwise confer.

material, and indeed material of the DR-promoting sort, that would license a strict internalism. If not, then we must be willing to give up that kind of constraint as inconsistent with our epistemic values. If a norm rules most or all of our beliefs as unacceptable, then it will not help us achieve any lasting truth for our beliefs; if a norm silences all or most of our statements to each other, then it will not aid the smooth conduct of our conversations.

First, might our psychological processes be sufficiently open to the inner eye to be considered internally available? This question clearly has a large contingent component, concerning our actual psychological make-up. And indeed the transparency of the mental has seemed a tempting thesis at times in the history of the philosophy of mind. Actually looking at the empirical literature, however, leads one to suspect that there is no comfort for the internalist here. We have overwhelming evidence that many basic cognitive mechanisms are predominantly unconscious. I will rely here on an *argumentum ex bibliographia*, listing a few paradigm references from the rather vast literatures here. Nisbett and Wilson (1977) launched the notion that humans are simply hopeless at telling what kinds of psychological processes underwrite their own reasoning. Going back at least to Helmholtz, psychologists have seen the conscious component of visual perception as representing a very slim portion of perceptual processing (for example, Crick and Koch 2000). Researchers such as Evans and Over (1996) and Sloman (1996) investigating deductive reasoning have argued for a 'dual process' theory: an unconscious, preattentive filtering process selects only certain possibilities as salient to the problem at hand, which it feeds to our conscious, analytic processes. Those latter processes cannot function properly when the former do not. Inductive reasoning is even more unconscious; Reber contends in his (1993) that not only do we learn various sorts of contingent correlations better implicitly than consciously, but also subjects provided with explicit hints about the correlation to be uncovered perform worse than subjects relying on more purely unconscious forms of learning! Our epistemic capacities in various domains from basic physics (Spelke 1990; Leslie 1982) to psychology (Premack 1990; Scholl and Leslie 1999) to morality (Shweder and Haidt 1993; Cummins 1996; Darley and Shultz 1990) appear to depend crucially on unconscious processes, whose workings are closed to the very subjects who are deploying them. Empirical scientific investigation builds upon our ability to theorize about natural kinds, which is rooted in a brute capacity for biological essentialism (Atran 1990; Keil 1989).

What about the belief or inference itself, as an internalist source of justification? Do we sometimes have a self-recommending component in our phenomenology, in which certain beliefs or inferences just strike us as necessary, or at least appropriate and credible? A positive answer to that question is not enough: such intuitive cognitions must also be of sufficient number and scope to provide the requisite internal buttressing to our otherwise unconscious cognitive infrastructure. I will grant here, for the sake of argument, that beliefs based directly on perception and memory have an appropriately phenomenological quality. But clearly those two sources of justification, as centrally important as they are, cannot pull all the weight of our cognition about the world. A vast proportion of our beliefs are about the unobserved (such as the future, or unsurveyable universal generalizations), or even unobservable (such as theoretic constructs or ethical principles). A strict internalism will require still further raw materials from within our introspective purview.

Intuitionists such as Bealer or BonJour have generally focused on the existence and cogency of rational intuition (or, in BonJour's terms, 'rational insight'). They have taken as their opponents the radical empiricist who would deny that we have any such completely non-perceptual forms of justification. I think their arguments are generally sound; I too would endorse a substantive category of the a priori (see below). But the question at hand is whether a strict internalism makes sufficient room for justified cognition, or whether instead it presents in fact too small a lot upon which to build cognition's house. If intuitionist internalism is to succeed, it must also address this further issue of not just the cogency but moreover the sufficiency of rational intuition.

And here I fear that they run aground. Perhaps we do have some such intuitions, in which the propositions have a phenomenology of rational compulsion—one of Bealer's favorite examples is DeMorgan's Laws. But these cases only go so far, and do not extend much beyond certain simple forms of deductive and mathematical reasoning. Not even all of those forms are generally available: the great majority of subjects do not recognize the validity of instances of *modus tollens*, for example. And our intuitive powers are especially weak in the domain of non-deductive inferences. BonJour strives valiantly in his (1998) to formulate a principle of induction that elicits this phenomenology, but they lack (for me, at least) that sense of rational necessity.[9]

Moreover, many propositions that have this phenomenological glow about them are just not the right kind. Our actual inductive intuitions are generally a mess, for example. Indeed, instances of the gambler's fallacy seem more compelling on their face than any formulation of a proper principle of induction (Garnham and Oakhill 1994)! Again, I am not arguing from the existence of such undesirable intuitions that we can never rely on intuitions; rather, I am claiming that we might not want to rest the entire weight of a priori justification upon them.

[9] Here's one such allegedly intuitive principle of induction in question: 'In a situation in which a standard inductive premise obtains, it is highly likely that there is some explanation (other than mere coincidence or chance) for the convergence and constancy of the observed proportion (and the more likely, the larger the number of cases in question)' (BonJour 1998: 208). Does this proposition really present us with the sort of luminous phenomenology that the intuitionist requires? It does strike me as a plausible sort of thing to believe, but of course most of the things we believe will strike us as such. And rational intuition ought, one would think, to have higher standards than just that very ordinary and ubiquitous appearance of *prima facie* plausibility. Otherwise, relying on it would not help us promote our DR goals—almost all our beliefs would be 'intuitive', so the internalist constraint would be trivially satisfiable. But see my discussion of the 'Global Justifier' argument below for reasons why such a trivial internalist constraint is worse than no internalist constraint at all.

I do not doubt that BonJour is sincere in his declaration that his formulations strike him as 'sufficiently obvious to require little discussion' (BonJour 1998: 208). I similarly do not doubt Bealer, when he claims in his (1996) to have a rational intuition to the effect that intuition is a good source of evidence. But again I do not find myself sharing the intuition. I take this divergence to be emblematic of a more general lack of phenomenological univocity, which points to a further difficulty with appealing to intuitions. As discussed earlier in the context of the case against IDR, we lack good tools to resolve conflicts in intuition. So not only are our intuitions insufficient in number and scope, and frequently inconsistent with diachronic reliability, but also a reliance on intuition would be deleterious to dialectical robustness as well. The internalist needs to argue that we can take the epistemic weight off of our tacit processes and place it on an introspectively-available structure. But given how massive that epistemic architecture is, intuition simply presents too thin a dialectical reed.

Another internalist strategy, which we might term inferentialism, seeks to find an argument to the conclusion that the outputs of our tacit psychological processes are rational and/or reliable. I have no doubt that some philosophers can make such a case, though it will not be a simple matter, given the presence in the literature of many arguments to the contrary (for example, Stein 1996), and it is indeed hard to see how it could be done noncircularly.[10] But put such concerns aside. What I question, however, is the relevance of such an argument to the issue at hand. For if such arguments are only available to the trained philosopher, then this strategy would entail that only we philosophers can have justified beliefs! I am here following Goldman (1999: 13), who has argued recently that '[i]t is very unlikely that someone who has never studied philosophy could produce a satisfactory justification for the reliability of his inductive or deductive inference procedures. To conclude from this, however, that ordinary, philosophically untrained people have no inferential warrant would be a dramatic capitulation to skepticism.' In our terms here, it would be a complete surrender of the DR desiderata. Surely it would be nice for everyone to be able to consciously defend their unconscious cognition. But it cannot, given the DR desiderata and the sorts of limited creatures we are, be an epistemic necessity.

Note that I am not suggesting that it is a problem that ordinary folks in general cannot, as a matter of epistemological principle, form an argument to the effect that they have epistemically successful faculties of non-empirical cognition without depending on such faculties in the argument. It is not obvious that the defender of a strict internalist condition needs to take on such baggage, which seems to require something tendentious like a JJ principle. What I am suggesting simply is that ordinary folks in general cannot, as a matter of psychological fact, form such an argument at all.

The internalist might try to reply that, even if most ordinary folks are utterly unprepared to argue for the epistemic success of their non-empirical cognitive

---

[10] Cf. the exchange between Boghossian (2003) and Williamson (2003).

faculties in particular, nonetheless they are surely capable of launching a general defense of their own cognitive capability. They could observe that they are basically successful in navigating the world—they do not (usually) walk into walls, or forget to come in out of the rain, and so on—and then they could take this success as evidence that they are at least moderately decent believers. A fortiori they could conclude that they are at least moderately successful in their non-empirically-based cognition. Call such an argument the 'Global Justifier' argument.[11]

But such an internalist reply would allow the ordinary folk to prove too much, and render the internalist constraint useless. I have been arguing that we would not want too strong a constraint, lest we place justification beyond the reach of most if not all humans. But we also have no use for too weak a constraint. Recall that the motivation for an internalist constraint was to require agents to remain in close cognitive contact with their specific sources of justification, such as our earlier example of the woman with the Microsoft-impaired brother. Internalism would not help her, if by relying on the Global Justifier she could satisfy the constraint without thereby improving her doxastic state, as measured by the DR desiderata. If all agents could make use of one big argument that justified all of their cognitive activity, then the original motivations for an internalist constraint would be vitiated. So we cannot allow merely possessing or deploying the Global Justifier argument to be sufficient for the justification of all of one's beliefs. To do so would be inconsistent with our goals in setting forth epistemic norms. Just as we must avoid setting the justificatory bar too high, lest no beliefs pass, we must also eschew placing it too low, lest all beliefs pass, without regard for whether they are the sorts of beliefs that the DR desiderata would have us promote.

II.C Prospects for a less-strict internalism

So at the end of day we will not be able to endorse a strict internalist constraint on justification: none of the three possible avenues of justification are sufficient, or sufficiently internalistically-acceptable. Our justificatory norms must allow some significant loophole by which enough of the beliefs produced by our unconscious cognitive infrastructure can be allowed to pass, even when introspection and reflection prove unable to produce for us any reasons for holding them. At the same time, we cannot allow ourselves in general to hold beliefs on no reason at all, merely because no reasons are forthcoming. A lack of reasons can hardly itself be a reason for holding a belief! That would be a sort of epistemic suicide, and would fail the DR desiderata as badly as strict internalism does. Rather, we require that the DR motivations still be addressed. Under what conditions can X's true-but-brute belief that p still comport with our desired diachronic reliability and dialectical robustness?

---

[11] Keith Lehrer in his (1997) seems to present something like this argument, when he invites us to accept that we are generally worthy of our own self-trust.

First, if the fact of whether-or-not-p were itself unlikely to change, at least in any environment X has any chance of finding herself in, then we needn't worry about X maintaining true p-beliefs over time. If p's truth is not at all variable, then it won't be hard to track that truth. It must also be unlikely that X will ever come across evidence against p, either, since without further reasons for p, such evidence should ideally compel her away from her initial belief. So X has less of a need for consciously-available evidence for p, since her right belief will not be subject to the epistemic vagaries of more changeable facts. Diachronic reliability would be guaranteed. When such conditions are met, let us call a belief that p *epistemically stable*.

Second, if most everyone else in X's epistemic community is also endowed with a similarly true-but-brute belief that p, then there will be no difficulty in integrating X's p-belief with her co-investigators'. X is unlikely to be challenged about her belief that p, since everyone else holds that belief as well, and so X has no need for any internally-accessible defense of p. Thus, under such conditions, dialectical robustness is not threatened by the absence of citable reasons. When this condition is met, we can consider a belief that p is *epistemically universal*.

So epistemic stability and universality together provide a sketch of a good candidate for the principled loophole we need in any internalist constraints on justification. These are generally rare doxastic properties, but rather common in an epistemic domain of great epistemological interest: the a priori. Epistemic stability and universality are easily found in such paradigm domains of a priori justification as arithmetic. That domain is clearly quite stable, since its truths are necessary; and we have been fortunate in that arithmetical dissention occurs extremely rarely. Indeed, necessity is a traditional hallmark of the a priori, and necessity entails epistemic stability; and going as far back as Plato, and still more recently (for example, Antony 2004), innateness has been cited as a sign of the a priori. So, even though rationalists might have thought themselves naturally allied with intuition-based methodologies, our reconstructive approach has revealed perhaps a closer relationship between rationalism and neopragmatism. In the areas in which we most clearly wish to claim a priori justification, our neopragmatist considerations suggest that we least clearly need to insist on imposing internalist strictures on that justification. (One might wonder, though, whether the results cited above might indicate that philosophy itself demonstrates insufficient universality as a domain for such exemption.)

III. CONCLUSION

We began by considering possible good-making features for a method in epistemology, and saw that reconstructive naturalism might be more desirable than either intuition-driven romanticism or metaepistemic naturalism. We applied RN to our norms of justification, and posited two general purposes for justificatory norms, diachronic reliability and dialectical robustness. These DR desiderata in turn motivated a general internalist constraint on justification. However, our best reasons for postulating the category of the a priori in the first place turned out to allow, perhaps even require, room for externalist sources of justification as well, in the special case of a priori knowledge. We can thus see how, on such age-old topics as internalism and rationalism, RN makes new positions available, and, moreover, provides a new way to make a case for such positions. By asking what we want from our epistemology, reconstructive naturalism can give us more of what we want from our metaepistemology as well.

REFERENCES

Allen, C. (forthcoming). 'Is Anyone a Cognitive Ethologist?' *Biology and Philosophy*.

Alston, W. (1989). *Epistemic Justification: Essays in the Theory of Knowledge*. Ithaca, NY: Cornell University Press.

Antony, L. (2004). 'A Naturalized Approach to the *A Priori*'. *Philosophical Issues*, 14: 1–17.

Atran, S. (1990). *Cognitive Foundations of Natural History: Trends in the Anthropology of Science*. Cambridge: Cambridge University Press.

Bealer, G. (1996). '*A Priori* Knowledge and the Scope of Philosophy'. *Philosophical Studies*, 81: 121–42.

—— (1998). 'Intuition and the Autonomy of Philosophy', in DePaul and Ramsey (1998), 201–39.

Blackburn, S. (1984). 'Knowledge, Truth, and Reliability'. *Proceedings of the British Academy*, 70: 167–87.

Boghossian, P. (2003). 'Blind Reasoning'. *Supplement to the Proceedings of The Aristotelian Society*, 77: 225–48.

BonJour, L. (1980). 'Externalist Theories of Empirical Knowledge'. *Midwest Studies in Philosophy*, 5: 53–73.

—— (1985). *The Structure of Empirical Knowledge*. Cambridge, Mass.: Harvard University Press.

—— (1998). *In Defense of Pure Reason: A Rationalist Account of* A Priori *Justification*. Cambridge: Cambridge University Press.

Craig, E. (1990). *Knowledge and the State of Nature: An Essay in Conceptual Synthesis*. Oxford: Clarendon Press.

Crick, F., and Koch, C. (2000). 'The Unconscious Homunculus', in T. Metzinger (ed.), *The Neuronal Correlates of Consciousness: Empirical and Conceptual Questions*. Cambridge, Mass.: MIT Press, 103–10.

Crowley, S. (manuscript). 'An Inadequate Epistemology of Animal Cognition'.

Cummins, D. (1996). 'Evidence For the Innateness of Deontic Reasoning'. *Mind and Language*, 11: 160–90.

Cummins, R. (1998). 'Reflections on Reflective Equilibrium', in DePaul and Ramsey (1998), 113–27.

Darley, J., and Shultz, T. (1990). 'Moral Rules: Their Content and Acquisition'. *Annual Review of Psychology*, 4: 523–56.

DePaul, M., and Ramsey, W. (eds.) (1998). *Rethinking Intuition: The Psychology of Intuition and Its Role in Philosophical Inquiry*. Lanham, MD: Rowman & Littlefield.

Evans, J. St.B., and Over, D. (1996). *Rationality and Reasoning*. Hove, UK: Erlbaum.

Fumerton, R. (1988). 'The Internalism/Externalism Controversy', in J. Tomberlin (ed.), *Philosophical Perspectives, 2: Epistemology*. Atascadero, Calif.: Ridgeview Publishing, 443–59.

Garnham, A., and Oakhill, J. (1994). *Thinking and Reasoning*. Oxford: Blackwell.

Gilbert, M. (1994). 'Remarks on Collective Belief', in Schmitt (1994a), 235–56.

Goldman, A. (1979). 'What is Justified Belief?', in G. S. Pappas (ed.), *Justification and Knowledge: New Studies in Epistemology*. Dordrecht: D. Reidel, 1–23.

—— (1999). 'A Priori Warrant and Naturalistic Epistemology', in J. Tomberlin (ed.), *Philosophical Perspectives, 13: Epistemology*. Oxford: Blackwell, 1–28.

—— and Pust, J. (1998). 'Philosophical Theory and Intuitional Evidence', in DePaul and Ramsey (1998), 179–97.

Greco, J. (1999). 'Agent Reliabilism', in J. Tomberlin (ed.), *Philosophical Perspectives, 13: Epistemology*. Oxford: Blackwell, 273–96.

Haack, S. (1993). *Evidence and Inquiry: Towards Reconstruction in Epistemology*. Oxford: Blackwell.

Hacking, I. (1990). *The Taming of Chance*. Cambridge: Cambridge University Press.

Hintikka, J. (1999). 'The Emperor's New Intuitions'. *Journal of Philosophy*, 96: 127–47.

Jackson, F. (1998). *From Metaphysics to Ethics: A Defence of Conceptual Analysis*. Oxford: Clarendon Press.

Katz, J. (1998). *Realistic Rationalism*. Cambridge, Mass.: MIT Press.

Keil, F. (1989). *Concepts, Kinds, and Cognitive Development*. Cambridge, Mass.: MIT Press.

Kim, J. (1988). 'What is "Naturalized Epistemology?" ', in J. Tomberlin (ed.), *Philosophical Perspectives, 2: Epistemology*. Atascadero, Calif.: Ridgeview Publishing, 381–406.

Kornblith, H. (2002). *Knowledge and Its Place in Nature*. Oxford: Clarendon Press.

Lehrer, K. (1997). *Self-Trust: A Study of Reason, Knowledge, and Autonomy*. Oxford: Clarendon Press.

Leslie, A. (1982). 'The Perception of Causality in Infants'. *Perception*, 11: 173–86.

Machery, E., Mallon, R., Nichols, S., and Stich, S. (2004). 'Semantics, Cross-Cultural Style'. *Cognition*, 92: B1–B12.

Moser, P. (1985). *Empirical Justification*. Dordrecht: D. Reidel.

Neta, R. (forthcoming). 'Epistemology Factualized: New Contractarian Foundations for Epistemology'. *Synthese*.

Nichols, S., Stich, S., and Weinberg, J. (2003). 'Metaskepticism: Meditations in Ethno-epistemology', in S. Luper (ed.), *The Skeptics: Contemporary Essays*. Burlington, VT: Ashgate, 227–47.

Nisbett, R., and Wilson, T. (1977). 'Telling More Than We Can Know: Verbal Reports on Mental Processes'. *Psychological Review*, 84: 231–95.

Plantinga, A. (1993). *Warrant and Proper Function*. New York: Oxford University Press.

Premack, D. (1990). 'The Infant's Theory of Self-Propelled Objects'. *Cognition*, 36: 1–16.

Pust, J. (2000). *Intuitions as Evidence*. New York: Garland Publishing.

Reber, A. (1993). *Implicit Learning and Tacit Knowledge: An Essay on the Cognitive Unconscious*. New York: Oxford University Press.

Rorty, R. (1989). *Contingency, Irony, and Solidarity*. Cambridge: Cambridge University Press.

Schmitt, F. (ed.) (1994a). *Socializing Epistemology: The Social Dimensions of Knowledge*. Lanham, MD: Rowman & Littlefield.

—— (1994*b*). 'The Justification of Group Beliefs', in Schmitt (1994*a*), 257–88.

Scholl, B., and Leslie, A. (1999). 'Modularity, Development and "Theory of Mind"'. *Mind and Language*, 14: 131–53.

Shweder, R., and Haidt, J. (1993). 'The Future of Moral Psychology: Truth, Intuition, and the Pluralist Way'. *Psychological Science*, 4: 360–5.

Sloman, S. (1996). 'The Empirical Case for Two Systems of Reasoning'. *Psychological Bulletin*, 119: 3–22.

Solomon, M. (1994). 'A More Social Epistemology', in Schmitt (1994*a*), 217–34.

Sosa, E. (1991). *Knowledge in Perspective: Selected Essays in Epistemology.* Cambridge: Cambridge University Press.

—— (forthcoming). 'A Defense of the Use of Intuitions in Philosophy', in M. Bishop and D. Murphy (eds.), *Stich and His Critics.* Oxford: Blackwell.

Spelke, E. (1990). 'Principles of Object Perception'. *Cognitive Science*, 14: 29–56.

Stein, E. (1996). *Without Good Reason: The Rationality Debate in Philosophy and Cognitive Science.* Oxford: Clarendon Press.

Stich, S. (1990). *The Fragmentation of Reason: Preface to a Pragmatic Theory of Cognitive Evaluation.* Cambridge, Mass.: MIT Press.

Weatherson, B. (2003). 'What Good Are Counterexamples?' *Philosophical Studies*, 115: 1–31.

Weinberg, J., Nichols, S., and Stich, S. (2001). 'Normativity and Epistemic Intuitions'. *Philosophical Topics*, 29: 429–60.

Williamson, T. (2003). 'Blind Reasoning'. *Supplement to the Proceedings of The Aristotelian Society*, 77: 249–93.

4

Inner Spaces and Outer Spaces: the New Epistemology*

Paul M. Churchland

1. SOME PARALLELS AND CONTRASTS WITH KANT

A novel idea is sometimes best introduced by analogy, or contrast, with ideas already familiar. Let us begin, then, with the Kantian portrait of our epistemological situation, and more specifically, with his characterization of the two faculties of empirical *intuition* and rational *judgment*. Most famously, Kant argued that both of these faculties constitute a human-specific canvas on which the activities of human cognition are doomed to be painted. Space and time were claimed to be the 'pure forms' of all *sensory* intuition—the abstract background forms, that is, of all possible human sensory representations. And the organized family of the various 'pure concepts of the understanding' were claimed to provide the inevitable framework of expression for any of the *judgments* that we humans ever make about the empirical world. Accordingly, while the world-in-itself (the 'noumenal' world) is certainly not 'constructed' by us, the world-as-perceived-and-thought-by-us (the 'empirical' world of three-dimensional physical objects) does indeed display a substantial component that reflects precisely the peculiar contributions brought to the business of cognition by our own internal cognitive machinery.

Kant, of course, had an agenda that we moderns need not share: namely, the desire to vindicate an alleged class of *synthetic* a priori truths (for example, geometry and arithmetic), and to explain in detail how such truths are possible. Beyond this, he had commitments that we moderns may wish to deny, such as the innateness of the 'pure forms and concepts' at issue, and the implasticity of the cognitive activities that they make possible. But his portrait still constitutes a useful starting-point from which a competing, and importantly different, portrait can be quickly sketched and readily grasped.

Consider, then, the possibility that human cognition involves not just *two* abstract 'spaces', of possible human *experiences* on the one hand, and possible

* Reprinted, with revisions, from *Proceedings and Addresses of the American Philosophical Association*, 76 (2002): 25–48 (Presidential Address, Pacific Division). This essay is an abridged version of the opening chapter of a book-in-progress bearing the same title.

human *judgments* on the other, but rather many *hundreds*, perhaps even *thousands*, of internal cognitive 'spaces', each of which provides a proprietary canvas on which some aspect of human cognition is continually unfolding. Consider the possibility that each such figurative cognitive space is physically embodied in the very real space of the possible *collective* activities of some proprietary population of appropriately devoted *neurons* within the human or animal brain.

To continue, suppose also that the internal character of each of these representational spaces is not *fixed* by some prior decree, either divine or genetic, but is slowly shaped or sculpted by the extended experience of the developing animal, to reflect the peculiar empirical environment and practical needs that it encounters, and the peculiar learning procedures embodied in the brain's ongoing business of synaptic modification. These internal spaces may thus be *plastic* in varying degrees, and may hold out the promise of an enormous *range* of conceptual and perceptual possibilities for one and the same species of creature, in stark contrast to the frozen conceptual prison contrived for us by Kant.

Consider also the possibility that the human brain devotes every bit as much of its cognitive activity to the production and administration of coherent *motor behavior* (walking, swimming, speaking, piano playing, throwing strikes, making a dinner, running a meeting) as it does to the perceptual and judgmental activities of typical concern to traditional philosophies. And note the possibility that such proprietary cognitive spaces, whose neuronal basis is located, for example, in the frontal cortex, the motor cortex, and the cerebellum, can successfully *represent* the complex motor-procedures and action-procedures listed above, by means of the muscle-manipulating *trajectories* of the collective neuronal activities within those motor spaces. Note also that such trajectories and limit-cycles within sundry *sensory* spaces can equally well represent complex *causal* processes and *periodic* phenomena, as externally encountered in perceptual experience, rather than as internally generated to produce bodily behavior.

So we begin by expanding the number of representational spaces, into the hundreds and thousands, far beyond the Kantian pair. We locate them in discrete anatomical parts of the brain. We make each one of them plastic and multipotent in its semantic content and its conceptual organization. And we reach out to include motor cognition and practical skills, along with perceptual apprehension and theoretical judgment, as equal partners in our account of human knowledge.

2. REPRESENTATIONS IN THE BRAIN: EPHEMERAL VERSUS ENDURING

But we have not yet confronted the single largest contrast that we need to draw, between the Kantian portrait above and the account to be pursued in this essay. For Kant, there is no question but that the fundamental unit of human cognition is the *judgment*, a unit that lives in a space of sundry logical relations with other actual and possible judgments, a unit which displays the characteristic feature of truth or falsity. However, on the account proposed in this essay, there is no question but that the 'judgment', as conceived by Kant and by centuries of other logicians, is *not* the fundamental unit of cognition, not in animals, and not in humans either. Instead, the fundamental unit of cognition, strictly, of occurrent or ephemeral cognition, is the *activation pattern* across a proprietary population of neurons. It is the activated *point* within any one of the many hundreds of representational spaces urged above.

This fundamental form of representation is one we share with all other creatures that possess a nervous system, and it does roughly the same job in every space and in every case. Such a representation lets the animal know—better, it constitutes the animal's knowledge—that its current location, in the space of possible situations comprehended by the underlying population of neurons, is *here* on the cognitive map embodied in that population. That activation point is rather like the brilliant dot of a laser pointer illuminating one tiny spot on an otherwise unlit highway map, a moving dot that continuously updates one's current position in the space of geographic possibilities represented by that map.

Since these thousands of spaces or 'maps' are all connected to one another by billions of axonal projections and trillions of synaptic junctions, such specific locational information within one map can and does provoke subsequent point-like activations in a *sequence* of downstream representational spaces, and ultimately in one or more motor-representation spaces, whose unfolding activations are projected onto the body's muscle systems, thereby to generate cognitively informed behaviors.

On this view, Kantian-style 'judgments', though entirely real, constitute a peripheral form of representational activity, marginal even for adult humans, and completely absent in nonhuman animals and prelinguistic children. How we humans manage to generate a 'language space', to sustain our speech production and speech comprehension, is an engaging scientific question to which we must, at some point, return. For now, let me announce that, for better or for worse, the view to be explored and developed in this essay is diametrically opposed to the view that humans are capable of cognition precisely because we are born with an innate '*language* of thought'.

Fodor has defended this linguaformal view most trenchantly and resourcefully in recent decades, but of course the general idea goes back at least to Kant and to Descartes. My own hypothesis is that all three of these acute gentlemen have been falsely taken in by what was, until recently, the only *example* of a systematic representational system available to human experience, namely, human language. Encouraged further by the structure of our own dearly beloved Folk Psychology,[1] they have wrongly read back *into* the objective phenomenon of cognition-in-general an historically *accidental* structure that is idiosyncratic to a single species of animal (namely, humans), and which is of profoundly secondary importance

---

[1] 'Folk Psychology' is the ordinary conceptual framework, comprehending notions like 'desires that P', 'believes that P', 'fears that P', 'intends that P', used by Everyman to explain and predict the behavior of other humans.

even there. We do of course use language—a most blessed development we shall explore in due course—but language-like structures do not embody the basic machinery of cognition. Evidently not for animals, and not for humans either, because the human neuronal machinery, overall, differs from that of other animals in various small degrees, but not in fundamental kind.

An account of cognition that locates us on a continuum with all of our evolutionary brothers and sisters is thus a prime desideratum of any responsible epistemological theory. And the price we have to pay to meet it is to give up the linguaformal 'judgment' or 'proposition' as the presumed unit of knowledge or representation. But we need no longer make this sacrifice in the dark. Given the conceptual resources of modern neurobiology and cognitive neuromodeling, we are finally in a position to pursue an alternative account of cognition, one that embraces some highly specific and very different units of representation. What I hope to show in this essay is that this initial investment in an unorthodox assumption, concerning the nature of our primary units of representation, will yield extraordinary dividends as we proceed.

One of those dividends emerges very early in our story, for the portrait of knowledge held out to us draws a fundamental distinction between the ephemeral vehicles of our knowledge of the fleeting-here-and-now on the one hand, and the comparatively stable and enduring vehicles of our *background* knowledge of the world's-general-structure-in-space-and-time on the other. As just suggested, the former vehicles are the fleeting activation-patterns across a given population of neurons; they are the ever-moving, ever-jumping points of here-and-now activation within their proprietary conceptual subspaces. Think again of the moving, darting laser-dot on the otherwise unlit road map.

The latter or 'background' vehicles are entirely different. At this level of *general* knowledge, the vehicle or unit of representation is *the entire conceptual framework*. It is the *entire activation space* for the relevant population of neurons, a space that has been sculpted by months or years of learning, a space that encompasses all of the possible instances of which the creature currently has any conception. Indeed, that space is precisely the background canvas on which each fleeting *instance* of any category gets 'painted', and that painting consists in nothing more nor less than an activation at a specific location within that sculpted space of *possible* activations. (To reprise the metaphor of the previous paragraph, the background conceptual framework is the entire *road map* at issue, the waiting space of all *possible* positions that the laser-dot might at some time illuminate.)

To illustrate with a simple and concrete example, consider the space of possible *color-experiences* portrayed in Figure 1. That space is said to embody every possible color-qualia of which the human visual system is capable, and that space is organized in a very specific way, a way common to all humans with normal vision. Barring some form of color-blindness, we all share the *same* family of distance-relations and betweenness-relations that collectively locate each color-representation within that space, relative to all of its sibling color-representations. To possess this

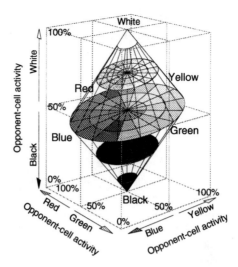

Figure 1 The human phenomenological space for representing objective colors

roughly double-coned space is to have the most rudimentary human knowledge of the general structure of the domain of objective colors. And to have a current activation vector at a specific point within this internal conceptual space (half-way up the central axis, for example) is to have a current representation or *experience* of a specific color (in that case, middle-*gray*).

A second example concerns one's internal conceptual space for representing human *faces*, as (speculatively) portrayed in the example of Figure 2. In fact, that three-dimensional space is a schematic of the activation space of a specific popula-tion of neurons within an *artificial* neural network, one that attempts to model the gross structure of the primary visual pathway in humans. That network was trained to discriminate faces from nonfaces, male faces from female faces, and to reidentify the faces of various named individuals across diverse photographs of each (Cottrell 1991).[2]

As you can see immediately, the training process has produced a hierarchical structure of distinct representational regions within the space as a whole. Sundry nonface images presented to the network's sensory neurons are repres-ented by sundry activation points close to the *origin* of this downstream con-ceptual space, and various faces are represented by various activation points within a much larger 'face region' away from the origin. That complementary region is itself split in two, into roughly equal regions for male faces and female faces, respectively. Within each gender-subspace lies a scatter of much smaller subspaces, each of which comprehends a cluster of closely proximate activation

---

[2] The artificial network actually had eighty neurons at the crucial representational layer, not three, as my three-dimensional diagram would suggest. I deploy this low-dimensional fiction to help make visual sense of what is happening in the more complex case of an eighty-dimensional space.

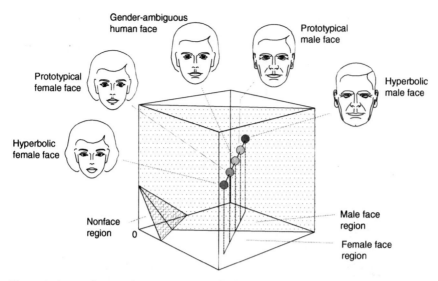

Figure 2 A neural-network activation space for representing human faces

points for representing distinct sensory presentations of the face of a single
individual.

Of course, *every* point in the larger region represents a face of some kind or
other, not just the points illustrated. But as one moves progressively farther away
from the solid straight line between the average or prototypical male-face point
and the average or prototypical female-face point (see again Figure 2), one
encounters representations of faces that are increasingly nonstandard or hyperbolic in various ways. Since such outlying points contrast maximally with the
more central points, they represent faces that 'stand out' from the crowd, faces
that differ maximally from what we expect in an average, humdrum face. And just
as the color space has a middle-*gray* at its central point, so does our face-space have
a gender-*neutral* face at its central point.

The evident structure of these two spaces, for colors and for faces, reveals itself
anew in some simple perceptual illusions. Fix your gaze on the ✕ at the center of the
reddish square on the right side of Figure 3 and hold it for ten seconds. Then fixate
on the ✕ in the central gray square immediately to its left. For a few brief seconds
you will perceive that hue-neutral square as being faintly green. A parallel experiment, beginning with the genuinely green square at the left of Figure 3, will make
that same central square look faintly red. If you look back to the color space of
Figure 1, you will notice that red and green are coded at opposite sides of that space,
with maximal distance between them. Forcing oneself into a protracted period of
steady neural activity, in order to code either one of these extremal colors, produces a
specific pattern of short-term 'fatigue' and/or 'potentiation' across the three kinds of
color-coding neurons that underlie our three-dimensional color space.

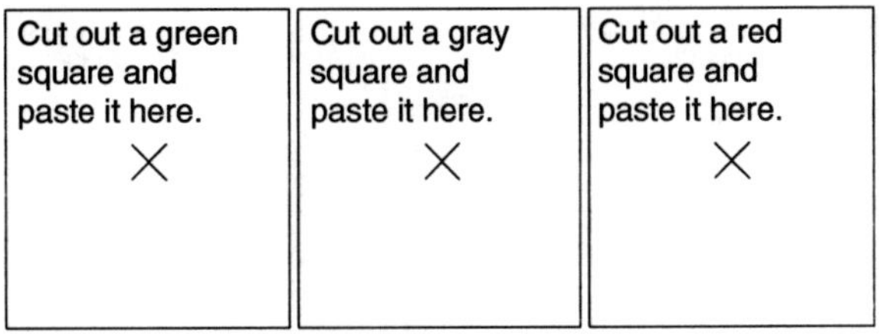

Cut out a green square and paste it here. X	Cut out a gray square and paste it here. X	Cut out a red square and paste it here. X

Figure 3 Polar-opposite colours flanking a hue-neutral test square

That fatigue induces those neurons, when finally relieved of their extremal burden, to fall back *past* their normal neutral points, that is, to relax back into a momentary activation pattern that briefly *mis*represents a *hue-neutral* perceptual input as if it were an input from the side of the color space exactly *opposite* from the original, fatigue-inducing stimulus. Hence the brief illusion of its exactly complementary color.

You may observe a similar short-term illusion concerning the *gender* of the face portrayed in the middle position of Figure 4. That deliberately gender-ambiguous, vector-average human face is flanked by a hyperbolic female face on the right, and a hyperbolic male face on the left. Use your hand to cover all but the male face, and fixate on the bridge of his nose for ten seconds. Then slide your hand to the right so as to reveal (only) the neutral face, shift your fixation suddenly to the bridge of *its* nose, and make a snap judgment as to the *gender* of that (objectively neutral) face. Since hyperbolic male and female faces (like red and green colors) are coded at opposite sides of the relevant activation space, the preceding color-experiment suggests that, thanks to a comparable fatigue or saturation effect, the neutral face will now look, if anything, to be faintly *female*. If your reaction is like mine, it does. And as with the color illusion, you can also perform the opposite experiment. Fixate for at least fifteen seconds on the isolated hyperbolic female face, and then suddenly refixate on the middle face to see if it subsequently looks, if only for a second or so, to be distinctly *male*. Be your own judge. (You may also notice an intriguing *age* effect. The central face appears as two entirely *distinct individuals* in the two conditions. When seen as male, it looks quite young, no more than twenty. When seen as female, it looks to be a much older person, no less than thirty-five. I'm still pondering that one.)[3]

[3] These two examples portend a multitude. Readers may remember the three buckets of water—one tepid, flanked by one hot and one cold—touted by Locke and Berkeley. The tepid one feels warm, or cool, depending on which of the two flanking buckets initially fatigued the thermal receptors within the testing hand. The 'waterfall illusion' provides a fourth example. Given three textured squares, a steadily down-flowing motion in the left square will induce, after saturation, an illusory *upward* motion in the motionless central square, and an upward-flowing motion in the right square will induce the opposite illusion. But these are both one-dimensional illusions. What is intriguing about the color and face illusions, as distinct from temperature and motion, is that they occur in a representational space of more than one dimension, three of them in the case of colors and probably many hundreds in the case of faces.

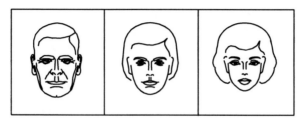

Figure 4 Polar-opposite faces flanking a gender-neutral face

There are many charming variations on these experimental themes, for both the color space and the face space, but we must here move on. That these spaces *exist*, that they display a determinate internal *structure*, and that they have an at-least-slightly *plastic* neuronal basis, are the suggestive lessons of this introductory discussion.

3. INDIVIDUAL LEARNING: SLOW AND STRUCTURAL

Still, one might ask, of these introductory spaces, if they are perhaps innate, that is, somehow specified in the human genome. Whatever the correct answer here, it is surely empirical. As for the human color space, the answer may well be positive. As we shall see, later in this essay, the probable neuronal and synaptic basis for the 3-D color solid discussed above seems to be anatomically simple, repetitive, and highly uniform across normal human individuals. It is therefore a fair candidate for being somehow specified in the human genome.

On the innateness of the human representational-space for *faces*, however, our judgment must incline to the negative, for several reasons. First, and unlike the three-dimensionality of both your color space and the (schematic) face space of Figure 2, the dimensionality of your brain's face space lies almost certainly in the hundreds and perhaps in the thousands. Second, the configuration of the synaptic connections that structure that face space must therefore include at least a million or so synaptic connections.[4] Unlike our color system, none of these connections are repetitive in strength or placement, so their genetic specification would be costly. And third, those connections are not uniform across individuals in any case. We already know that the metrical structure of an individual person's face-representing space *varies* substantially as a function of which culture she grew up in, specifically, as a function of which racial or ethnic group happened to exhaust or dominate her childhood experience with human faces. (It is sometimes called, inaccurately, the 'other-race effect'.) In sum, the basis of our face space is complex,

---

[4] On average, each neuron in the brain enjoys in excess of 1,000 synaptic connections with other neurons.

not recursively specifiable, and highly variable across individuals. It is therefore a most unlikely candidate for being coded in the genome.

Of course, the sheer *existence* of a neuronal population primed to take on the job of parsing faces is likely something that *is* genetically specified. After all, each of us has an inferotemporal cortex (the presumed region of the brain that supports facial recognition), and all normal infants fixate on face-like stimuli from birth. But the adult structure of that space, its idiosyncratic dimensions, and its internal similarity-metric are all features that are *epi*genetically determined. By far the greater part, and perhaps even all, of what anyone knows about faces has its origins in one's post-natal experience with faces.[5]

Such an anti-nativist conclusion, concerning the neuronal and synaptic basis of the brain's representational spaces, is appropriate for almost all of the many spaces that the brain comprehends. The only likely exceptions will be those occasional spaces, such as our color space, perhaps, that directly code the behavior of our various sensory neurons. There is a rule here that cannot be too far wrong. Specifically, the greater the *distance* between a given neuronal population and the body's sensory neurons—as measured by the number of successive synaptic connections that have to be traversed for an axonal message to get from the one population to the other—the exponentially greater is the likelihood that the target population embodies a representational space that has been structured by *learning*.

The fact is, the modification, extinction, and growth of new *synaptic connections* is the single most dramatic dimension of structural change within the brain, from birth onwards. Creating and adjusting the precious configuration of one's 10^{14} synaptic connections is the very essence of learning in one's infant and childhood stages, for it is the collective configuration of the synaptic connections onto any neuronal population that *dictates* the family of categories embodied in that population's proprietary activation space. As our artificial neural-network models reveal, that collective configuration of synaptic connections is what *shapes* the web of similarity and difference relations that unite and divide the categories within the resulting activation space. And that same collective configuration of synaptic connections is what *transforms* any incoming activation pattern (from, for example, an earlier population of sensory neurons) into a new activation pattern located at a specific location within this carefully sculpted secondary space. Those assembled connections are thus central to *both* the relatively enduring conceptual framework that is acquired by the learning individual in the first place, *and* to its subsequent moment-to-moment activations by ephemeral

---

[5] One's prenatal *motor* and *proprioceptive* experience with one's own face, lips, and tongue may give one a leg up on the post-natal *visual* processing of post-natally encountered faces. For those 'visual' faces are homomorphic structures subject to homomorphic behaviors. But the 'knowledge' involved here is still *epi*genetic, even if acquired while still in the womb. The fact is, fetuses are highly active in the late stages of pregnancy: they move their tongues and mouths, and even suck their thumbs and fists. These experiences are importantly instructive.

sensory inputs. These synaptic connections are, simultaneously, the brain's elemental information *processors*, as well as its principal *repository of general information* about the world's abstract structure.

Accordingly, the establishment of one's myriad synaptic connections, and the fine-tuning of their individual strengths or 'weights', constitutes the focal and primary process of learning that anyone's brain undergoes in its first twenty years of life, and especially in the first ten, and most especially in the first five. For it is during these periods that one's background conceptual framework is slowly established, a framework that is likely, with only minor modifications, to remain with one for the rest of one's life.

Notably, and despite its primacy, that synapse-adjusting/space-shaping process is almost wholly ignored by the traditions of academic epistemology, even into these early years of our Third Millennium. This is perhaps not too surprising. The profound inaccessibility of the brain's microprocesses, the absence of compensatory computer models thereof, the focus of professional concern on normative matters, and the tyrannical primacy of folk-psychological conceptions of cognitive activity, collectively contrive for *past* theorists an acceptable excuse for this monumental and crippling oversight. But the validation-dates on these several excuses (as in, 'use before 01/01/2001') have all run out.

Beyond conventional microscopy, an ever-growing armory of experimental techniques and instruments—such as the selective staining of neurons and their connecting pathways, electron microscopy, single-cell microelectrodes, patch-clamps, genetically modified mice, CAT scans, PET scans, MRI scans, and fMRI scans—now provide us with an overlapping set of windows onto the brain's physical structure and its neuronal activities, from the subcellular details of its molecular activities up to the molar-level behavior of its brain-wide neuronal networks. The brain is no longer an inaccessible black box. On the contrary, the steady stream of experimental data just mentioned provides an ever-expanding set of empirical *constraints* on responsible cognitive theorizing. It also makes possible the invaluable sorts of back-and-forth interactions, between theoretical suggestions on the one hand and experimental probings on the other, that have proven so successful in other scientific endeavors. Theories can suggest and motivate experiments that might never have been tried, or even conceived, in their absence. Equally, experimental results can force needed modifications in the theories being tested. And the cycle begins anew.

Artificial neural networks, as realized directly in electronic hardwares, or as modeled at one remove in conventional computers, provide us with a second way of formulating and testing theories of how cognitive activities can arise from interconnected sets of neuron-like elements. Unlike biological networks, the artificial networks can be as simple and as well controlled as we wish. We can monitor their every connection, their every twitch, and their every change, without killing, damaging, or interfering with the network elements involved. Since, being electronic, they also run much faster than do their biological namesakes, we can also perform and complete experiments on their 'learning' activities within *hours*, experiments that would take months or years to perform on a biological brain. This means, of course, that we can often learn very swiftly that our initial attempt to model some brain function or other is just *wrong*. We can thus go back to the empirical brain for renewed theoretical inspiration, and then go back to the drawing board in hopes of constructing a more faithful artificial model.

This activity has already yielded the rough outlines of a competing conception of cognitive activity, an alternative to the 'sentential' or 'propositional-attitude' model that has dominated philosophy for the past 2,500 years. This newer conception is important for a number of reasons, not least because it finally makes some explanatory contact with the physical and functional details of the biological organ, the brain, that sustains our cognitive activity. But it is important for many other reasons as well, perhaps the first of which is the novel account it provides of the *origins* of any individual's conceptual framework.

This is an issue that is mostly ignored, submerged, or finessed with a stick-figure theory by the philosophical tradition. Two styles of 'solution' have dominated. The writings of Plato, Descartes, and Fodor illustrate the first great option: since one has no idea how to explain the origin of our concepts, one simply pronounces them innate, and credits either a prior life, almighty God, or fifty million years of biological evolution for the actual lexicon of concepts we find in ourselves. The works of Aristotle, Locke, and Hume illustrate the second great option: point to a palette of what are taken to be sensory 'simples', such as the various tastes, smells, colors, shapes, sounds, and so forth, and then explain our base population of simple concepts as being faint 'copies' of the simple sensory originals, copies acquired in a one-shot encounter with such originals. Nonsimple or 'complex' concepts are then explained as the recursively-achieved concatenations and/or modulations of the simple 'copies' (and never mind the origins of *that* constructive machinery).

Both options are hopeless, and for interesting reasons. If we put God and Plato's Heaven aside as nonstarters, the preferred (i.e., the evolutionary) version of the first option confronts the difficulty of how-on-Earth to code for the individual connection-places and connection-strengths of fully 10^{14} synapses—so as to sculpt the target conceptual framework—using the resources of an evolved genome that contains only 30,000 genes, ninety-nine percent of which (all but a paltry 300 of which) we share with *mice*, with whom we parted evolutionary company over fifty million years ago. The problem here is not so much the nine-orders-of-magnitude gap between these two numbers (in principle, a recursive procedure can bridge a gap of any size), though that yawning gap does give pause for thought. The real difficulty is the empirical fact that each person's matured synaptic configuration is radically different from anyone else's. It is utterly unique to that individual. That synaptic configuration is thus a hopeless candidate for being recursively specifiable as *the same* in all of us, as it must be if the numbers gap just noted is to be recursively bridged, and if the same conceptual framework is thereby to be genetically recreated in every normal human individual.

The second option is little or no better. Empirical research on the neuronal coding strategies deployed in our several sensory systems reveals that, even in response to the presumptively 'simplest' of sensory stimuli, the sensory messages sent to the brain are typically quite complex, and their synapse-transformed vector-offspring—that is, the downstream conceptualized representations into which they get coded—are more complex still, typically *much* more complex. The direct-inner-copy theory of what concepts are, and of how we acquire them, is a joke on its face, a fact reflected in the months and years it takes any human infant to acquire the full range of our discriminatory capacities for most of the so-called 'simple' sensory properties. (It takes *time* to configure the brain's 10^{14} synapses, even to comprehend the allegedly 'simple' properties at issue.) Additionally, and as anyone who ever pursued the matter was doomed to discover, the recursive-definitions story suggested for 'complex' concepts was a crashing failure in its own right. Try to construct an explicit definition of 'electron', or 'democracy'—or even 'cat' or 'pencil', for that matter—in terms of concepts that plausibly represent sensory simples.

Perhaps the strongest argument that either side—Blanket Nativist versus Concatenative Empiricist—could adduce in its own favor was the evident poverty of the opposing view. Given the depth of their poverties, each had a nontrivial point, so long as these alternatives were seen as exhausting the possibilities. But of course they do not. For as our artificially trained models illustrate, we already possess a workable story of how a neuronal activation space can be slowly sculpted, by experience, into a coherent and hierarchical family of prototype regions. This story also accounts for the subsequent and context-appropriate *activation* of those concepts, activations made in response to sensory instances of the categories they represent. And this same neurostructural and neurofunctional framework sustains penetrating explanations of a wide variety of perceptual and conceptual phenomena, including the profile of many of our cognitive *failures*. It forms the essential foundation of the larger epistemological theory here being introduced.

4. INDIVIDUAL LEARNING: FAST AND DYNAMICAL

But *only* the foundation. Adjusting trillions of synaptic connections is not the only way to engage in a process worthy of the term 'learning', and boasting a well-tuned configuration of such connections is not the only way to embody systematic 'knowledge' about the world. To this basic dimension of learning—the dimension of *structural* changes in the brain—we must add a second dimension of learning: the dimension of *dynamical* changes in the brain's typical or accustomed modes of operation. These dynamical changes can take place on a much shorter time scale (seconds and less) than the structural changes we have been discussing (weeks, months, and years), and they typically involve no structural changes whatever, at least in the short term. But this dimension of cognitive development is at least as important as its structural precursor, as we shall see.

To a first approximation, one can conceive of the brain's dynamical activity as a single moving point in the brain's all-up neuronal activation space, a point in ceaseless motion, a point that spends its time, marble-like, rolling merrily around the almost endless hills and valleys of the conceptual landscape that the basic or structural learning process has taken so long to sculpt. This landscape analogy is accurate enough, in that it rightly suggests that one's unfolding cognitive state tends to favor the 'valleys' (the acquired prototype regions or categories) and to slide off the 'hills' (the comparatively 'improbable' ridges between the 'more probable' valleys). But it fails adequately to suggest the spectacular *volume* of the brain's 'all-up' activation space (the assembled sum of the thousands of vaguely Kantian *sub*spaces). Let us do a brief accounting.

If we assume, very conservatively, that each neuron in the brain admits of only ten different functionally significant levels of activity—ten steps between a minimum spiking frequency of 0 Hz and a maximum of 90 Hz, for example— then, since the brain has 10^{11} neurons, we are looking at a space of 10 to the $10^{11\text{th}}$ power or $10^{100,000,000,000}$ functionally distinct, a priori possible global activation states. (For comparison, the accessible Universe contains only about 10^{87} cubic meters.) It is within this almost incomprehensible volume of distinct activational possibilities that a given individual's moving activation-point must craft its one-shot, three-score-and-ten years, idiosyncratic cognitive excursion, that indi- vidual's conscious (and unconscious) life.

That space is far too large to explore any significant portion of it in a human lifetime ($\approx 2 \times 10^9$ seconds). If one's activation point were to streak through the possible points at a rate of 100 per second, a lifetime's exploration would touch only 2×10^{11} distinct points, leaving fully $5 \times 10^{99,999,999,988}$ points unvisited.

This accounting is roughly accurate, but it concerns only the a priori volume of the human neuronal activation space, that is, its potential volume if each neuron's activities were independent of every other's. By contrast, its a posteriori volume, if still mind-boggling, is substantially smaller, for a reason you will already appreciate. The whole point of the synapse-adjusting learning process discussed above was to make the behavior of neurons that are progressively higher in the information-processing hierarchy profoundly and systematically *dependent* on the activities of the neurons variously below them. Accordingly, that learning process shrinks the space of (empirically) possible global activation points dramatically.

More specifically, it shrinks the original space to a set of carefully contrived internal subspaces, each of which is an attempt to represent, via its acquired internal structure, some proprietary aspect or dimension of the external world's enduring structure. Being devotedly general in their representational significance, these subspaces therefore represent the brain's conception of the *possible* ways in which the world may present itself to us in our singular, ongoing perceptual experience. For example, the color space of Figure 1 attempts to represent the range of all possible colors. The face space of Figure 2 attempts to represent the range of all possible human faces. A third space might represent the range of all possible projectile motions. A fourth, the range of all possible voices. And so on. Collectively, these many subspaces specify a set of 'nomically possible' worlds, worlds that instantiate the same categories and share the enduring causal structure of our own world, but differ in their initial conditions and ensuing singular details.

As stated earlier, one's inner cognitive narrative is a specific trajectory through such an antecedently sculpted all-up activation space. But even given such a well-informed space, the path of that cognitive trajectory is not dictated by one's sensory experience alone. Far from it. As we shall see, your next activation-point, within your global activation-space, is always dictated (1) partly by your current sensory inputs, (2) partly by the already acquired profile of your background conceptual framework (that is, by the lasting configuration of your synaptic connections), but also, and most importantly, (3) by the concurrent activation-state of your *entire neuronal population*, a complex factor that reflects your cognitive activity immediately preceding the present computational interaction. This arrangement makes the brain a genuine *dynamical system*, a system capable of a great range of possible behaviors, much of which is unpredictable even in principle.

Once again, a Kantian parallel may help to illuminate the claims here being made, by the contrasts required as well as by the similarities in place. It is arguable that Kant embraced a third great canvas of cognitive activity, distinct from Intuition and Judgment. This was the faculty of Imagination, whose hallmark feature was the *spontaneity* of the cognitive activities there displayed. Unlike Kant, we shall not postulate a distinct space or canvas to sustain the activities of the imagination. On our view, those activities take place in the very same family of neuronal activation spaces discussed earlier. What distinguishes imaginative activity from other forms of cognition is not its location, but its cause. Imaginative cognitive activity arises not from ascending inputs from the several sensory modalities, but from descending or recurrent inputs from neuronal populations higher up in the brain's information-processing hierarchy. It is initiated and steered by brain activity from above rather than by sensory activity from below.

On the matter of spontaneity, however, we line up with Kant. And with good reason. The brain is a dynamical system of unparalleled complexity. It is a continuously varying physical system with many billions of degrees of freedom—the activation levels of its billions of neurons, for starters. It is a system whose dynamics are decidedly nonlinear, which means that, for many regimes of activity, infinitesimally small differences in one's current cognitive state can snowball exponentially into very large differences in the brain's subsequent cognitive state. This puts inescapable limitations on the degree to which we, or any other conceivable physical device for that matter, can *predict* any brain's unfolding cognitive activities, even on the assumption that the brain's behavior is rigorously deterministic. The problem is that, for such a system, effective prediction requires, first, infinitely perfect information about the brain's current structural and dynamical state, and second, infinitely accurate computations concerning its law-governed development into subsequent states. Neither requirement can be met in this world, nor even relevantly approximated.

The result is a system whose cognitive behavior, in general, simply cannot be predicted, not by itself, and not by anything else either. This need not mean that *no* regularities will display themselves to the casual eye. To the contrary, when the brain is in the midst of some prototypical activity, such as brushing one's teeth, dealing a deck of cards, or sipping a cup of coffee, its specific motor behavior can be reliably predicted for several seconds or so into the future. And if we look at behavior as reckoned over days and weeks, we can reliably predict that, if the environment remains normal, people will take dinner about six o'clock, go to bed around ten, and get up around six or seven. The details of such periodic behaviors may be beyond us. (Will he have sausages, or fish? Will he wear the green pyjamas, or the blue? Will he get up on the right side of the bed, or the left?) But even a nonlinear system can display roughly stable, if endlessly variant, orbits or cycles. Beyond these two exceptions, however (very short-term behaviors and long-term patterns), a person's cognitive and motor behavior is deeply unpredictable. It displays a spontaneity that reflects its origins in an unmonitorable and ever-shifting mix of mercurial microprocesses.

But let us return to the topic of learning. Beyond a welcome measure of spontaneity, what the recurrent or descending neuronal pathways also make possible is the ongoing *modulation* of the brain's cognitive response to its unfolding sensory inputs. The details of that modulation reflect the ever-changing dynamical state of the brain as a whole; it reflects all of the acquired here-and-now contextual information embodied in the brain at the time of the sensory inputs in question. Most importantly, the current context into which each sensory input arrives is never exactly the same twice, not twice in a lifetime. For even with the brain's synaptic connection-weights fixed in their mature configuration, the brain's *dynamical* state, its all-up pattern of current neuronal activation-levels, provides an ever-moving, never-repeating cognitive context into which its every sensory input is interpretively received. Accordingly, one never has a truly identical cognitive response on two different occasions, even if the total sensory inputs should happen to be identical on those two occasions. Identical rocks, thrown sequentially into this internal Heraclitean river, will never make exactly the same splash.

To be sure, the resulting differences are usually small, and their downstream cognitive consequences are typically small as well. The brain, like the Solar System, is at least a quasi-stable dynamical system. But sometimes the downstream differences are substantial, and reflect a changed outlook on the world, as when a trusted friend suddenly mistreats an innocent colleague horribly. Though the friend may return to normal in the days and weeks that follow, his smiles and greetings and other social exchanges never look quite the same to you again. Your perceptions, anticipations, and interactions, at least where he is concerned, are permanently altered: you have learned something about his character.

More specifically, that experience has kicked your cognitive trajectory into an importantly different and hitherto unvisited region of your antecedently sculpted neuronal activation space. In the vast majority of that space's many dimensions, your trajectory remains in familiar territory. But in at least a handful of the available dimensions, that trajectory is now exploring new ground.

Strictly, it should be said, that trajectory is *always* exploring novel territory, since it never intersects itself *exactly*. (For an isolated dynamical system, such a perfect return would doom the system to an endless and unchanging periodicity.) But sometimes the novelty of one's activation-space position is not minor: it is substantial. Occasionally, one's redirected trajectory takes one out of a familiar and much-toured basin of dynamical attraction, over a local ridge of relative improbability, and into a new and quite different basin of attraction, a basin in which *all* sensory inputs of a certain kind now receive an importantly different regime of conceptual interpretation. If that new regime happens to yield an increased capacity for anticipating and manipulating one's environment, or some specific aspect of it, then it is appropriate to credit the creature with a new insight into the world. Though no *structural* changes have taken place in one's nervous system, such a case is still a clear instance of learning—*dynamical* learning.

The example of the misapprehended and then reapprehended friend is a deliberately mundane example of the process. That process will loom larger in importance when one appreciates that most cases of major scientific insight or so-called 'conceptual revolution' are also instances of dynamical learning in particular. Consider, for example, Newton's famously sudden realization (the falling apple incident at Woolsthorp) that the Moon's orbit is just another case of *projectile motion*, governed by the same laws as a stone thrown here on Earth. Consider Darwin's realization that the origin of distinct species might be owed to an entirely natural analog of the *artificial selection* long practiced in animal husbandry. Consider Torricelli's insight that we are all living at the bottom of an *ocean of air*, and the test of that hypothesis with a (steadily falling) barometer lugged manfully up a mountainside. Or consider Bernoulli's, Maxwell's, and Boltzmann's conjecture that a gas is just a cloud of *tiny ballistic particles* in rebounding collision with each other, and with the walls of whatever container might confine them.

In all of these cases, and in many others, the decisive cognitive change effected lay not in the reconfiguration of anyone's synaptic weights. The cognitive changes at issue happened much too swiftly for that molasses-like process to provide the explanation. Rather, the change consisted in the dynamical redeployment of conceptual resources already in place, resources learned years ago and in other contexts entirely, resources *originally* learned by way of that slower synaptic process here found wanting. What is novel in the historical examples above is not the concepts deployed (*inertial projectile, selective reproduction, deep ocean,* and *swarm of ballistic particles*), but rather the unusual target or circumstance of their deployment: namely, the *Moon, wild animals*, the *atmosphere*, and *confined gases*, respectively. In each case, an old and familiar thing came to be understood as an unexpected instance of a quite different category, a category hitherto employed in quite different circumstances, a category that makes new and systematic sense of the old phenomenon. To borrow a notion from Biology, we are here looking at a variety of *cognitive exhaptations*, cognitive devices initially developed in one environment that turn out to serve unusually well for a different purpose in a different environment.

As the reader may begin to surmise, this account of dynamical learning contains the resources for a new account of what theoretical hypotheses are, of what explanatory understanding consists in, and of what explanatory unification or 'intertheoretic reduction' consists in. Its classical adversaries are the *syntactic* account of theories ('a theory is a set of sentences'), with its appropriately *deductive* accounts of both explanation and intertheoretic reduction, and the *semantic* view of theories ('a theory is a family of homomorphic models'), with its appropriately *model-theoretic* accounts of explanation and reduction. Both of these classical accounts are inadequate, I shall argue, especially the older syntactic/sentential/propositional account. For, among many other defects, it denies any theoretical understanding whatever to nonhuman animals, since they do not traffic in sentential or propositional attitudes.

That classical account is deeply inadequate for humans also, since it wrongly attempts to apply *linguistic* categories, appropriate only at the social level, to the predominantly *non*linguistic activities of individual brains, activities better described in terms of *unfolding activation vectors* than in the procrustean terms of sentential or propositional attitudes. There is ample room for sentential representations within the epistemological story to be presented below, and important work for them to do. But their proper home lies in the social world, in the shared space outside of the human brain, in the space of public utterances and the printed page, not inside the individual human head.

The semantic view of theories is mistaken also, but of these two classical adversaries, it comes much closer to the truth of the matter. That view deserves discussion, but on this occasion space demands that I pass it by. Let me move directly to a different parallel, which comes closer still to the truth of the matter. The view of theories here to be defended is a neurally-grounded instance of the tradition represented by Mary Hesse, Thomas Kuhn, Ronald Giere, and Nancy Cartwright. That tradition focuses on the role of models, metaphors, paradigms, and idealized 'nomological machines' in the business of scientific theorizing.[6]

---

[6] This list is confined specifically to philosophers of science, but the theoretical tradition here drawn upon reaches beyond the confines of that particular subdiscipline. 'Cognitive Linguistics', as represented by the work of linguists such as J. Elman, E. Bates, R. Langacker, G. Lakoff, and G. Fauconier, is a different but salient branch of the same tree. 'Semantic-Field Theory', as represented by the work of philosophers such as E. Kittay and M. Johnson is another. And so is the 'Prototype Theory' of conceptual organization explored by an entire generation of psychologists.

In some respects, this is a highly diverse group. Famously, Kuhn's focus lay at the social level; Giere's focus lies firmly at the psychological level; and Cartwright tends to focus on the metaphysical nature of objective reality. But they are all united in seeing our scientific endeavors as dependent on the artful *assimilation* of complex and problematic phenomena to some special phenomena that are familiar, tractable, and already well understood. It is the neurocomputational *basis* of precisely such assimilative processes that I aim to capture as instances of dynamical learning.

The proper formalism to achieve this end is not the Predicate Calculus of the syntactic approach, nor Set Theory, as on the semantic approach. The proper formalism is *vector algebra* and *high-dimensional geometry*. And the proper deployment of this formalism is the story of how vector coding and vector processing are realized in the vast network of the biological brain. This allows us, among other things, to bring a dynamical dimension into our account of human scientific theorizing—it is, after all, a causal process unfolding in time—a dimension largely or wholly absent from the original syntactic and semantic accounts.

Before leaving this introductory discussion of dynamical or second-level learning, it is worth mentioning that one further major problem in the epistemological tradition is going to show up in a new and potentially more tractable guise, namely, the problem of the underdetermination of theory by evidence, and the status of broadly Realist versus broadly Instrumentalist interpretations of the enterprise of science. The underdetermination problem does not disappear, far from it, but it does assume a different form, and it heralds, I shall argue, a philosophical lesson somewhat different from that urged by either of these traditional adversaries. For one thing, as you may appreciate, the 'evidence' relation needs to be reconceived entirely, since the parties to it are no longer the 'theoretical' and the 'observational' sentences of the syntactic view, nor the set-theoretic structures and their 'observational substructures' embraced by the semantic view. For another, we are going to find that underdetermination infects the domain of all possible *evidence* no less than the domain of all possible theories, with consequences we shall have to evaluate. And for a third, we shall rediscover another old friend—'incommensurability' (also reconfigured)—as we confront the practical-infinity of neurocognitive alternatives potentially vying for human acceptance as the preferred vehicle of our global understanding. Despite these familiar bogeymen, it will be a recognizable version of Scientific Realism, as I see it, that best makes sense of the overall situation.

5. COLLECTIVE LEARNING AND CULTURAL TRANSMISSION

If it is important to distinguish a brain's *dynamical* adventures (in trying to apply its concepts to an ever-expanding experience of the world) from its more basic *structural* adventures (in slowly shaping a useful framework of concepts in the first place), then it is equally important to distinguish both of these originally individual activities from a third major level of learning: the level of *cultural* change and *collective* cognitive activity. For it is the institution of this third level of learning that most surely distinguishes the cognitive adventure of humans from that of any other species. To a first approximation, that third-level activity consists in the cultural assimilation of individual cognitive successes, the technological exploitation of those successes, the transmission of those acquired successes to subsequent generations, and the ever-more-sophisticated *regulation* of individual cognitive activities at the *first two* levels of learning.

The existence and overwhelming importance of this third level of cognitive activity will be news to no one. But the proper characterization of that collectivized process is still a matter of substantial dispute. Is it the journey of Geist toward complete Self-Consciousness, as Georg Hegel surmised? Is it the reprise of selective evolution at the level of linguistic items, a ruthless contest of selfish 'memes', as Richard Dawkins has suggested? Is it the convergent March of Science toward the Final True Theory, as some Pragmatists and Logical Empiricists dared to hope? Is it just the meandering and ultimately meaningless conflict between fluid academic fiefdoms competing for journal space and grant money, as some skeptical Sociologists have proposed?

A wry answer might be that it is all of these, and more. But a more considered and more accurate answer would be that it is none of the above. Nor will the true nature of this third-level process ever become clear until we appreciate the manifold ways in which the various mechanisms of human culture serve to nurture, to regulate, and to *amplify* the cognitive activities of individual humans at the *first two* levels of learning, the levels we share with nonhuman animals.

As the off-hand list of the preceding paragraph will attest, there is no shortage of philosophical theories about the structure, dynamics, and long-term future of cultural or third-level learning. They are many and various. But if the proposal here on the table is correct, that the central *function* of these cultural mechanisms is the detailed regulation and exploitation of learning at the first two levels of learning, then none of the familiar theories can hope to be anything more than incidentally or accidentally correct in their portrayals of the human epistemic adventure. For no epistemology or philosophy of science prior to the present period has had any interest in, or any clear conception of, these first two kinds of learning: namely, the generation of a hierarchy of prototype-representations via gradual change in the configuration of one's synaptic weights (first-level learning), and the subsequent discovery of successful redeployments, of that hard-earned framework of activation-space representations, within novel domains of experience (second-level learning).

Indeed, those original and more basic levels of representation and learning have been positively *mis*characterized by their chronic portrayal as just hidden, inward versions of the *linguistic* representations and activities so characteristic of cognitive activity at the third level. As noted earlier, Jerry Fodor (1975) is the lucid, forthright, and prototype felon on this particular score, for his theory of cognitive activity is that it is explicitly language-like from its inception. As you can already begin to appreciate, this view fails to capture anything of the very different, *sub*linguistic styles of representation and computation revealed to us by the empirical neurosciences and by artificial neuromodeling. Those styles go wholly unacknowledged. This would be failure enough. However, the 'Language of Thought' hypothesis fails in a second monumental respect, this time, ironically enough, by *under*valuing the importance of language. Specifically, it fails to acknowledge the extraordinary cognitive *novelty* that the invention of language represents, and the degree to which it has launched humankind on an intellectual trajectory that is impossible for creatures denied the benefits of that innovation, that is, for creatures confined to only the first and second levels of learning.

What I have in mind here is the following. With the emergence of language, the human race acquired a public medium that embodied, in its peculiar lexicon and in its accepted sentences, at least some of the acquired wisdom and conceptual understanding of the adults who share the use of that medium. Not *all* of that acquired wisdom. Not by a long shot. But enough of it to provide an informed template to which the conceptual development and dynamical cognition of subsequent generations could be made to conform. These subsequent generations of language-learners and language-users are thus the heirs and beneficiaries of at least some of the cognitive achievements of their forebears. In particular, they do not have to sculpt a conceptual space entirely from scratch, as nonlinguistic animals do, and as prelinguistic humans must have. To the contrary, as human children learn their language, from their parents and from the surrounding community of conceptually competent adults, they can shape their individual conceptual developments to conform, at least roughly, to a hierarchy of categories that has already been proven pragmatically successful by a prior generation of cognitive agents.

At that point, the learning process is no longer limited to what a single individual can learn in a single lifetime. That collective medium of representation—language—can come to embody the occasional cognitive innovations of many different human individuals, and it can accumulate those innovations over hundreds and thousands of lifetimes. Most importantly, the conceptual template that the language embodies can slowly *evolve*, over historical periods, to express a different and more powerful view of the world than was expressed by its more primitive precursors.

It is important not to overstate this point. Almost *all* of anyone's acquired wisdom goes with him to the grave, including his inevitably idiosyncratic command of the resources of human language. There is no realistic hope of recording the specific configuration of anyone's 10^{14} synaptic weights, and no realistic hope of tracing the dynamical history of anyone's brain-wide neuronal activations, and thus no realistic hope of recreating, exactly, one's current brain-state within the skull of another human. But one can hope to leave at least something of one's acquired understanding behind, if only a faint and partial digest thereof, through the 'communities of conversation and shared conceptual practice' that one's speech behavior, whether live or printed, has helped to shape.

This said, it is equally important not to *under*state the importance of language. Being a public institution whose current lexicon, grammar, and network of broadly-accepted sentences are under no individual's exclusive personal control, a living language thereby constitutes a sort of 'center of cognitive gravity' around which individual cognitive activities may carve out their idiosyncratic but safely stable orbits. Being also a cultural institution that long outlives the ephemeral individual cognizers that sequentially pass through it, a language embodies the incrementally-added wisdom of the many generations who have inevitably re-shaped it, if only in small ways, during the brief period in which it was theirs. In the long run, accordingly, that institution can aspire to an informed structure of categories and conventional wisdom that dwarfs the level of cognitive achievement possible for any creature living outside of that transgenerational framework. Large-scale *conceptual* evolution is now both possible and probable.

Everyone will agree, of course, that a species with some mechanisms for historical recording can achieve more than a species with no such mechanisms. But I am here making a rather more contentious claim, as will be seen by drawing a further contrast with Fodor's picture of human cognition. On the Language of Thought (LoT) hypothesis, the lexicon of any *public* language inherits its meanings directly from the meanings of the innate concepts of each individual's innate LoT. Those concepts derive *their* meanings, in turn, from the innate set of causal sensitivities they bear to various 'detectable' features of the environment. And finally, those causal sensitivities are fixed in the human genome, according to this view, having been shaped by many millions of years of biological evolution. Accordingly, every normal human, at whatever stage of cultural evolution, is doomed to share the *same* conceptual framework as any other human, a framework that the current public language is therefore secondarily doomed to reflect. Cultural evolution may therefore *add* to that genetic heritage, perhaps considerably, but it cannot undermine it or supercede it. The primary core of our comprehensive conception of the world is firmly nailed to the human genome, and it will not change until that genome is changed.

I disagree. The lexicon of a public language gets its meanings not from its reflection of an innate LoT, but from the framework of broadly accepted or culturally entrenched sentences in which they figure, and by the patterns of inferential behavior made normative thereby. Indeed, the sublinguistic categories that structure any individual's thought processes are shaped, to a significant degree, by the official structure of the ambient language in which she was raised, not the other way around.

To raise an even deeper complaint, the meaning or semantic content of one's personal cognitive categories, whether innate or otherwise, derives not from any feature-indicating nomic relations that they may bear to the external world, but from their determinate place in a high-dimensional neuronal activation-space, a space of intricate and idiosyncratic similarity relations, a space that embodies a highly informed 'map' of some external domain of properties. Evidently, the correct account of first-level learning requires us to put aside any form of atomistic, externalist, *indicator*-semantics in favor of a decidedly holistic, internalist, *domain-portrayal* semantics.

This means that both the semantic content of public languages, and the semantic content of individual conceptual frameworks, are not in the least bit 'nailed' to a fixed human genome. Both are free to vary widely, as a function of local epistemic circumstance and our individual and collective cognitive histories. But whereas each person's acquired conceptual framework is doomed to wink out after roughly three-score-and-ten years, the off-loaded, public structures of one's then-current language are fated to live on, in pursuit of an epistemic adventure that has no visible limits. Certainly this third-level world-representing process is not required to cleave to some Paleolithic or pre-Paleolithic conceptual framework somehow dictated by the human genome.

On the contrary, and given time, this third-level process opens the door to systematic reconstructions of our practical undertakings, and to systematic reconceptions of even the most mundane aspects of our practical and perceptual worlds. We can put out an Initial Public Offering on the NYSE, to support a company's plan to build a nuclear power plant to smelt aluminum from bauxite with megawatt applications of electric power. We can start a phone-campaign to marshal registered Democrats to vote against the anti-Choice initiative, Proposition 14, on the ballot of this year's State Elections. We can aspire to write a thirty-two bar tune in the key of G, based on the same chord sequence, appropriately transposed, as Harold Arlen's popular hit, 'Stormy Weather'. We can destroy the bacteria in a foul dishwashing sponge by boiling its residual water with magnetron-generated microwaves in the counter-top oven. We can marvel as we watch the spherical Earth rotate at fully fifteen degrees per hour, on its north-south axis, as the Sun 'sets' at the western horizon and the full Moon simultaneously 'rises' at the eastern horizon. Thoughts and undertakings such as these are simply beyond the conceptual resources of a stone-age community of human hunter-gatherers. On the other hand, being the beneficiaries of their own third-level history, that stone-age group has thoughts and undertakings, concerning such things as fire manipulation, food preparation, weapons technology, and clothing manufacture, that are equally inconceivable for the members of a baboon troop. We differ from the stone-age humans by being at a very different rung on the long-term conceptual ladder that the institution of language provides. The baboons differ from us both, in having no such ladder to climb.

The institution of language is, however, only the first of many powerful mechanisms at this third and supra-individual level of learning. My hope, in later essays, is to provide a novel perspective on all of them by exploring their roles in the regulation, amplification, and transmission of human cognitive activities at the first two levels of learning, as conceived within the neurostructural and neurodynamical frameworks outlined above. The payoff, if there is one, lies in the multi-level coherence of the portrait of human cognition that slowly emerges, and in the fertility of that portrait in grounding novel explanations of various aspects of human cognitive activity found problematic by our existing epistemological tradition. In short, I shall try to tell a new story about some old problems. In the meantime, I hope to have whetted your appetite for the larger program.

REFERENCES

Cottrell, G. (1991). 'Extracting Features from Faces Using Compression Networks: Face Identity, Emotions, and Gender Recognition Using Holons', in D. Touretzky, J. Elman, T. Sejnowski, and G. Hinton (eds.), *Connectionist Models: Proceedings of the 1990 Summer School*. San Mateo, Calif.: Morgan Kaufman, 328–37.
Fodor, J. A. (1975). *The Language of Thought*. New York: Crowell.

5

How to Know (that Knowledge-that is Knowledge-how)

Stephen Hetherington

In this paper I revive, refine, and apply an idea that has received undeservedly little epistemological attention over the past forty or so years. It concerns the nature of knowledge; and if it is correct, then knowledge is fundamentally not what most contemporary philosophers seemingly take it to be. I will try to render the basic idea more appealing, by showing how to embed it quite deeply within epistemology, and thereby how to redirect some core epistemological discussions. In short, I will suggest why the idea in question deserves to be more prominent in epistemology's future than it has been in epistemology's past.

1. THE RYLEAN DISTINCTION

Over half a century ago, Ryle (1949: ch. II; 1971) attracted epistemological attention with his distinguishing between *knowing-that*—propositional or factual knowledge, knowing that such-and-such is so—and *knowing-how*—practical knowledge, knowing how to do something.[1] Accompanying that distinction was Ryle's argument for the falsity of *intellectualism* about knowledge-how. His contention was that knowing how to do A need not include having some guiding knowledge that p.[2] An intelligently performed action need not be preceded and powered, let alone at all constituted, by consideration of some proposition, let alone by knowledge of the proposition's being true.

Ryle's analysis engendered two dominant reactions. The first has been to accept that knowledge-that and knowledge-how are metaphysically asunder:

Knowledge-that is a cognitive state in which one accurately represents or reflects or reports some aspect of reality; knowledge-how is not. Knowledge-how is an ability, a not-necessarily-cognitive capacity to do or act; knowledge-that is not.

---

[1] Smith (1988: 15 n.2) suggests that Dewey was the first modern philosopher to articulate the distinction.

[2] When I talk of knowledge-how, I am not talking of knowing how it is that p, for example. This is a kind of knowledge-that, as Franklin (1981: 194) explains. (And in section 11 that distinction will matter.)

There have also been attempts to refute Ryle. Almost unfailingly, these have sought to show that knowledge-how is a kind of knowledge-that—in effect, to keep some version of intellectualism alive, according knowledge-that that kind of conceptual centrality.

However, there is a further possible reaction to Ryle's challenge. Maybe (as Ryle thought) knowledge-how is not a kind of knowledge-that. Yet maybe (and contrary to what Ryle thought) knowledge-that and knowledge-how are not wholly distinct. I will argue that knowledge-that and knowledge-how are not distinct, because a reduction of the one to the other *is* possible. But it is not the reduction that is generally contemplated. I will show that it is knowledge-*that* which can be reduced—to knowledge-how. To know that *p* is to know how to perform various actions; or so I will contend.

2. THE RYLEAN ARGUMENT

I begin by defending Ryle against a recent attempted reduction—by Stanley and Williamson (2001)—of knowledge-how to knowledge-that.[3] Appropriately, their initial goal is to establish, swiftly and emphatically, that Ryle's reasoning fails. But their anti-Rylean argument fails, also swiftly and emphatically. In part, that is because they misunderstand how Ryle was reasoning. In part, it is because Ryle was right in this respect.

Stanley and Williamson present Ryle's argument as having two premises and a *reductio* assumption (413–14):[4]

1. For any action *F*: If one *F*s, one employs knowledge how to *F*.
2. For any *p*: If one employs knowledge that *p*, one contemplates the proposition that *p*.

RA For some φ: Knowledge how to *F* is knowledge that $\varphi(F)$.

By 1, if one *F*s (for some particular *F*), one employs knowledge how to *F*. Hence, by RA, there is some φ such that one has knowledge that $\varphi(F)$. By 2, one therefore contemplates the proposition that $\varphi(F)$. But contemplating a proposition is an action itself. Consequently, 1—and then RA, and then 2—also applies to that action, thereby generating a *further* action of contemplation, to which 1—and then RA, and then 2—will apply, thereby generating... and so on, *ad infinitum*. We thus embark upon a vicious infinite regress, with an infinite number of increasingly complex acts of contemplation being required if even the initial action *F* is to be performed. No such action, therefore, *is* performed, if each of 1, 2, and RA is true. Yet we know that actions *are* performed. Consequently, the conjunction of 1, 2, and RA is false. Given 1 and 2, RA is false.

---

[3] Snowdon (2003) helps to prepare the conceptual way for approaches such as theirs.

[4] In 1 and 2, I make explicit, via initial quantification, what Stanley and Williamson leave implicit.

That is Ryle's argument, as reconstructed by Stanley and Williamson. Now, they wish to retain RA (with the rest of their paper being an attempt to model it). So, how can they reject Ryle's argument while leaving RA intact? Their answer (414–16) is simple. If 1 is to be true, it must be restricted to intentional actions, because otherwise actions such as digesting one's food falsify 1. But once the argument is restricted in that way, 2 is false, because many exercises of knowledge-that are not accompanied by an intentional action of contemplating a proposition.[5] In short, at least one of 1 and 2 is false. Hence, RA need not be classified as false, even given Ryle's argument.

Unfortunately for Stanley and Williamson's project, however, they have misunderstood both the focus and the form, let alone the force, of Ryle's reasoning.

For a start, central to Ryle's discussion is the assumption that not all actions are exercises of knowledge-how: not all are intelligently performed actions. He distinguishes (1949: 28–9, 45–7) between actions which manifest knowledge-how and ones which do not. Accordingly, he would not accept 1 (en route to rejecting RA). What Ryle does rely on, I suggest, is this intellectualist premise (where, in effect, R(1) replaces Stanley and Williamson's 1 and RA, and R(2) replaces their 2):

R For any action F, and for some content φ describing a sufficient criterion of how to do F: If (when doing F) one knows how to F, then (1) one already has knowledge that $\varphi(F)$, which (2) one knows how to, and one does, apply so as to do F.

R(1) says that some appropriate knowledge-that's presence is required for there to be a given case of knowledge-how. R(2) describes how the knowledge-that's presence is then involved in bringing about the given exercise of that knowledge-how. And that R reflects both the spirit and key details of Ryle's thinking is shown by this representative passage (1949: 31):

According to the [intellectualist] legend, whenever an agent does anything intelligently, his act is preceded and steered by another internal act of considering a regulative proposition appropriate to his practical problem.... Next, supposing that still to act reasonably I must first perpend the reason for so acting, how am I led to make a suitable application of the reason to the particular situation which my action is to meet?... [T]he absurd assumption made by the intellectualist legend is this, that a performance of any sort inherits all its title to intelligence from some anterior internal operation of planning what to do.

R then allows the Rylean anti-intellectualist argument to proceed along these lines:

If one knows how to F, then one does F only if (for some content φ describing a sufficient criterion of how to do F):
one already has knowledge that $\varphi(F)$, which one knows how to, and one does, apply so as to do F.

[5] Stanley and Williamson (2001: 415) cite Ginet's (1975: 7) example of one's (i) manifesting the knowledge that the door is opened by turning the handle without (ii) contemplating any proposition to this or a similar effect.

But if one already knows how to—and one does—apply one's knowledge that $\varphi(F)$ so as to do F, then this is a *fresh* instance of both performing and knowing how to perform a specific action. At which point, R is again applicable; and so the foregoing form of reasoning recurs. We thereby begin a regress (a vicious infinite one) of more and more instances of increasingly complex regulative knowledge-that being needed and applications of them being performed—all of this, before one can perform even one action which manifests knowledge-how. Given R, therefore, we are unable to perform even one such action in the first place. Yet we *can* do so. Hence, R is false.

However, R is intellectualism-as-applied-to-our-intelligently-performed-actions, which is to say that it *is* intellectualism. Consequently, intellectualism is false.

And what, now, of Stanley and Williamson's objection to what they believe to be Ryle's reasoning? Does their objection also undermine the revised Rylean argument?

Not at all. None of us, I take it, knows how to digest food; we just do it, with the pertinent parts of our bodies functioning appropriately. So, that kind of case is irrelevant to R, even if it falsifies Stanley and Williamson's 1. And cases in which a person uses some knowledge that p without contemplating the proposition p, even if they falsify Stanley and Williamson's 2, leave R untouched. For although R(2) talks of *applying* one's knowledge that $\varphi(F)$ so as to do F, this does not entail that an act of *contemplating* or *considering* is involved. The application could be quite automatic and unconscious.

Thus, Stanley and Williamson have not done justice to the Rylean reasoning. Correlatively, they have not shown that the logical space exists within which to locate their anti-Rylean reduction of knowledge-how to knowledge-that. Others, such as Koethe (2002), Schiffer (2002), and Rumfitt (2003), have commented critically upon the latter analysis. Yet for all that Stanley and Williamson have shown to the contrary, we *already* know—courtesy of our Rylean argument— that their analysis cannot be correct. Knowledge-how is not simply, or even complicatedly, knowledge-that.

3. THE KNOWLEDGE-AS-ABILITY HYPOTHESIS

But it does not follow, from that Rylean success, that knowledge-that is as distinct from knowledge-how as Ryle took it to be. On the contrary; here is why we should investigate the possibility of knowledge-that *being* a kind of knowledge-how.[6]

Whenever you know that p, you have an *ability*—in that sense, you know how—to represent or respond or report or reason accurately that p (where in

---

[6] This idea's initial (albeit brief) formulation seems to have been by Hartland-Swann (1956; 1957), perhaps inspired by some Wittgensteinian thoughts. It is a conception of knowledge which is all-but-invisible in contemporary epistemology. The most similar version to the one I will present is by White (1982: 115–21). A recent advocate is Hyman (1999), whose emphasis is slightly different to mine. He aims to determine 'how [knowledge, if it is an ability] gets expressed in thought and behaviour' (438). My focus will be on how, if knowledge is an ability, various central epistemological problems about knowledge would be recast—and even solved.

general these potential outcomes need not be publicly verifiable). Whenever you also happen to *be* representing or responding or reporting or reasoning accurately that *p*, are you *only then* knowing that *p*? Traditionally, epistemologists would imply so, telling us, for example, that knowledge that *p* is some apt sort of accurate representation that *p*. On that traditional way of thinking, therefore, the *ability* to represent or report or respond or reason accurately is not the knowledge; it only accompanies or generates the knowledge. Rather (on such thinking), that ability's *manifestation* on a specific occasion—that instance of accurately representing or reporting or responding or reasoning—is the knowledge. (One knows that *p* at time *t* only insofar as at *t* one has the accurate representation that *p*, say.) However, this implies that to have an ability to know that *p* is neither thereby, nor even impliedly, to know that *p*, because not all abilities are ever manifested. Yet that implication is mistaken. If you know how to know that *p*, then you *do* know that *p*.

Having said that, though, two points of clarification are needed. First, in mentioning your knowing how to know that *p*, I am not talking of your knowing how to know that *p* in the sense of knowing how to *find* someone who knows whether *p*, for instance (and who will tell you whether *p*). In that circumstance, it would *not* follow that you do know that *p*. But if you know how—by having the ability *within yourself*—to know that *p*, you do know that *p*.[7] It is that sense of knowing how to know that *p* of which I am speaking. Second, we need to be careful here about temporal indexing. I am not saying that if you are able now to observe tomorrow that *p*, for example, you know now that *p*. What I am claiming is that if you are able now to observe *now* that *p*, say, you know now that *p*.[8]

So, with those two qualifications being taken for granted, this simpler interpretation suggests itself:

> Your knowing that *p* *is* your having the ability to manifest various accurate representations of *p*. The knowledge as such is the ability as such.

[7] Here is a possible objection to that claim: 'A person could know how to proceed in order to know that *p*, by (for instance) knowing what kind of evidence is needed, where to locate it, and so forth. Yet suppose that, perhaps through lack of interest, she declines to pursue that path of inquiry. She therefore knows how to know that *p*, even as she does not know that *p*.' But that objection relies upon a misinterpretation. As described, the person knows how to know *whether p*, not how to know *that p*. In contrast (and as I claim), she already knows how to know that *p*, only if she already knows that *p*. (To this, the objector might reply as follows: 'If she knows how to know whether *p*, she knows how to know that *p and* how to know that not-*p*.' That is not so, though. At best, she knows how to know-that-*p-if*-at-a-later-time-she-is-to-know-that-*p*; and she stands analogously to knowing that not-*p*. Yet this does not entail her now knowing *simpliciter*, unconditionally, how to know now that *p*.)

[8] 'Right now, you cannot see the chewing gum beneath your table. Yet you are *able* to observe it, because you can proceed to look under the table. This falls short of your knowing now of the gum's presence, though.' But that suggested analysis does not threaten the hypothesis I am developing. Because I am not now looking under the table, I am able *now* to observe the gum only *later*, rather than to observe it now. (Nor can I remember it now. I have not previously looked under the table.) My knowing now of the gum's presence is my being able now to observe it now.

I will call this the *knowledge-as-ability* hypothesis (and in a moment I will generalize it somewhat).[9]

It is an hypothesis that clashes with the usual epistemological claim that knowledge is a kind of belief. But that usual claim might not be true, even if belief is allowed to be either occurrent or dispositional. If the knowledge-as-ability hypothesis is correct, then knowledge is not an occurrent belief. And it might not even be a dispositional belief.[10] For, given that hypothesis, no occurrent belief is knowledge; it is at most a *manifestation* of knowledge. And a dispositional belief can be knowledge only if the disposition amounts to an ability to represent or respond or report or reason. However, this conceives of belief more broadly than is standard. Generally, epistemologists would say that the knowledge that *p* is the belief that *p*—and that there are *also* associated abilities to reply or report or reason that *p*, for example. This offers us a needlessly fragmented analysis, though. Even if we leave in place that distinction between belief (as some kind of representation) and replies or reports or reasonings, we may still *link* them via knowledge. And we need not regard *only one* of them, such as belief, as being the knowledge. Each of them could just be a way of manifesting the knowledge that *p*, where this is not something else *like* them (a further kind of mental or verbal act or state), but is instead the ability *to* be manifested in such ways.

There is significant theoretical unification in that sort of analysis. We may acknowledge the existence of several ways to manifest the knowledge that *p*, with true belief being only one such way. True acceptance is another, as is one's solving a theoretical problem to which *p* is the correct answer. There is also one's answering correctly—to oneself or others—when asked—by oneself or others—whether it is true that *p*. Arguably, there is even the phenomenon of performing actions which would not be appropriate unless *p* were true. And why should a state of believing that *p* be accorded a special status amongst these, and other, possible manifestations of what would appear to be an underlying ability to generate these responses or representations? Why should knowledge that *p* be only a belief, for instance, rather than any of these other possible ways of registering that *p*?[11] Collectively, they may readily be interpreted as constituting a theoretically unified body of possible manifestations of knowledge that *p*. No one member of the collective deserves to be singled out as being the knowledge—with the others being mere manifestations of it. Accordingly, we may conjecture that the knowledge that *p* lies *beyond* them,

[9] This hypothesis should be distinguished from an analysis like Sosa's (2003: ch. 9), for example, according to which a true belief is knowledge when it results from an exercise of a cognitively virtuous faculty or capacity. According to Sosa, having such a capacity or ability is necessary to a true belief's being knowledge. Yet he allows that the knowledge as such *is* the belief (one possessing some favoured features, such as that of being accurate). As I am about to explain, that is not how I conceive of knowledge.

[10] Might it be a disposition *to* believe, though? (On this distinction, see Audi 1994.) See note 37 on why I will not be focussing on dispositions. And as to belief, I am about to explain why belief is merely one among several phenomena to which knowing can be constitutively related.

[11] A few epistemologists, such as Lehrer (1990: 10–11, 26–36), have advocated conceiving of knowledge as being an acceptance, not a belief. And Cohen (1992: ch. IV) has described possible

without being *like* them (that is, just one more *of* them). Specifically, they would be manifestations of it; and it would be the ability *to* generate such manifestations. Once more, then, my hypothesis is that knowledge that p is the ability—the know-how—to respond, to reply, to represent, or to reason accurately that p.[12] (For short: it is the ability—the knowledge-how—to *register* accurately that p.)[13]

4. JUSTIFICATION

The first goal of our knowledge-as-ability hypothesis must be to show that it allows us to model, and, if possible, to explain, knowledge-that's having various key features. The hypothesis already characterises knowledge-that as an ability to register *accurately* that p. From the outset, therefore, knowledge's traditional *truth* condition is retained. In this section, I consider the equally traditional *justification* component within propositional knowledge. Does our ability analysis of knowledge model that component? It does indeed.[14]

First, an ability might be quite pronounced—enough so to be a *skill*. (And in the rest of this paper that is how I will understand the term 'ability'.) Hence, there is no problem in principle with this kind of ability's having precisely the *strength*—whatever, precisely, the degree of strength is—that justificatory support within knowledge is supposed to have.[15] Your having justification for a belief that p (as part of knowing that p) might be your having strong evidence supporting that

---

roles within knowledge for both belief and acceptance. I am spreading knowledge's metaphysical net even farther afield.

[12] Or maybe more besides; I leave open how representational and discursive any manifestations of this ability have to be. I also leave open the answer to this question: 'What of those times when I am unconscious, unable to observe or recall or reflect? Do I lack all knowledge then?' Maybe I do. When asleep, say, I have the ability to wake, and *then* to know, at *that* time by having pertinent further abilities.

[13] Of course, we could retain knowledge's being a belief in particular, so long as we build these further features into our concept of belief. But then beliefs, on our view of them, would *be* abilities. My hypothesis would be avoided only in name, not substance.

[14] But it also allows for the possibility of justification *not* always being required within knowledge, a possibility argued for by Hetherington (2001a: ch. 4). If the relevant kind of ability to register accurately that p requires only a mere physical capacity to reply accurately, say, then this ability might lack both the normative dimension and the counterfactual strength that epistemologists routinely expect knowledge's justification component to provide. In this paper, I leave open, by providing a quite schematic analysis, the issue of whether knowledge can ever be so weak. The issue arises no more problematically for my analysis than for comparatively standard ones. What mine needs to do is, like other analyses, to *allow for* the issue to arise; and this it does.

[15] How strong *is* knowledge's justificatory component? Where, exactly, is the justificatory boundary between knowing that p and not knowing that p? In this paper I offer no answer to that difficult (and underdiscussed) question; here, it amounts to asking how much of a *skill* the ability needs to be. (Must it make the knower an expert, say—even if only an expert at accurately registering now that p?) The suggestion to be made in section 5 will at least accommodate this *issue* more simply and naturally than can be accomplished within a more traditional epistemology. On what that epistemological problem is, see BonJour (2002: 43, 46, 48–9; 2003: 21–3) and Hetherington (2001a: 124–6, 143–5). And on why the non-traditional idea in section 5 improves significantly on traditional epistemology in this respect, see Hetherington (forthcoming).

belief's being true. And the presence of such evidence could either make you, or reflect your being, *strongly* able to register accurately that *p*, such as by being able to do this reliably, in a wider range of apt circumstances.

Second, abilities can take different *forms*. (i) Some are manifested in a partly or wholly 'automatic' way. For instance, when a batter is well able to play a particular sort of shot, his exercising this ability could require him not to think, or even to be able to think, about playing the shot when doing so. The shot must be performed, not only in apt circumstances, but *wholly unreflectively*.[16] Any accompanying reflection—even the person's still being *able* to reflect at that moment—would interfere with his playing the shot well, no matter how otherwise apt the circumstances happen to be. Now imagine an ability, having that kind of structure, being directed at accurately registering that *p*. This would make any such registering justified in an *externalist* way. For example, there would be an actual *reliability*— and without any accompanying reflection on that reliability—in the person's ability to register accurately that *p*. (ii) Some abilities, in order to be exercised effectively, *do* involve either the actuality or the availability of mental monitoring— checking, evaluating, reasoning, and so forth. An ability like this, when directed at accurately registering that *p*, will make any such registering justified in an *internalist* way.[17] For example, good evidence would be used reflectively in generating, and in evaluating whether to maintain, the registering.[18]

5. GRADES OF KNOWLEDGE

It is routine for epistemologists to agree that the justification which helps to constitute a piece of knowledge that *p* can be more or less strong, providing better or worse support for the truth of the belief that *p*. Hence, epistemologists readily accept that there could be two pieces of knowledge that *p*, each including sufficient justification, with one of these bodies of justification being stronger than the other. Yet it is also standard for epistemologists not to accept that the better justified one of these two pieces of knowledge is thereby stronger itself, simply *as* knowledge that *p*. Even if justification is gradational, knowledge is not (say epistemologists in general): in this sense, knowledge that *p* is absolute. Elsewhere, though (2001*a*), I have argued that there is no such structural disparity between justification and knowledge: *each* is gradational. There are different ways to describe this aspect of knowledge. The better justified piece of knowledge that *p* might be called either *better* knowledge that *p* (2001*a*) or *less fallible* knowledge that *p* (2002*b*), for example.

[16] This could be so even if he would not have been able to play the shot so well without previously reflecting on how to play it.

[17] On the difference between epistemic externalism and epistemic internalism, see Hetherington (1996*a*: chs. 14, 15) and Kornblith (2001).

[18] Craig (1990: 157) apparently endorses a similar view of some quite discursive cases of knowledge-that—namely, as crucially involving some intellectual knowledge-how.

And the knowledge-as-ability hypothesis coheres well with those independently supported ways of talking about knowledge. After all, an ability can be stronger or weaker, more or less well developed. In general, abilities are gradational. So, the same is true even of a particular case of knowledge that p, insofar as it is an ability. This is especially true, given how *complex* the relevant ability is. It can be more or less strong in *many* respects. For instance, your ability to register accurately that p can be more or less psychologically resilient in the face of questioning; it can be more or less sensitive to a more or less wide range of actual and counterfactual circumstances; it can be more or less imaginative in thinking of possible questions itself to which it can then be more or less thorough in responding; it can be more or less fast at doing any of this; and so forth.[19] Given the knowledge-as-ability hypothesis, therefore, it is wholly appropriate to accord your knowledge that p a gradational quality, reflecting these and kindred possibilities. Any given case of knowledge that p is thus a more or less well developed and complex ability—a stronger or weaker instance of knowledge-how.

Accordingly, when there are two cases of knowledge that p, with one of them being better justified than the other, the knowledge-as-ability hypothesis allows us to regard the better justified piece of knowledge that p as being a *stronger* or *better* or *less fallible* ability to register accurately that p. Section 4 implies that we may readily regard the knowledge that p's strength *qua* knowledge that p as being constituted by the strength of its justification component. And now we see in more detail what this involves. In various ways that reflect the different kinds of ability involved, your knowledge that p can be more, *or* it can be less, strong. The knowledge-as-ability hypothesis provides further support for saying that you thereby know more, or you know less, *well* that p.[20]

6. SCEPTICAL CHALLENGES

The knowledge-as-ability hypothesis equates knowledge that p with an ability to *register* accurately that p. And (as section 3 explained) that ability can include the ability, for example, to *respond* accurately that p. Such responses could be given to isolated or to sustained questions, to simple questions or to subtle and complicated ones. Consequently, the responses might not—but might—involve the careful use of evidence and reasoning. And among the more subtle questions

---

[19] For some indication of the possible dimensions of such complexity, see Elgin (1988) and Goldman (1986: Part II).

[20] Hyman (1999: 439) overlooks this aspect of the ability analysis of knowledge. Rightly, he realises that having the ability in question does not entail being able to manifest the ability in *all* of the relevant possible ways. He also says that being able to produce *one* such manifestation does not entail that the ability in question is present. What does follow, then? There is some inescapable vagueness. And is this a problem for the knowledge-as-ability hypothesis? We now see that it need not be, because we may allow that any case of knowledge that p is an ability which is more, *or* it is less, well developed.

which might need to be carefully answered, by using good evidence and reasoning, are *sceptical* ones. Is there knowledge? Could there be some? Are people at all rational? Is there knowledge of a physical world? Does anyone have moral knowledge? Such questions are easily posed, less easily understood or well answered. Nonetheless, in this section I offer some possible non-sceptical cheer. (And in the next section I supply some more.) I will indicate how, given the knowledge-as-ability hypothesis, sceptical questions about knowledge might even *help* us as putative knowers.

First of all, not everyone doubts equally well, and not all sceptical questions are of equal difficulty and depth.[21] You can question the truth of, or the support for, a view more *or* less deeply, searchingly, and accurately.[22] And insofar as knowledge is an ability to register accurately, a particular instance of knowledge is a *stronger* ability to register accurately (other things being equal) insofar as it includes the ability to answer sceptical questions which are themselves stronger—more probing and intelligent doubts and challenges. Correlatively, one way to *improve* a given case of knowledge is by subjecting it to sceptical questions—indeed, ones which are stronger, not weaker. You would improve your instance of knowledge by taking the sceptical questions seriously, engaging with them, and answering them in ways that establish your having the knowledge in question. Section 5 argued that in principle it is possible to improve a piece of knowledge (by strengthening the ability which constitutes that knowledge). One possible way of doing so is by both encountering and countering sceptical questioning.

Popper might well have approved of this picture. For there is also a real risk of *not* satisfactorily answering the sceptical questions. One might not defeat a given sceptical doubt even to one's own satisfaction, let alone to widespread epistemological applause. In effect, therefore, sceptical questions can function as potential *falsifiers* of one's claims to have either some particular item of knowledge or some stated kind of knowledge. This is especially true of some sceptical doubts—those which are quite strong. Even if one's knowledge that *p*—the relevant ability—survives a less searching sceptical question, there is a chance of its succumbing to a more powerful one. Should we therefore seek to *evade* those sceptical questions, particularly the powerful ones? Well, a safe life need not be a significant or strong one; and much the same is true of knowledge. Whenever one's knowledge that *p*—the relevant ability—is grappling with sceptical questions, *at least it is being tested.* And there is a sense in which the sceptical questions thereby become *part* of the knowledge, the ability, itself. This does not occur automatically; simply hearing and replying to a sceptical question need not include genuinely testing one's ability to register accurately. Still, whenever one *is* seriously subjecting that ability

---

[21] Less skilful sceptical questioning can be rather like a child's relentless *why*ning—'Why? Why?'.

[22] Often, education is partly a matter of enriching this sort of ability. For each person in turn, there can be beliefs whose truth would, prior to appropriate education, have seemed beyond the reach of real doubt. Reasons for doubting would not have occurred to the person; they would not have been taken seriously; or they would not have been well understood.

to sceptical scrutiny, one is living a core Popperian moral: one is treating one's knowledge-claims as being open to possible falsification. And whenever that ability survives a specific sceptical test (if indeed it does), this is a survival with a Popperian ramification. Just as specific sceptical questions may be thought of as testing a specific instance or kind of ability to register accurately, that ability may be regarded as becoming *stronger* with any survival of such a test. As I acknowledged, there is always the chance of a particular instance or kind of knowledge *not* surviving that sceptical test. That knowledge could be lost entirely, such as when sceptical possibilities intrude too significantly upon one's ability to focus one's thoughts upon what is true. This remains a risk you take in attempting such testing; sceptical doubts *can* become psychologically real for us. But again, the Popperian moral is that wherever there is such a risk, a correlatively powerful *gain* is also possible. If your knowledge does survive, then not only is it still present; its gradational dimension is now enhanced. It is stronger; it has improved; it has grown.

This possibility imparts extra epistemic urgency to much *epistemological* debate, too. For it is within epistemology, most obviously, that sceptical questioning is contemplated, understood, and discussed.[23] And thus, we now find, such epistemological debate provides a special opportunity of *improving* particular cases or kinds of knowledge, as we confront our knowledge-claims with adventurous and striking sceptical questions which we endeavour to answer non-sceptically and successfully. Yet, by the same token, epistemological inquiry can be epistemically dangerous. To let sceptical questions loose among our knowledge-claims might be to startle the latter into retreat. We might *lose* the knowledge which we were testing via these sceptical subtleties. This is so, even though that same knowledge might not have been dislodged if we had not exposed it to those sceptical thoughts. Still, we can console ourselves with the aspirational thought that if the knowledge does manage to survive the sceptical examination, then (other things being equal) it is now *stronger* than it would otherwise have been. If it had not undergone that testing experience, then (all else being equal) it would have continued to exist, *but in a less impressive form*. It would have been comparatively impoverished *qua* knowledge that *p*, say. It would have been a *lesser* piece of knowledge that *p*, qualitatively speaking, than it becomes if it survives the sceptical questioning (again, all else being equal). Gradationally, there would have been stasis, not growth, in that piece of knowledge. So, if the putative knowledge

[23] This does not entail that, within epistemology, sceptical questions *always* are, or need to be, present in these ways, contrary to what Lewis (1996) claims. He believes that to do epistemology is automatically to be enmeshed in a sceptical web, attending to sceptical possibilities: 'Do some epistemology. Let your fantasies rip. Find uneliminated possibilities of error everywhere .... [I]t will be inevitable that epistemology must destroy knowledge' (559–60). But Lewis is both descriptively and normatively mistaken about that. It is central to his paper's most striking claim, namely, 'That is how knowledge is elusive. Examine it, and straightway it vanishes' (560). However, at most Lewis has shown that (given his theory of knowledge) to think somewhat sympathetically about scepticism—which, I am saying, is *not* essential to doing epistemology—is to lack knowledge when doing so. And that is a far less disturbing conclusion than Lewis claims to have gained.

does engage successfully with sceptical ideas, it is strengthened as the knowledge it thereby continues to be. It is strengthened, precisely because the relevant ability to continue registering accurately will have improved. It will now be a more fully and subtly developed ability to register accurately, even in response to more difficult and challenging sceptical questions. These are questions with which many people's pieces of knowledge do not engage, thereby missing that Popperian, hence risky, opportunity to *improve* as knowledge.

7. SCEPTICAL LIMITATIONS

Sceptics will interpret those Popperian possibilities rather less optimistically. They will emphasise the risks, dismissing the opportunities. They will assure us that, because sceptical questions cannot be answered adequately, there is no knowledge, let alone (as I was urging in section 6) any *improved* knowledge as a result of adequately answering the sceptical questions.

However, the knowledge-as-ability hypothesis provides a means of evading that sceptical pessimism. For example, suppose that, when confronted by the sceptical question of whether you know that you are not dreaming that p, you retain your skill at registering accurately that p. Everything else being equal, the knowledge-as-ability hypothesis would therefore accord you the knowledge that p. Even so, the knowledge-as-ability hypothesis remains able to explain how this survival of your knowledge might reflect, in part, what a sceptic would view as a *limitation*, not purely an achievement, on your part. You might have the knowledge, in part, because of your not being a sufficiently subtle thinker to enter imaginatively and deeply into the sceptic's thinking. You hear the sceptic's question; you answer briskly, even brusquely, and non-sceptically, while retaining the ability which is your knowing that p. You have kept that knowledge that p, in part by reacting to the sceptic as if you had *not* been listening to her. Yet the knowledge-as-ability hypothesis allows us to say that this could *be* one of the many—perhaps the infinitely many—possible ways of knowing that p. Is that assessment by the knowledge-as-ability hypothesis a mistake, a failing? No, because the assessment will also include your being deemed to know that p only unsubtly, unimaginatively, shallowly. Must we infer that therefore you would *not* know that p? Again, no: you would lack *good* knowledge that p, *impressive* knowledge that p. Nevertheless, section 5 argued that knowledge can be qualitatively gradational: it is possible for an instance of knowledge that p to be more—*or* to be less—good or impressive as knowledge that p than is some other piece of knowledge that p. And section 6 described how sceptical questions, in particular, present us with opportunities to *make* our knowledge of a specific fact more impressive, all else being equal. But if you do not take those opportunities (perhaps because, as we imagined occurring, you have not seriously engaged with the sceptic's way of thinking), it does not follow that you *lack* the knowledge which was being sceptically questioned. All that *follows* is that you would lack the improved knowledge which could have been formed by your replying well to those sceptical questions. However, in general you do not *fail* to know that *p* simply because there are ways in which, in theory, you could know *better* that *p*.[24] Thus, we find that the very same feature (outlined in section 6) which makes sceptical questions epistemically tempting also lessens their epistemic danger. For insofar as answering a sceptical question well would (other things being equal) improve one's knowledge that *p*, one's not answering it well would (other things being equal) either extinguish, *or* lessen the quality of, one's knowledge that *p*. Sceptics (like non-sceptics responding to them) discuss only the former—pessimistic—alternative. In contrast, I am saying that the latter one should not be overlooked. If I am right to do so, then the traditional—pessimistic—sceptical interpretation is conceptually optional at best.

Still, the knowledge-as-ability hypothesis does not preclude sceptical victories. It easily accommodates the possibility that a skill can disappear. You could cease being sufficiently accurate in registering that *p*, for instance, if the sceptic happens to instil enough actual doubts in your mind as to *p*, perhaps enough doubts to make you hesitate, shift your focus, and observe the relevant aspects of the world less directly and accurately. Think of how an athlete's skill in performing some movement can be weakened by her not closing her mind to various distracting thoughts. These need not even be irrelevant thoughts. They could be about her technique, say, these being thoughts which she *should* have at some other times. But they can also include thoughts about mistakes which she might make, possible ways for her not to make the movement so well. And when performing the action, these are not thoughts she should have. Presumably, the 'flow' of her performance would falter, impinging upon the 'zone' within which she is manifesting her ability. If this happens too often, the ability itself could be weakened. And now let us return to the case of sceptical questions. For that kind of 'thoughtful distraction' problem (as we may call it), concerning an athlete's maintaining her ability to make some special movement, is analogous to how sceptical questions can affect the ability which is one's knowing that *p*. Those questions highlight possible ways in which one could be mistaken; and a perpetual focus upon such possibilities might well divert one's attention from what is true, leading to one's making clumsy or mistaken cognitive 'movements'. It could disrupt one's 'flow', impinging upon one's 'zone', as an observer of, and thinker about, whether it is true that *p*. It could weaken one's ability to register accurately that *p*, as one begins thinking about how one might *not* be registering accurately that *p*. In such ways, then, sceptical questions can weaken your pertinent knowledge-how—which is to say, your knowledge-that. A real skill might really deteriorate.[25]

[24] At the very least, by giving little attention to the sceptical questions, you would fail to know *perfectly* that *p*. Yet how many abilities or skills are ever perfect? Imperfection rarely turns a putative ability into an inability.

[25] This is a special case of the oft-made claim that one's becoming overly reflective or intellectual can deprive one of knowledge of the world. Usually, it seems, the claim is interpreted as saying that

Again, though, this does not automatically occur whenever no intellectually compelling reply to a sceptical argument is presented.[26] The knowledge-as-ability hypothesis offers us an array of possible outcomes other than the sceptical one. If you cannot provide a rationally compelling direct answer to the sceptic's challenges, then (other things being equal) you thereby do not *improve* your knowledge that *p*. But you need not thereby *lose* your knowledge that *p*. It is possible, now that you are aware of the sceptic's questions, that your inability to improve your knowledge that *p* by fully disposing of those questions will somewhat *lessen the quality* of your knowledge that *p*. This does not entail the demise of that knowledge, though. That depends on further factors, pertaining to whether you are able to maintain the relevant skill. To take one pertinent example:

> Students who enter an epistemology classroom, confidently knowing that there is an external world, might leave that classroom still confidently knowing that there is an external world. But in fact (without their realising it) that knowledge might now be somewhat less proficient or strong than it was previously. Other things being equal, this *is* the result if the students have now heard—with some interest, but without really disposing of—some searching sceptical questions posed by the teacher. Accordingly, their knowledge as such can continue to be present, even if in a less impressive way than the students assume is the case.[27]

So, sceptical questions, if not answered adequately, can at least *weaken* our knowledge. And they might, *or* might not, thereby eliminate it.[28]

---

one would know less of the world due to one's knowing more of 'unworldly' matters instead. But another possible interpretation is that one could know less of the world due to knowing less of everything—as one never focusses determinately upon a particular truth, due to one's perennially considering *alternative* possibilities.

[26] Is such a direct and intellectually effective reply to sceptical questions possible anyway? Elsewhere (2001*a*: 37–40; 2002: 95–7; 2004), I have tried to provide that sort of answer to sceptical challenges, an answer which does not presuppose this paper's ability analysis of knowledge. That answer confronts sceptical questions by arguing that they fail to constitute real challenges to our having knowledge. They do not describe genuinely independent and prior possibilities—defeaters—that need to be eliminated *before* there is any knowledge that *p* present at all, let alone present and able to be improved.

[27] I am not saying that this is the only possible result in such a situation. For example, if the sceptical questions are accompanied by reasoning which, unbeknownst to the students, is fallacious, then a student's external world knowledge might be better if she ignores that reasoning than if she does not. ('Is inattention therefore being recommended as an epistemic strategy?' Not as such: the student would probably not know that her ignoring the sceptical reasoning could have this benefit. It will do so, only when the sceptical reasoning *is* flawed in itself; and she has not attempted to discover whether the reasoning is like that. Moreover, if she were not to ignore the sceptical reasoning, indeed if she were to engage with it so as to reveal its fallaciousness, then, other things being equal, she could know the external world even better still.)

[28] For more on how a conception of knowledge as being gradational undermines sceptical arguments, see Hetherington (2001*a*: ch. 2). The present section has shown, more specifically, how an analysis of knowledge as being gradational-*because-knowledge-is-an-ability* lessens the power of sceptical challenges.

8. HELPFUL GETTIER CASES

Any analysis of knowledge, even a schematic one such as this paper's, needs to be tested against the phenomenon of Gettier cases. Originated by Gettier (1963), two main categories of Gettier case have been developed: *helpful* Gettier cases and *dangerous* ones, as they can be called (Hetherington 2001*a*: 73–4). I discuss the former kind in this section, and the latter kind in section 9. In each section, I will be asking whether the knowledge-as-ability hypothesis helps us to understand or resolve such cases.

Chisholm's (1989: 93) sheep-in-the-field case is a representative (helpful) Gettier case. Here it is, in a slightly expanded version:

> Standing outside a field, you see what looks like a normal sheep. You therefore have good sensory evidence of there being a sheep in that field. So, you infer that *S*, that there *is* a sheep in the field. And you are correct, because there is indeed one there. What *you* see, however, is a dog, disguised as a sheep. The real sheep in the field is hidden from your gaze.

Is your belief that *S* knowledge? It is true. It is justified, too, insofar as apparently decent sensory evidence justifies such a belief. Epistemologists have no hesitation, though, in denying that it is knowledge. In general, they have taken that denial to challenge, fundamentally and freshly, our understanding of what knowledge is.

So, let us see how the ability analysis might apply to the case. I will use it to derive two possible, but contrary, interpretations. The first, in (A), respects the usual assessment of the case (according to which your belief that *S* is not knowledge). However, we will also see why that assessment need not force us to reassess the nature of knowledge. Next, in (B), I show how, using the ability analysis, we might reject that usual assessment of the case anyway.

(A) *Lack of knowledge.* The case juggles two main components. (1) Normally, when seeming to yourself to be seeing a sheep in a field, you have an accompanying ability to register accurately that *S* (that is, that there is a sheep in that field). But in this case you see only a disguised dog—apparently a sheep, really a dog. And we might think of this *problematic* circumstance (as it may be termed) as weakening what would otherwise, given the same sensory evidence, be your ability to register accurately that *S*. That ability's being weakened would not entail that you *cannot* register accurately that *S*, even in that setting. The point would be that you are *unlikely*, given that problematic circumstance, to be doing so: you would lack the ability, the skill. (2) The case also includes a *fortuitous* circumstance—the fact of there being a sheep elsewhere in the field, out of your sight. This fortuitous circumstance makes your belief that *S* true: you *are* registering accurately that *S*.

So much for the case's circumstances; what epistemic effects do they have? Section 4 indicated how the ability analysis allows knowledge to include justification, both internalist and externalist justification. That analysis is therefore able to regard the case's problematic circumstance (the disguised dog) as depriving you of good *justification*—good externalist justification, at least—for your belief that *S*. Admittedly, you have what would normally be good justification supporting that belief. But Gettier cases are far from normal. *Apparently* there is justification as you survey the field. Normally, there would thereby *be* justification. Yet, given the case's problematic circumstance, your apparent justification has a significant chance of being mistaken. You are not aware of this; nor can you be, while within the Gettier case. So, it is an externalist failing, inflicted upon your evidence by the hidden problematic circumstance. This is already enough, though, to *dissolve* the Gettier case as such. For it means that externalist criteria of justification allow us to regard the case as one from which either all justification, or a required aspect even of internalist justification, is missing.[29] And if there is a lack of justification, there is no Gettier case in the first place; in which event, our understanding of knowledge is not threatened by what was purportedly Gettier's distinctive challenge. The case's knowledge-denying aspects are included in its problematic circumstance. And the way in which these deny the presence of knowledge may be explained, we have seen just now, by regarding them as denying the presence of justification. The additional inclusion within the case of the fortuitous circumstance (the hidden sheep) simply reminds us that once there is insufficient justification for a particular belief, even the belief's being true does not make it knowledge.

But that allows us to regard the standard interpretation of such cases (namely, as not containing knowledge) as merely giving voice to (i) a general reluctance among epistemologists to attribute knowledge when there is *a significant chance of the person's belief being mistaken*, and (ii) how this remains so, even if her belief is not mistaken. The standard interpretation, therefore, does not entail that Gettier cases like this one reveal some notably new way for a belief not to be knowledge. Gettier, in contrast to what epistemological orthodoxy assumes, has not presented such a radical challenge to our conception of knowledge.

(B) *Presence of knowledge.* Might the standard interpretation of these Gettier cases be wholly mistaken? Might the cases not even be ones from which knowledge be absent? After all (and contrary to what (A) argued), within this representative case you *do* have an ability to register accurately that *S*. Remember (from section 3) that the accurate registering which manifests your knowing that *S* need not be restricted to your representing that *S*, let alone your representing that *S* in response to immediate sensory evidence. For instance, it can include your *answering questions* as to whether *S* is true; and given that (due to the fortuitous circumstance) *S* is true, your answer will always be correct. Similarly, your ability could include your *recalling* your representation of *S*; and (other things being equal) this

---

[29] The required aspect in question is that of not-being-significantly-likely-to-be-mistaken. Even internalists require justification to have this property. Otherwise, only merely-apparent justification is being discussed.

will always be accurate. All things considered, therefore, if you are in a Gettier case like this one, you do have an ability which may be regarded as constituting knowledge. Perhaps this knowledge would lack a strong justificatory *pedigree*. But if the ability analysis is correct, that kind of pedigree is not always required by knowledge.[30] The ability which is the knowledge that *S* can, yet need not, supply its manifestations (such as a belief that *S*) with that kind of history.

Still, perhaps there *is* some notable, even if generally overlooked, justification present within these Gettier cases. In this particular case, your representing that *S must* be accurate, *given* your being in a Gettier case. For it is essential to such a case that the belief in question be true. As we saw in (A), epistemologists say that within Gettier cases there is a significant chance of being mistaken (so that it is really only through luck that the belief is not mistaken). However, that standard epistemological interpretation takes into account only the case's problematic circumstance, thereby failing to analyse the case *as* a Gettier case. Fortuitous circumstances are no less essential to this kind of Gettier case than are problematic ones. And relative to both circumstances—which is to say, within this case *as* a Gettier case—it *follows* that your belief is true. Although Prob(*S*/the problematic circumstance) is low, Prob(*S*/[the problematic circumstance] & [the fortuitous circumstance]) is not. Indeed, the latter value is 1. It could not be higher. Insofar as you are in a Gettier case, therefore, you *do* have an ability which may readily be deemed to be knowledge. From (A), externalist factors seem to deprive you of it (by depriving you of justification); now, in (B), we find them restoring it.[31]

9. DANGEROUS GETTIER CASES

The other category of Gettier case comprises *dangerous* ones. Probably, this category's most famous instance is the fake barns case, first published by Goldman (1976). Again, you are outside a field. This time, you seem, to yourself, to be

[30] On the idea that knowledge need not include a justificatory pedigree, see Levi (1980: 1–2).

[31] 'Is there something suspiciously strong about that argument from probability? Does it imply, surprisingly, that you have knowledge that *S*, in part by according you *perfect* justification for your belief that *S*?' No. The justification is not perfect, because there can be more to justification than that kind of probability measure. Even so, the probability assignment is of some justificatory significance. That argument from probability does entail that, given your being in a Gettier situation, your belief that *S* has to be true. But that entailment is trivially appropriate: by definition, any Gettiered belief is true. And this should alert us to something more substantive. It shows that, in order to lack the knowledge in question within a Gettier case, one needs not to know *that* one is within that Gettier case as such. If you were to know, while inquiring within the sheep-in-the-field Gettier situation, that you are inside that Gettier situation as such, you would thereby know that *S*. You would know that your belief that *S* is true, because, definitionally, within any Gettier situation the belief in question is true. The lack of the knowledge of being in a particular Gettier case is thus necessary to lacking knowledge within one. Yet this entails that the fact simply of being in a Gettier situation—having a justified true belief, in the presence of a hidden fortuitous circumstance—should not be thought of as depriving one of the knowledge that *p*. Accordingly, epistemologists have long been misreading the significance of Gettier cases. (But I will not develop that point any further in this paper. For a related analysis of the Gettier challenge, see Hetherington 2001*b*.)

seeing a barn. Accordingly, you believe that *B*—that you are seeing a barn. And your belief is true.[32] However, once more there is a *problematic* circumstance. This time, it is the fact of there being many fake barns in the vicinity—papier maché barn facades, indistinguishable (when viewed from outside their respective fields) from a real barn. Does that circumstance prevent your belief that *B* from being knowledge, even while leaving in place the belief's being justified and true? Most epistemologists would say so; are they right?

I suspect not. If dialectical charity is to accord the problematic circumstance maximal epistemic impact, we should suppose that you *will* proceed to be deceived by one or more of the fake barns. Yet, even then, the problematic circumstance would still only stand right now to your belief that *B* much as does the fact (supposing it to be one) that tonight, while not seeing a barn, you will have a wholly convincing *dream* that *B*, a dream that will be subjectively indistinguishable for you from your present experience as of seeing a barn. And does the latter circumstance—your misleadingly, albeit convincingly, dreaming later tonight that *B*—prevent your belief that *B* from being knowledge right *now*? Surely not; in which case, the fact that you *will* be deceived by a fake barn does not deprive you of knowledge right now of seeing a barn. Hence, a fortiori, the mere fact of there existing those fake barns right now, regardless of whether you will ever be deceived by them, also does not deprive you of the present knowledge of seeing a barn.

The ability analysis accords well with that view of the case.[33] The existence of the fake barns—like the fact that tonight you will dream that *B*—leaves unimpaired your ability to register (by representing, responding, replying, or reasoning) accurately right now that *B*. This is especially so, given that (contrary to the supposition in the previous paragraph) the mere existence of the fake barns does not entail that you will ever be deceived by them: you might never see them at all. And even if you *are* ever deceived by them, your thereby failing to know at those moments that you are seeing a barn is due simply to knowledge's requiring truth. It does not reflect some hitherto hidden feature of knowledge, one which necessitates a newly complex analysis of knowledge.

Of course, there is another way for the problematic circumstance to have epistemic influence. If you were to be expected to *know* that you are not looking at one of the fake barns right now, with the penalty for lacking that knowledge being your not knowing that *B*, they would in effect be functioning as *sceptical* possibilities in relation to your knowing right now that *B*: each fake barn would represent a possible way of being deceived, one which you need to know is not being actualised.[34] However, sections 6 and 7 showed (as follows) how the ability analysis can weaken the epistemic impact of sceptical doubts and questions. If you were to know that you

---

[32] It is true in a normal way. This kind of case includes no notably or unusually fortuitous circumstance. (On the other hand, we will see, no such circumstance is needed, because the case's problematic circumstance never actually misleads the case's believer.)

[33] It is a view that is argued for in more detail elsewhere. See Hetherington (1998).

[34] For more on how a sceptic might wish to use Gettier circumstances as sceptical possibilities, see Hetherington (1996*b*).

are not looking at a fake barn, you would have survived a potential falsifier of your claim to know that *B*; and the latter knowledge would thereby be (gradationally) *strengthened*.[35] By the same token, though, if you cannot provide what that sceptical questioning seeks, you might be sacrificing *only* that strengthened knowledge that *B*, rather than the knowledge that *B* as such. You might now possess *weakened* knowledge that *B* (especially if you realise that you are aware of not directly confronting the possibility of being deceived by a fake barn). Nevertheless, having even weakened knowledge that *B* is better than not having the knowledge at all. And the latter lack *could* arise, if you lose your epistemic nerve or confidence, say, proceeding to relinquish the belief that *B* in the face of the sceptical thinking.

10. EPISTEMIC AGENTS

Epistemologists generally attribute knowledge to epistemic subjects. But the term 'epistemic subject' could well reflect some substantive, even false, theoretical commitments. Wilfrid Sellars once asked me, when I was a postgraduate student, why I was referring to epistemic *agents*. I had no answer to him. So, I began following his advice, talking only of epistemic subjects. However, the ability analysis suggests that he was mistaken. If that analysis is right, then knowledge, at any rate, is sometimes the preserve of epistemic agents. For knowledge is an ability to perform various actions: to represent or reply or respond or reason accurately.

Even an ability to represent that *p*, including the ability to believe that *p*, makes one an agent. It need not make one a reflective or self-aware agent. Nonetheless, it is a function of acting, rather than of being acted upon, whereas the concept of an epistemic subject is wholly a concept of someone upon whom the world acts. Thinking of knowledge as possessed only by epistemic subjects conveys a picture of knowers—*qua* knowers—as mere recipients. And there is an historical irony in that. Famously, Sellars (1963: ch. 5) argued against the myth of the sensorily given. Yet to attribute knowledge to epistemic subjects bespeaks some commitment to a more *general* myth of the given, according to which to know is to be in a *state* of being *subject* to information. The ability analysis implies that we should discard that remnant of that epistemic myth.

It is a myth that sits ill with our often attributing a responsibility to knowers that is more than merely causal, such as when we talk of someone's being either morally or epistemically responsible for what she knows. Usually, when this way of talking is resisted, its supposed failing is the conjunction of the following two theses: (i) knowledge is a belief; and (ii) because doxastic voluntarism is false, no one has the

---

[35] Even this accords sceptics too much. Your knowing that you are not looking at a fake barn is your knowing that your sensory evidence right now—apparently of a barn—is of a real barn. Yet this just *is* your knowing that *B*. Hence, it is not *further* knowledge which could sensibly be required by the sceptic (if you are to know that *B*). For more on this weakness in sceptical thinking, see Hetherington (2001*a*: 37–40; 2002: 95–7; 2004).

control over her beliefs that makes it appropriate to hold her either epistemically or morally responsible for having them. But the knowledge-as-ability hypothesis, with its denial of (i), makes it possible to distinguish between knowledge and belief in that respect: if (i) is false, then (ii), even if true, might be irrelevant to the epistemic and moral evaluation of knowledge. Even if a person cannot be epistemically or morally responsible for having a given belief, this need not be true of her having a particular piece of knowledge. We face the intriguing prospect of being epistemically and morally responsible (other things being equal) for at least some of our *knowledge*, even if never for our *beliefs*. For example, if (ii) is true, then you could fail to be epistemically responsible for a belief that *p* (which, on the ability analysis, is a *manifestation* of your knowledge that *p*) which you could not help but have. Nonetheless, if (i) is false, you might somehow be epistemically responsible for the *ability* which is your knowledge that *p* in the first place. At any rate, the falsity of doxastic voluntarism would not absolve you of the latter responsibility.

What form might that epistemic responsibility take, though? Your knowledge that *p* is an ability to register accurately that *p*, where the registering might well involve non-doxastic and eminently controllable states. Even if there is no epistemic responsibility for believing that *p*, there could be for accepting or answering that *p*, say. Still, the latter remain manifestations of a knowledge-ability; they are not the ability itself. And if epistemic responsibility is to be only for such manifestations, is there to be no epistemic responsibility for the knowledge as such? Is there to be none simply for *having* some knowledge? In a sense, yes: only epistemic *subjects* as such are categorically apt for being epistemically responsible (if indeed they ever are) for *receiving* or *having* information; only epistemic *agents* as such would be categorically apt for being responsible for what they *do* with their knowledge-abilities. Their responsibility would not be for *having* the knowledge that *p*; it would be for *using* the knowledge that *p*. In this way, epistemic responsibility, if it exists, would be 'forward looking', pertaining only to actions.[36]

I lack the space here to defend these thoughts in more detail; I offer them as a somewhat supported conjecture, ripe for testing.

11. ABILITIES

So far, I have allowed knowledge-how to be an ability.[37] Ryle viewed it in that way, too. Yet Stanley and Williamson (2001: 416) regard Ryle's analysis of knowledge-how as being seriously flawed:

According to Ryle, an ascription of the form '*x* knows how to *F*' merely ascribes to *x* the ability to *F*. It is simply false, however, that ascriptions of knowledge-how ascribe abilities. . . . For

---

[36] The same is true of moral responsibility, as Hetherington (2003) explains. (But are epistemic responsibility and moral responsibility wholly analogous? Hetherington (2002*a*) doubts that they are.)
[37] Why have I talked of abilities, not dispositions? Some abilities are dispositions; some are not. As White (1982: 114–15) notes, all dispositions, unlike some abilities, imply *tendencies*. However,

example, a ski instructor may know how to perform a certain complex stunt, without being able to perform it herself.

But Stanley and Williamson's objection does not show that a Rylean account is not true of *some* kinds of knowledge-how, including the kind discussed in this paper. On the ability analysis, your knowing that p is your knowing how to register accurately that p. And you cannot know how to do this, without thereby being able to do so. The ski instructor could know how to perform the stunt without being able to perform it, because she could have various apt mental characteristics even while being physically unable to perform the stunt. However, that disparity is absent when the skill in question is constituted *by* those apt mental characteristics.[38] Hintikka (1975: 11) says that 'what is confusing about the locution "knowing how"' is its being ambiguous between (i) a skill sense and (ii) a 'knowing the way' sense. On (i), '*a* has the skills and capacities required to do *x*, i.e., . . . he can do *x*.' On (ii), '*a* knows the answer to the question: How should one go about it in order to do *x*?' In criticising Ryle, Stanley and Williamson adopt interpretation (ii). Yet that is knowledge-how only in the sense of knowing how it is that p, which is knowledge-that. In contrast, I am adopting interpretation (i). And when (i) is used, knowing how to register accurately that p *does* entail being able to do so.

This does not require there to be an underlying physical essence to knowing. It allows knowing to have a nature, though. Knowing that p is not the obtaining of a *random* assortment of conditional facts. There can be significant structural features linking the various possible ways of manifesting a particular knowledge-ability, features which allow us to model many important kinds of claims about knowledge. And that is precisely what we have found throughout this paper. We need to revise the metaphysics that underlies our analytical descriptions of knowledge, even when we need not revise the claims themselves.

12. RYLEAN MISTAKES

This paper has sought to build upon a Rylean insight. Yet Ryle himself would not have accepted this paper's analysis. As we saw in section 1, he argues that knowledge-how need not include knowledge-that. He also seeks to show that 'knowing-that presupposes knowing-how' (1971: 224): knowledge-how is involved in *gaining* knowledge-that (ibid.), and knowledge-how is required for effectively *using* knowledge-that (224–5). How, then, does Ryle claim to keep knowledge-that distinct from knowledge-how?

requiring the presence of a tendency to register accurately that p would restrict the generality of my analysis, because tendencies are conceptually linked to *frequency* of performance in a way in which abilities are not.

[38] For this same reason, Snowdon's (2003: 8–11) counterexamples to knowing-how's being an ability do not undermine my use of that thesis. None of his cases are about wholly cognitive abilities or knowledge-how.

He purports to find the following differences between them (1949: 59). (1) There can be *partial* or *limited* knowledge of how to *F*, whereas there cannot be partial or limited knowledge that *p*. (2) Learning how—coming to know how—is *gradual*, whereas learning that—coming to know that—is 'relatively sudden'.

Is Ryle right about that? Do (1) and (2) undermine the ability analysis of knowledge-that? I do not believe so; I will discuss these claims in turn.[39]

(1) Insofar as there can be partial knowledge how to *F*, there *is* still knowledge how to *F*. The requisite ability merely happens to be less exhaustive or strong—it is weaker—than it might have been. For example, there are situations where attempting to use it will not be successful: you try to play the shot, and you fail. But in that sense of limitation, there *can* be partial knowledge that *p*. The knowledge would be fallible, say, having a less exhaustive—a weaker—justificatory component than it might have had. So, there are situations where that same justification will lead you astray: you believe that *p*, on this occasion mistakenly.

(2) Coming to know that *p* need not occur quickly. It might involve learning much else besides. Yet this *is* one's acquiring an ability—the ability to register *p* accurately, in a wider, rather than narrower, range of circumstances. Conversely, the acquiring of an ability, like gaining some knowledge-that, can occur speedily. For example, you could rapidly gain perceptual knowledge of your surroundings, thereby coming to know, equally speedily, how to register them accurately.

13. CONCLUSION

None of this proves that the knowledge-as-ability hypothesis is true. It remains an hypothesis. But I hope to have shown that it could well be true, even though it is at odds with some theses that are currently favoured by epistemologists. In any case, what currently seems plausible to epistemologists might easily, had philosophical history proceeded slightly differently, have *been* something like this paper's analysis. We have seen that Ryle came close to adopting such an analysis. And if he had done so, others might have followed his lead. It is not too late for us to do so now. It is *never* too late to be open to an epistemological idea.[40]

REFERENCES

Audi, R. (1994). 'Dispositional Beliefs and Dispositions to Believe'. *Noûs*, 28: 419–34.
BonJour, L. (2002). *Epistemology: Classic Problems and Contemporary Responses*. Lanham, MD: Rowman & Littlefield.

[39] For more detailed discussion, see Hetherington (2001*a*: 13–15).

[40] I am grateful to Anne Newstead, Paul Snowdon, two anonymous Oxford University Press referees, and the members of an audience at the University of Melbourne for their thoughtful reactions to earlier versions of this paper.

—— (2003). 'A Version of Internalist Foundationalism', in L. BonJour and E. Sosa, *Epistemic Justification: Internalism vs. Externalism, Foundations vs. Virtues*. Malden, Mass.: Blackwell, 3–96.

Chisholm, R. M. (1989). *Theory of Knowledge* (3rd edn.). Englewood Cliffs, NJ: Prentice Hall.

Cohen, L. J. (1992). *An Essay on Belief and Acceptance*. Oxford: Clarendon Press.

Craig, E. (1990). *Knowledge and the State of Nature: An Essay in Conceptual Synthesis*. Oxford: Clarendon Press.

Elgin, C. Z. (1988). 'The Epistemic Efficacy of Stupidity'. *Synthese*, 74: 297–311.

Franklin, R. L. (1981). 'Knowledge, Belief and Understanding'. *The Philosophical Quarterly*, 31: 193–208.

Gettier, E. L. (1963). 'Is Justified True Belief Knowledge?' *Analysis*, 23: 121–3.

Ginet, C. (1975). *Knowledge, Perception, and Memory*. Dordrecht: Reidel.

Goldman, A. I. (1976). 'Discrimination and Perceptual Knowledge'. *Journal of Philosophy*, 73: 771–91.

—— (1986). *Epistemology and Cognition*. Cambridge, Mass.: Harvard University Press.

Hartland-Swann, J. (1956). 'The Logical Status of "Knowing That" '. *Analysis*, 16: 111–15.

—— (1957). ' "Knowing That"—A Reply to Mr. Ammerman'. *Analysis*, 17: 69–71.

Hetherington, S. (1996a). *Knowledge Puzzles: An Introduction to Epistemology*. Boulder, Colo.: Westview Press.

—— (1996b). 'Gettieristic Scepticism'. *Australasian Journal of Philosophy*, 74: 83–97.

—— (1998). 'Actually Knowing'. *The Philosophical Quarterly*, 48: 453–69.

—— (2001a). *Good Knowledge, Bad Knowledge: On Two Dogmas of Epistemology*. Oxford: Clarendon Press.

—— (2001b). 'A Fallibilist and Wholly Internalist Solution to the Gettier Problem'. *Journal of Philosophical Research*, 26: 307–24.

—— (2002a). 'Epistemic Responsibility: A Dilemma'. *The Monist*, 85: 398–414.

—— (2002b). 'Fallibilism and Knowing That One Is Not Dreaming'. *Canadian Journal of Philosophy*, 32: 83–102.

—— (2003). 'Alternate Possibilities and Avoidable Moral Responsibility'. *American Philosophical Quarterly*, 40: 229–39.

—— (2004). 'Shattering a Cartesian Sceptical Dream'. *Principia*, 8: 103–17.

—— (forthcoming). 'Knowledge's Boundary Problem'. *Synthese*.

Hintikka, J. (1975). 'Different Constructions in Terms of the Basic Epistemological Verbs', in *The Intentions of Intentionality and Other New Models for Modalities*. Dordrecht: Reidel, 1–25.

Hyman, J. (1999). 'How Knowledge Works'. *The Philosophical Quarterly*, 49: 433–51.

Koethe, J. (2002). 'Stanley and Williamson on Knowing How'. *Journal of Philosophy*, 99: 325–8.

Kornblith, H. (ed.) (2001). *Epistemology: Internalism and Externalism*. Malden, Mass.: Blackwell.

Lehrer, K. (1990). *Theory of Knowledge*. Boulder, Colo.: Westview Press.

Levi, I. (1980). *The Enterprise of Knowledge: An Essay on Knowledge, Credal Probability, and Chance*. Cambridge, Mass.: MIT Press.

Lewis, D. (1996). 'Elusive Knowledge'. *Australasian Journal of Philosophy*, 74: 549–67.

Rumfitt, I. (2003). 'Savoir Faire'. *Journal of Philosophy*, 100: 158–66.

Ryle, G. (1949). *The Concept of Mind*. London: Hutchinson.

—— (1971). 'Knowing How and Knowing That', in *Collected Papers*, vol. II. London: Hutchinson, 212–25.

Schiffer, S. (2002). 'Amazing Knowledge'. *Journal of Philosophy*, 99: 200–2.

Sellars, W. S. (1963). *Science, Perception and Reality*. London: Routledge & Kegan Paul.

Smith, B. (1988). 'Knowing How vs. Knowing That', in J. Nyiri and B. Smith (eds.), *Practical Knowledge: Outlines of a Theory of Traditions and Skills*. London: Croom Helm, 1–16.

Snowdon, P. (2003). 'Knowing How and Knowing That: A Distinction Reconsidered'. *Proceedings of the Aristotelian Society*, 104: 1–29.

Sosa, E. (2003). 'Beyond Internal Foundationalism to External Virtues', in L. BonJour and E. Sosa, *Epistemic Justification: Internalism vs. Externalism, Foundations vs. Virtues*. Malden, Mass.: Blackwell, 97–170.

Stanley, J., and Williamson, T. (2001). 'Knowing How'. *Journal of Philosophy*, 98: 411–44.

White, A. R. (1982). *The Nature of Knowledge*. Totowa, NJ: Rowman & Littlefield.

6

Epistemology and Inquiry: the Primacy of Practice

Christopher Hookway

1. EPISTEMIC EVALUATION: THE DOXASTIC PARADIGM

Epistemology, like ethics, studies part of our evaluative practice. We can provisionally characterize this practice by saying that it regulates our attempts to avoid error and arrive at accurate representations of reality, or perhaps by saying that it guides our search for knowledge of ourselves and of our surroundings. This characterization is provisional because part of our task here is to identify just what this practice regulates and to describe the vocabulary it should use in making these evaluations. It is also provisional because the evaluations we make use of in regulating this practice are not all epistemic: we can be concerned with whether particular beliefs are interesting or important, about whether methods of inquiry are ethical, about whether it would benefit us to believe some proposition for which we lack evidence, and so on. Thus we should also be interested in what it is that makes an evaluation distinctively 'epistemic'. Our conclusion will be that insights drawn from the pragmatist tradition can help us to arrive at a distinctive way of addressing these issues, one that promises progress in thinking about important epistemological issues.

Our vocabulary of epistemic evaluation is wide-ranging and various and, in setting out an epistemological theory, it is natural to concentrate on a range of *fundamental* epistemic evaluations, anticipating that what we learn in studying these can be applied to illuminate the wider range of evaluations that we actually employ. We may also find that this vocabulary is fundamental because it is implicated in the distinctively philosophical problems that arise about this practice. However important to us the other evaluations may be, we should focus on those that are controversial or philosophically puzzling. So one issue to be addressed when we begin to do epistemology concerns the identification of this favoured set of fundamental evaluations. And a common strategy is to identify a distinctive and fundamental vocabulary, the set of words or concepts that are centrally implicated in our practice. This parallels the position in ethics when theorists hope that an examination of evaluations expressed in terms of 'good' or 'right' can provide the core of an adequate account of ethical evaluations; and philosophical debates can be concerned with how far this emphasis is correct. In arriving at a set of favoured evaluations, we need to provide a descriptively adequate account of:

(1) What sorts of states or activities provide the targets of epistemic evaluation? What do we evaluate?

(2) In evaluating these states or activities, what sort of vocabulary of evaluation do we employ?

(3) What criteria do we use in applying this evaluative vocabulary? How does this evaluative vocabulary work?

(4) How successful are we in executing this evaluative practice? Do the target states and activities possess the evaluative properties we normally take them to have?

We can identify a standard set of answers to these questions, the answers presupposed by much research in epistemology and presented in textbooks introducing students to the area. This holds that the targets of epistemic evaluation are beliefs, and other propositional attitudes as well as the propositions which they can involve. It also holds that the fundamental vocabulary that we use in evaluating these states employs words like 'knows', 'is justified in believing', and so on. Our evaluative practice is thus manifested when we describe our own beliefs, or those of other people, as *justified* beliefs or perhaps as *knowledge*. So we are concerned with evaluating knowing subjects: which of their beliefs are justified? Do they know what they think they know? And, in the course of doing this, we evaluate propositions: Are they well supported by a particular body of evidence or by an argument or proof? Generally, we assume that a person will be justified in believing some proposition on the basis of a body of evidence only if the proposition itself is supported by that evidence. To this end, much research in epistemology is directed at providing theories of justification or knowledge, accounts of the conditions that must be satisfied if people are to count as knowing something or as being justified in believing it. Many of the debates that have been fundamental to recent research in epistemology have concerned the formulation, defence, and criticism of such theories of knowledge and justification. Such theories have often been tested by investigating how far the claims they make match our intuitive judgements about when someone possesses knowledge of, or justified belief in, some proposition.

We can call this the *doxastic paradigm*: epistemic evaluation is fundamentally concerned with evaluating *beliefs* and their objects, by establishing whether they are justified or by establishing whether they constitute knowledge. The doxastic paradigm seems to employ the idea that the person as studied in epistemology is, primarily, a holder of beliefs: we can characterize someone's epistemic position at some time by listing the propositions that they believe or know at that time. The evaluations are targeted on someone's corpus of beliefs at a particular time. While, in the course of making these evaluations, we may refer to the processes of reasoning that led up to the acquisition of the belief, our primary interest is in the resulting belief rather than the process of reasoning.

Before introducing a contrasting 'paradigm', I want to comment on how three important epistemological problems are likely to be formulated from the perspective we have just described. The first, the problem of scepticism, questions whether we *really* possess knowledge and whether our beliefs are *really* justified. We have to address the challenge that, once we reflect on our beliefs in the light of our best epistemological theories, it will turn out that, when cases are examined more carefully, we don't possess knowledge when we intuitively take ourselves to do so.

Another fundamental philosophical issue arises here, one that has not been much discussed. This is what has been called the 'value problem' (Greco 2003; Zagzebski 2003). Given the fundamental vocabulary employed, this view faces an important (and little discussed) question about just why justified belief (and knowledge) are better than beliefs that do not meet the conditions for knowledge or justification. As Socrates asked in the *Meno*: why is knowledge better than mere true opinion? We can also ask why knowledge should be valued above beliefs which are both true and justified but which do not count as full-blooded knowledge. Candidate answers suggest that knowledge is a more reliable guide to conduct than mere true belief (a claim which Socrates denied), or that knowledge is less likely to be given up for bad reasons (Socrates's own suggestion). Much epistemology assumes that knowledge is good, and, when it relies on our intuitive judgements of what is known, it assumes that we are generally sensitive to this value, whatever is. But it is striking that, until very recently, the issue has been little explored.

At this stage I want to mention a further question, one that has dominated the epistemology of the last twenty years. This concerns whether an externalist approach to justification (or knowledge) is possible, or whether only an internalist account is acceptable. Roughly speaking, an internalist account holds that whether a belief is justified is determined by considerations (reasons, evidence, etc.) which are internal to (perhaps available to) the believer. It is not enough that the belief be formed in a reliable manner (for example) if the subject can offer no reason for thinking that the method was reliable, and is not warranted in her confidence that relying on the methods will promote her cognitive ends. As with the analysis of knowledge, much discussion of this topic has relied upon speaker intuitions: would we intuitively *say* that someone knew or was justified in believing when there was no 'internalist' justification available?

In the following section, I shall offer a different way of thinking about the fundamental targets of epistemic evaluation and the fundamental vocabulary that is employed. And I shall argue, in support of this perspective, that it offers a better way of thinking about the three issues I have just described: scepticism, the value problem, and internalism vs. externalism. As we shall see, one way in which this perspective is preferable is that it enables us to raise questions about (for example) knowledge and justified belief which focus on the concepts in these areas that we *ought* to have rather than describing the concepts we actually possess. By enabling us to think about the value of knowledge and about the importance of justification, we shall be in a position to critically evaluate the concepts we actually have and better understand the challenge of scepticism.

2. EPISTEMOLOGY AS THEORY OF INQUIRY

I shall now provide a preliminary characterization of an alternative to the doxastic paradigm which I shall call 'epistemology as theory of inquiry'. In subsequent sections I shall explore how adopting this perspective affects our thinking about scepticism, about the value problem, and about the issue of internalism.

We noted above that a belief's justification will often depend upon processes of reasoning or inquiry that lead us to adopt it: if beliefs result from poor reasoning or badly directed inquiry, then they will not be justified. The doxastic picture recognizes this but holds that the justification of belief (or the possession of knowledge) provides our primary evaluative focus. The challenge of scepticism was that, perhaps, we possess no knowledge or justified beliefs at all. The alternative picture gives much greater weight to the fact that theoretical deliberation and public *inquiries* are themselves regulated in accord with some complex systems of normative standards. These are goal-directed activities and we often need to be reflective and disciplined in the ways in which we carry them out. When we want to reach a settled belief on some matter, we set ourselves cognitive goals, we consider how best to achieve these goals, and then we reflect on our progress, revising our strategies and monitoring our progress until we are satisfied that we have achieved our goal. The goal of the activity is usually set by a problem or question to which we seek an answer, and reflection focuses on the merits of that goal, upon how best to achieve it, and upon evaluating progress towards it. The target for epistemic evaluations lies in our ability to carry out inquiries, to reason effectively and solve problems, rather than in how far our beliefs are justified, or whether we possess knowledge.

Consider a simple example:

Suppose I want to know whether some number (say 71) is prime: I ask the question 'Is 71 prime?'. In thinking about this question perhaps I first note that it is an odd number, that it is not divisible by 2. I then work through the known small primes: it is not divisible by 3, or by 5, or by 7. I then see that this is enough to show it is prime, since if it has a prime proper factor greater than 7, then it will also have a proper factor of 10 or less and hence a prime factor of 7 or less.

Of course, this is just one example and many other inquiries will introduce many layers of complexity that are absent from this one. However, it is sufficiently simple and representative for our purposes. In describing the case, we should distinguish some different elements. For example:

(i) What is the goal of the reasoning; what problem am I trying to solve?

(ii) What strategy do I employ in order to solve that problem? How effective is this strategy?

(iii) How did I plan to execute the strategy? Is that an effective way to execute the strategy? Did I execute it as I planned to?

(iv) What (intellectual capacities) did I make use of in executing my strategy?

In this case the answers are:

(i) The goal is to establish whether 71 is prime.

(ii) The strategy is to establish by considering individual cases that it is not divisible by any number less than the square root of 71. This is an effective strategy.

(iii) The chosen means of carrying out this strategy is to see if it is divisible by any odd prime below 10. This is a good way of carrying out the strategy and is successfully executed.

(iv) In solving this problem, I rely upon my abilities to do mental arithmetic, to identify small prime numbers, to keep track of results of earlier computations, etc. These abilities may involve detailed systematic knowledge of (for example) arithmetic but are also likely to involve reliable heuristics, reliable habits of computation, etc.

In this case, the reasoning is carried out by a single individual and, as Wilfrid Sellars often put it, the reasoning can all occur '*in foro interno*'. It is easy to see that this is not a necessary feature of the case. I could have employed pen and paper, or a calculator, as props to facilitate the reasoning involved in this case; in more complex cases, my reasoning could involve observation or experimental interventions in my surroundings, or conversation and discussion with others. Although we *may* not use the word 'reasoning' for these cases, it is clear that they are structurally similar to the cases where reasoning does occur *in foro interno*. Some philosophers use the word 'inquiry' to describe the genus of cases which fit this sort of structural pattern: the important point here is that, from a philosophical point of view, the similarities between these cases are more striking than the differences.

So reasoning is a kind of goal-directed activity; and the demands of rationality require us to reason in a disciplined way. The important point to register here is that, since reasoning is a goal-directed activity, the norms that govern reasoning and inquiry will include norms of *practical* reason: we are evaluating strategies for solving problems, the effectiveness of agents at putting their strategies into effect, and so on. My emphasis on the theory of inquiry is in line with Paul Grice's suggestion that much philosophical work on rationality fails to take seriously the fact that 'reasoning is an activity, something with goals and purposes' and fails to take account of the connection of reasoning with the *will* (Grice 2001: 16). One is reminded here of Peter Railton's claim that judgements about what it is rational to believe are always judgements of practical rationality (2003: 44–5): although deductive logic tells us about the relations between the truth values of different propositions and must inform our alethic judgements, logic does not tell us what inferences to draw and what beliefs to form. The latter reflects which true propositions are worth attending to, which of them are likely to be relevant to our other concerns, and how ready we are to risk conclusions that will subsequently turn out to be incorrect.

Two clarifications should be made here. First, as our example indicates, the fact that inquiry is a goal-directed activity does not entail that it is always done *for practical reasons*. I can reason about what to believe as well as about what to do. The goals of our inquiries can be intellectual, theoretical, scientific, etc.; the motives for inquiry can include disinterested curiosity. For present purposes, what is important is that there are interesting questions about how we can succeed in our inquiries about what to believe: how can we have confidence that we are adopting good strategies for alethic inquiries? How can we be sure that we are capable of executing such strategies in a disciplined and responsible manner? What is the basis of our confidence that we can carry out inquiries successfully?

Second, I am not defending the claim that *all* of our justified beliefs result from inquiry. Perceptual beliefs are likely to occur to the reader as one counterexample to that claim. Even in the case of perception, we should not lose track of the importance of experiment in scientific observation and of the fact that obtaining reliable perceptual knowledge often requires appropriate regulation of attention. We are not wholly passive in securing perceptual beliefs, and in subsequently reflecting on their credentials. But the focus on the practice of inquiry is not restricted to its role in *obtaining* reliable beliefs. In order to understand the epistemic role of perceptual beliefs, we have to understand their role as resources for further inquiry and investigation and we have to consider how this further role influences the ways in which we reflect upon them and sometimes seek further support for them. We also have to consider the role of perception in, for example, tracking objects and enabling us to acquire further information about the *same* things.

If we return to our schematic characterization of epistemology in the previous section, we can describe this approach as follows: the targets for epistemic evaluation are inquiries, activities of trying to solve problems of a distinctive kind. We are concerned with how far strategies and methods enable us to achieve our intellectual goals. Clarifying what this requires must await an investigation of the vocabulary to be employed in describing cognitive problems and their solutions and also an investigation of the overall structures of inquiries of different kinds. If words like 'knows' and 'is justified in believing' are important (as they surely must be), their role will emerge from an examination of their role in reflective inquiry and how best they can fulfill that role. The core question concerns how it is possible to be good at inquiry rather than, more simply, what it is to have justified beliefs or knowledge.

It may be thought that the difference between these perspectives is small: our aim in inquiry is always to obtain knowledge, almost certainly by seeking justification or warrant for beliefs. The first picture is the fundamental one, and the second picture simply alerts us to the complexities that we have to deal with when we try to apply this system of evaluations in practice. It directs us to address the instrumental issues of: how can we obtain knowledge in practice?; and how can we find justifications for our beliefs in practice? When we examine the systems of norms and standards that regulate inquiry and deliberation, we are investigating ways of obtaining knowledge and justified belief. I shall make a couple of observations about this now. The most important of these is to note that the second perspective enables us to confront some questions which the doxastic perspective begs: how far is it true that our most fundamental epistemic evaluations can be presented using the vocabulary of 'knowledge' and 'justification'?; and, if these terms are indeed as important as they seem to be, just why is this the case? It is a corollary of this that we are encouraged to consider just what we take to be the fundamental epistemic goods: what are our goals in inquiry and deliberation? What lies behind our desire to be 'good inquirers'? Perhaps we seek *wisdom* or *understanding*; perhaps we seek to contribute to the growth of flawed and fallible systems of ideas; perhaps other answers will be forthcoming.

I am not claiming that concepts like *knowledge* and *justified belief* are not important and interesting. Ernest Sosa encourages us to distinguish animal knowledge from reflective knowledge (Sosa 2003, for example), and the concept of knowledge can be useful for many explanatory, as well as evaluative, purposes. My concern here is with how we should think about the subject matter of epistemology, an area of philosophy that is concerned with our practice of epistemic evaluation and with meeting familiar sorts of sceptical challenges. When we study the history of our engagement with scepticism, our familiar concept of knowledge is not much in evidence: Plato appears to take it seriously, and it becomes important again in the twentieth century, especially in the work of Roderick Chisholm and those influenced by him. Although we often use the concept when we teach our students the lessons of Descartes's *Meditations*, it is very implausible that this is how Descartes presents his ideas. So it remains a question for discussion just why (and how) that concept features in our practice of epistemic evaluation. I shall say something about this in section 4, below.

3. HISTORICAL DIGRESSION: PRAGMATISM AND SCEPTICISM

These issues about the possibility of effective reasoning/inquiry appear to be epistemological questions. And this is a point of connection with the pragmatist tradition. John Dewey's great treatise on what he called logic, and we might think of as epistemology, was called *Logic: The Theory of Inquiry* (1938). He treats inquiry as a problem-solving activity, governed by norms of practical reasoning: successful inquiry (whatever its subject matter) begins when we find ourselves confronting a problem (we are in an 'indeterminate situation'), and it comes to an end when we have a solution to the problem (the situation has been rendered 'determinate' again). And Peirce's writings on epistemological matters are also focused on the norms that govern inquiry, which is described as a struggle to replace doubt by settled belief. The writings and Peirce offer many insights, but here I will just make some general observations.

First, they both regard issues about inquiry or theoretical deliberation as the fundamental ones. Inquiry is not seen simply as a means of acquiring 'justified beliefs' or 'knowledge' and, indeed, those concepts have little role in their work, other than as relics of a rejected Cartesian approach to epistemology. We might try to understand some of these concepts by seeing how (for example) claims about knowledge function *within* inquiry, but it would then be wrong to treat them as a distinct, semi-autonomous system of evaluation which can be understood in abstraction from the context of inquiry. Or we may find that other vocabularies for describing states will serve best the needs of inquiry, as when Dewey claims that inquiry issues in states of 'warranted assertibility'.

Second, and this is one further respect in which the outlook is 'pragmatist', they help us to undermine the radical dichotomy between the 'theoretical' and the 'practical', underlining the 'primary of practice' (Putnam 2002 *passim*; 1994: 152). One way to do this is to emphasise that much inquiry is carried out for the sake of the practical value of the results it obtains. However, the more fundamental pragmatist move, exploited here, is to note that even theoretical inquiry is a practice, an activity. Theoretical norms are the norms that guide inquiry, reasoning, theoretical deliberation; and the sorts of capacities that are invoked in explaining the nature of our practical activities generally can also be invoked when we study the practice of inquiry.

As this indicates, it is one mark of the pragmatists' approach to philosophy that they take these issues about reasoning and inquiry seriously; and it is another such mark that they seem to treat these issues as the most fundamental ones for epistemology or for what they call 'logic'. It is easy to see how this may be. Much epistemology is governed by the way epistemological issues are set up at the beginning of Descartes's *Meditations*. Abstracting from Descartes's own distinctive motivations for doing this, we can describe this approach by saying that the individual steps back from the concerns of life and surveys the opinions which he already possesses: for each belief we possess, we can ask such questions as:

- Do I know this?
- Am I justified in believing this?
- Can I be certain of this?
- Do I have any conceivable reasons for doubting this?

This is a very distinctive (very philosophical) kind of reflection and involves taking a sort of snapshot of one's current corpus of beliefs and then, using the favoured vocabulary, making evaluations of each member of that corpus.

The pragmatists remind us that this is not our normal context of epistemic reflection. We engage in such reflection when we are facing problems, trying to solve problems, and when we are considering questions about why these problems are important, what sorts of solutions of them we should take seriously, what methods we should employ in trying to deal with them, whether our engagement with these problems should lead us to re-examine aspects of our background knowledge, and so on. Reflection arises in connection with particular inquiries that arise within distinctive contexts, and it is an open question whether responsible inquiry can ever require us to engage in the sort of detached survey of our beliefs that the Cartesian approach encourages. Although the doxastic perspective can be detached from the sorts of motivations that governed Descartes's own work, it is striking that its chosen vocabulary for epistemic evaluation is designed for the evaluation of stable *states* rather than for the regulation of *activities*. The pragmatists encourage us to recognize the primacy of the latter.

This description might suggest that the approach I favour is robustly internalist, unable to take seriously the sorts of considerations and intuitions that have informed externalist approaches to epistemology. This is not so, for an examination of our practices of inquiry and deliberation enables us to see that, although reflection and the giving of reasons has a primary focus for epistemology, reasoning and reflection tend to be shallow. Our ability to reason rests upon a system of habits, capacities, traits and virtues, skills and attitudes, subdoxastic processes which serve as enabling conditions for reflection. Much of this is opaque to us, but unless we can trust the reliability and proper functioning of all of these capacities, we could not reason responsibly and effectively. One motivation for the project is that it suggests ways of understanding how internalist themes (reflecting and giving reasons) and externalist themes (conditions upon which our reasoning depends) are related. The limits of internalism can be recognized, so far as they do not prevent our being able to trust our abilities to inquire, reason, and deliberate.

The shift in perspective offers a distinctive way of thinking about the challenge of scepticism, indeed one that is more true to the historical origins of scepticism. As we noticed above, the doxastic paradigm encourages us to formulate the problems of scepticism in terms of knowledge and *justified* belief: sceptical challenges are taken to suggest that, contrary to appearances, we have no knowledge and none of our beliefs are justified. The challenges are then introduced in terms of the 'surveying' picture or philosophical reflection on our beliefs. If the second perspective is adopted, then we can formulate the problems of scepticism in a different way: sceptical challenges suggest that it is not possible for us to regulate our inquiries and deliberations in a responsible and effective manner. In 1990, I expressed this by saying that scepticism suggests that autonomous, responsible inquiry is not possible (see Hookway 1990 *passim*; 2003a: 196–7).

In fact, the argument of the *Meditations* can itself be understood from this perspective. The method of doubt is initially motivated by the fear that our most certain beliefs are corrupted by errors whose spreading influence in our corpus of opinions will prevent our identifying errors and thus making progress. Unless we obtain a positive result from our attempt to survey our current epistemic position we will not be able to make lasting contributions to scientific knowledge; we will have no basis for confidence that we can inquire responsibly and effectively. In modern epistemology, the 'surveying' style of reflection has taken on a life of its own: the doxastic paradigm encourages us to think that this is the starting point for epistemology. Once we reformulate problems about scepticism along the lines I have suggested here, then we are open to the possibility that successful inquiry depends upon a range of practical capacities and skills and that surveying reflection will conceal from us how strong our epistemic position is. If that style of reflection is not required by the best strategies for carrying out inquiries in a responsible manner, then it may not be a source of sceptical anxieties. We *may* be rightly confident in our ability to inquire well and responsibly even if we have no direct answers to the familiar sceptical challenges. And if this is not the case, this reflects requirements for responsible inquiry; unless it is ratified by requirements of this kind, the fact that reflection on why we are justified in our everyday beliefs fails to provide such a justification need not be a source of sceptical concern. This too is a theme that is echoed in the writings of the classical pragmatists.

4. THE VALUE OF KNOWLEDGE

Earlier in the paper, I suggested that epistemology should study our practice of epistemic evaluation by exploring how we are able to carry out inquiries and theoretical deliberations in a well-regulated manner. I said that this meant that the concept of *knowledge* was not used to formulate the fundamental problems of epistemology, but I also said that the approach might promise a better understanding of the evaluative role of that concept. We should seek such an understanding by exploring how the concept is used in making evaluations within our practice of inquiry. In this section I want to make some suggestions about this. Why is it epistemologically important that we possess knowledge? What can the answer to this question teach us about the sort of concept of knowledge that we need? It is a merit of the inquiry-based approach that we can see that knowledge can relate to inquiry in two very different ways. First, as is obvious, knowledge can be the result of inquiry and deliberation. Whether a state is described as knowledge can depend upon features of the processes of reasoning and investigation that contributed to its acquisition. The insights to be obtained from this may be limited because much of our knowledge, for example much perceptual knowledge, does not issue from reflective activities of inquiry. Second, knowledge is available as a resource for inquiry. That something is knowledge has forward-looking epistemic implications as well as backward-directed epistemic credentials. Unless we think about how we can use knowledge in further inquiry, we shall not understand the epistemic value and importance of knowledge.

From the 1960s until the 1980s, a major focus for epistemology was the attempt to provide a reductive analysis of the concept of knowledge. The struggle to find an analysis of knowledge which avoided counterexamples of the sort that Edmund Gettier introduced has thrown up a lot of conceptions which have been valuable in understanding epistemic matters, from Dretske's conclusive reasons, through the idea of tracking, to a concern with defeaters and relevant alternatives. Their interest is clear, however limited our confidence may be that the Gettier problem can actually be solved. We may suspect that the concept of knowledge is primitive and unanalyzable, or suspect it lacks the unity required to be a candidate for a serious analysis. What we should notice here is that features that have been taken to be characteristic of knowledge have been backward-looking: they have concerned the history of the candidate belief or the kind of justification that the believer (already) possesses for it. Hence when we ask what value attaches to states of knowledge, it is natural to give that question a backward-facing cast: why is it good to have cognitive states with *this* kind of history? And if we are working within the doxastic paradigm, it appears that the value of the state must somehow consist in its having such a history. If we take seriously Plato's demand, in the *Meno*, that we explain why it is better to have knowledge than mere true belief, then what we must explain is what is good about having this kind of backward-facing characteristic. This has led philosophers such as Linda Zagzebski (2003) and John Greco (2003), among others, to conclude that knowledge is of value because it is the kind of thing for which the knower deserves 'credit': somehow the belief reflects well on them; they have done well, epistemically speaking, in acquiring this belief. This may often be true (although surely not always: see Lackey [unpublished]). But I suspect it needs to be supplemented by a more forward-looking answer. Knowledge is epistemically good, at least in part, because of its role as a *resource* for the further growth of knowledge, for further successful inquiry.

One promising way of approaching such issues is to ask why it may be important to identify beliefs and believers that have these different properties while carrying out inquiries and investigations. If Williamson is correct in his claim that our knowledge comprises our evidence, that we should not use something as evidence unless it is known, then it is easy to see why it is important that we possess knowledge. It can be put to uses, within inquiry, to which mere true belief cannot be put (Williamson 2000: 184ff.). Unless we have knowledge, we shall have no evidence that can be employed in trying to discover what is true. Alternatively, we might hold that one use we make of knowledge ascription is to identify sources of information (see Craig 1990 *passim*). When we recognize that someone knows when the train leaves, or that they know how Powerpoint works, or why water expands on freezing, then we acknowledge that we obtain such knowledge for ourselves by using their testimony. And then we might ask what features a concept of knowledge must have if it is to be usable in this way: for a start, we must be able to establish that their answers to these questions are the correct ones independently of identifying which answers they would defend (see Hookway 1990: ch. IX; Schaffer [forthcoming]). In each case, we examine uses of knowledge within inquiry in order to understand why it is valuable and to see what sorts of features it must have. The value of knowledge is traced to factors that are internal to the process of inquiry.

Some recent discussions have identified this sort of issue by exploiting a problem for fallibilism, originally posed by Stewart Cohen (1988). The problem is that if we can acquire beliefs that can count as knowledge through inductive reasoning, in spite of the fact that such reasoning is fallible, we may have false beliefs whose inductive justification is just as good as that of clear cases of knowledge. Ernest Sosa offers the example of someone who drops a bag of garbage down the garbage chute of her apartment building. Shortly after, relying on past experience and on her reliable background knowledge, she concludes that the bag has reached the garbage room in the basement. We happily accord her knowledge although she cannot rule out the unlikely possibility that, for example, the bag has caught on a nail on the way down. It is possible, but very unlikely, that the belief she has formed is false (Sosa 2000; Greco 2003: 112). We might say that she knows whether the bag is at the bottom of the chute, although we would not say that she knows whether it has caught on a nail. Further paradox arises when the same person buys a ticket in a lottery where the chances of winning are one million to one. She too, on excellent inductive grounds, forms the true belief that her ticket will not win. In each case, our subject has an inductively grounded belief with a very high probability of truth. Some hold that, although she *knows* that the garbage is in the garbage room, her true belief that her ticket will lose does not count as *knowledge* (for extended discussion, see Hawthorne 2004). Whatever the source of these intuitions, it is natural to conclude that the differences between these cases are relevant to the value that we attach to knowledge: an account of the value of knowledge ought to explain just *why* we distinguish these cases as we do. Our question is: what do cases like this teach us about the special value we attach to knowledge? As Greco argues in 'Knowledge as credit for true belief', a range of standard accounts of knowledge fail to make sense of these differences (2003: 112–15).

There is space here to make only a very few observations. There are clear differences in what we can do with these two pieces of information. Our belief that the ticket-holder will not win does not provide us with any evidence that she is unlucky, whereas our belief that the bag is in the garbage room does provide evidence that it is no longer in the kitchen. We cannot infer from the belief that the ticket-holder will lose that everyone else's chances of winning have increased, albeit by a minuscule amount. Another clue is that, in the garbage case but not in the lottery case, it makes sense for the subject to proffer her testimony to someone else, saying 'You can take my word for it.' Perhaps we can't take her word for the fact that she will not win the lottery and this is partly because the fact has not yet been fixed. But that seems implausible because we would have the same intuitions if the winning number had already been selected but we had no clue as to what it was. Still, she is not a conduit through which the fact is transmitted to us, as she is in the case of the garbage chute. But given that the methods of inquiry she employed are highly reliable, she is certainly using information that would be valuable as a basis for our own further actions: her testimony would give us information that could certainly be used as the basis of a bet against her winning, for example. Something is distinctive about her inquiry that limits the uses we can make of the information, and a description of her as possessing knowledge can mislead us into supposing that the information had a greater general applicability as a resource for inquiry that it in fact has. Although this does not prevent her report being highly reliable and highly valuable, she cannot be seen as serving as a conduit by which the information is passed on to us for further cognitive purposes.

Indeed, if we claim knowledge that the lottery ticket will lose, we make a stronger claim than we are strictly entitled to, and, for the sorts of reason suggested by Grice, we implicate that we have additional reasons for thinking that our own ticket is less likely to win than the others (see Grice 1989: 30ff). In fact, of course, S has no better reason to think that *she* won't win than to think that anyone else (including the eventual winner) won't win. She doesn't believe that she won't win because she believes of some other person that they will; and nor does she believe of anyone else that they are less likely not to win than her. The role of chance in determining the winner explains why *this* is so, and maybe this is the core phenomenon that leads us to deny that she has knowledge of her upcoming lottery loss.

This means that if, in the case described, we claim knowledge that the ticket will lose, we implicate that we should adopt this claim as a resource for inquiry rather than the fact that there is very little chance of our ticket winning. Most likely we implicate that we have a special reason for ruling out the possibility that this ticket will win, a kind of reason that we could not introduce for all tickets. I do not pretend that this is any sort of solution to the lottery problem or to the value problem for knowledge: to find a solution would be a large task that cannot be attempted here. What these remarks are intended to do is illustrate that some relevant considerations can be identified by considering what can be done with the information, by considering the ways in which it can be used as a cognitive resource to be used in further inquiry.

5. THE PRIMACY OF PRACTICE: THE LIMITS AND VARIETIES OF INTERNALISM

We have already noticed two respects in which pragmatists emphasize that 'practice is primary in philosophy' (Putnam 1994: 152): cognitive activities are often to be understood as part of our attempts to interact with the world in solving problems and pursuing our goals; and epistemology is generally concerned with *activities* of inquiry and deliberation. In this concluding section, I want to identify a third dimension of the primacy of practice. Our participation in activities generally depends upon mastery of a practice: education provides us with a body of habits, routines, dispositions, which enable us to engage in activities without reflecting upon what to do at each turn. Indeed, the knowledge of how to proceed that is implicit in our habitual practices often far outreaches what can be made explicit through reflection. As Quine has said, reflection is essentially shallow: we are consciously guided by our sense of what is plausible, sensible, deserving of doubt, and, in doing this, we are trusting habits, dispositions, judgements which are the product of education and training. We are confident that our practical capacities will enable us to inquire well, in spite of the fact that we cannot formulate or defend the standards and principles that we follow (Quine 1960: 19; Hookway 2003*b*: 78ff.). Perhaps, as philosophers, we can make this implicit knowledge explicit (Brandom 1994: ch. 1), but our normal inability to do this is no loss; indeed it probably contributes to our success. Confidence in our practical capacities does not require us to be able to articulate what is going on and understand how they work. We exercise our judgement in thinking about what to do without being able to identify the principles on which we depend, and this is not a cognitive failing. These platitudes about how we carry out practical activities generally can cast illumination on the internalism/externalism debate.

Let us return to the 'Cartesian' exercise of stepping back and surveying the beliefs that belong to our current corpus, asking which count as knowledge or which are justified. We can carry out this activity only if all the information that is relevant to the epistemic status of these opinions is available to us: if we cannot *decide* which beliefs are justified, then we cannot carry out this distinctive kind of inquiry. So the surveying kind of inquiry requires that whether our beliefs are justified, or whether they count as knowledge, is available to us. One way of formulating internalism is that all the considerations that are relevant to the epistemic status of our beliefs are accessible to us, and it seems that the surveying enterprise (especially if undertaken in Descartes's solitary spirit) makes sense only if internalism is correct.

Once we recognize the role of (for example) habits in enabling us to carry out activities (including epistemic activities) effectively, then, the crucial question becomes one of whether we can be confident in our practices, in our ability to inquire well. It is not a necessary condition of our possessing this kind of confidence that we have access to how these habits and dispositions work; we do not need to be able to identify all of the factors which these habits and capacities enable us to be sensitive to. Training and education, as well as our innate endowments, can ensure that we are well adjusted to our cognitive needs without demanding that we must be able to access all those considerations that are responsible for our cognitive successes. Reliance on such habits does not make it a matter of *luck* that our cognitive ventures succeed. In that case, abandoning internalism need not leave us dependent upon luck for the success of our inquiries. Indeed, since these habits and capacities are the product of our experience, education, and training, it is not absurd to think of them as (in a very different way) internal to us. They may reflect our characters, and we can be held responsible for the effects of our reliance upon them: if my inquiry fails because I have relied upon bad epistemic habits and capacities, it is not absurd that I should be blamed for the failure. The inquiry-based approach thus casts a different light upon how we should think about the internalism/externalism debate.

At the same time as it does this, it also adjusts the way in which we think about the role of reflection in our inquiries. The capacity to reflect, or to reason consciously, is just one of the capacities we make use of in carrying out our inquiries. How reflective we should be, how far we should be aware of how our methods of inquiry work and raise questions about which methods are appropriate to particular inquiries, is not a matter to be settled a priori. It does not follow from reflection on the nature of knowledge or the nature of justification that we should reflect in one way rather than another. The fundamental question is how reflective we should be (and what capacities for reflection we need to have) if we are to be able to inquire responsibly and effectively on the sorts of matters that concern us. Inquiry can suffer from our trying to be too reflective, just as it can suffer from our being too trusting of our capacities.

I have tried to describe a distinctive approach to epistemological questions, one that owes a lot to the pragmatist tradition. Epistemology is primarily concerned with how it is possible for us to engage in activities such as inquiry and deliberation, and questions about knowledge and about justification should be seen as subordinate to these concerns. I have tried to suggest that adopting this perspective can affect the ways in which we formulate and think about a number of issues that are central to epistemology: the nature and value of knowledge, the challenge of scepticism, and the issues that are involved in the internalism/externalism debate.

REFERENCES

Brady, M., and Pritchard, D. (eds.). (2003). *Moral and Epistemic Virtues*. Oxford: Blackwell.

Brandom, R. (1994). *Making It Explicit: Reasoning, Representing, and Discursive Commitment*. Cambridge, Mass.: Harvard University Press.

Cohen, S. (1988). 'How to be a Fallibilist', in J. Tomberlin (ed.), *Philosophical Perspectives, 2: Epistemology*. Atascadero, Calif.: Ridgeview Publishing, 91–123.

Craig, E. (1990). *Knowledge and the State of Nature: An Essay in Conceptual Synthesis*. Oxford: Clarendon Press.

DePaul, M., and Zagzebski, L. (eds.). (2003). *Intellectual Virtue: Perspectives from Ethics and Epistemology*. Oxford: Clarendon Press.

Dewey, J. (1938). *Logic: The Theory of Inquiry*. New York: Holt, Rinehart & Winston.

Greco, J. (2003). 'Knowledge as Credit for True Belief', in DePaul and Zagzebski (2003), 111–34.

Grice, P. (1989). *Studies in the Way of Words*. Cambridge, Mass.: Harvard University Press.

—— (2001). *Aspects of Reason*. Oxford: Clarendon Press.

Hawthorne, J. (2004). *Knowledge and Lotteries*. Oxford: Clarendon Press.

Hookway, C. (1990). *Scepticism*. London: Routledge.

—— (2003*a*). 'How to be a Virtue Epistemologist', in DePaul and Zagzebski (2003), 183–202.

—— (2003*b*). 'Affective States and Epistemic Immediacy', in Brady and Pritchard (2003), 75–92.

Lackey, J. (unpublished). 'Why We Don't Deserve Credit for Everything We Know'.

Quine, W. V. (1960). *Word and Object*. Cambridge, Mass.: MIT Press.

Putnam, H. (1994). *Words and Life*. Cambridge, Mass.: Harvard University Press.

—— (2002). *The Collapse of the Fact/Value Dichotomy and Other Essays*. Cambridge, Mass.: Harvard University Press.

Railton, P. (2003). *Facts, Values, and Norms: Essays Toward a Morality of Consequence*. Cambridge: Cambridge University Press.

Schaffer, J. (forthcoming). 'Knowing the Answer'. *Journal of Philosophy*.

Sosa, E. (2000). 'Skepticism and Contextualism'. *Philosophical Issues*, 10: 1–18.

—— (2003). 'Knowledge, Animal and Reflective: A Reply to Michael Williams'. *Proceedings of the Aristotelian Society*, Supp. Vol. 77: 113–30.

Williamson, T. (2000). *Knowledge and its Limits*. Oxford: Clarendon Press.

Zagzebski, L. (2003). 'The Search for the Source of Epistemic Good', in Brady and Pritchard (2003), 13–28.

7

Knowing What to Think about: when Epistemology Meets the Theory of Choice

Adam Morton

TWO MOVING TARGETS

A very traditional epistemology studies changes in belief, given the information and reasoning available to a person, but ignoring her desires and values. A somewhat more realistic epistemology studies changes in belief, given information and reasoning and some relevant desires and values. The question in both cases is: if some of your beliefs change how should you change the rest? Parallel to this, a standard approach to rational decision will study changes in intention given a person's beliefs and desires. Counting intentions as a special kind of desire the question is: if some of your desires change how, given your beliefs, should you change the rest? But in reality we can hold neither beliefs nor desires constant while changing the others. We change both simultaneously. We move from one complex of beliefs and desires to another, hoping that both the transition and the final state have some relation to how they ought to be. The distinction between epistemology and decision theory, the theory of change of belief and the theory of change of desire, is not a very natural or helpful one. Both should gain from being part of a single theory of change of intentional state.

What would such a theory look like? Might some traditional epistemological topics look different from this perspective? In this paper I cannot do more than suggest how complicated and interesting the questions that arise are. I shall focus on two closely related mysteries. First, the factors that determine what combinations of belief- and decision-directed strategies will pay off. We really know very little about what these combinations are, and if we understood them better we would have a better grasp on what makes a reasonable belief and a sensible choice. We might even be able to say something useful to people pursuing epistemic-practical projects. Second, the characteristics of agents that allow them to negotiate these combinations. I do not think we can have an adequate account of reliability, intellectual virtue, or rationality until we have an informative model of how a creature generally like a human being can distribute its limited resources between competing and interlocked cognitive demands.

THE RATIONALITY OF STRATEGIES

One does not simply open one's eyes and record how the world seems; one does not open one's box of whims and consider what one might do. One follows *strategies* of investigation, which in part determine what evidence gets considered, and one follows strategies of choice, which in part determine what options get considered. Some belief-acquiring strategies are more reasonable than others. (Or more promising, less insane—not to get hung up on any particular loaded terms.) Which ones they are clearly depends on one's aims and needs. If your car is stalled on the railroad tracks you should not be pondering the twin primes conjecture. Nor should you be thinking about whether to shift the balance in your retirement portfolio. A special case of this fact is recognized in contemporary epistemology as the distinction between error avoidance and ignorance avoidance, or equivalently informativeness versus accuracy. The idea is that a completely safe, error-free, method of acquiring beliefs is unlikely to answer the questions that most interest us. In order to relieve our ignorance on matters of intellectual or practical concern we will have to take some risk of acquiring some false beliefs along with the true ones. A Cartesian project of guaranteed accurate and informative beliefs is simply not achievable by finite human beings in the likely span of human history. So, as a matter of general intellectual strategy and on a topic-by-topic basis, one has to decide what risk of false beliefs one is willing to take in order to satisfy one's desires for particular kinds of true ones.[1]

The error/ignorance balance one strikes will depend on one's desires, for knowing truths of a certain kind and not believing falsehoods. This may be a very practical matter. Suppose you are preparing chemicals to use in a demonstration for a school chemistry class and you want to know how pure the magnesium powder is, because if it is not then the demonstration will fizzle and the students will make fun of you. You will take some care, but you will want a method that gives an answer within half an hour. If it is likely to take longer you can do a different demonstration. But suppose on the other hand that you are analyzing the substratum for a batch of vaccine, and if it is not pure then the vaccine will be dangerous. Then you take much more care; you are willing to follow a procedure that won't give any answers for a week. As is often remarked, you will be willing to accept a conclusion on the basis of weaker evidence in the first case than the second, but it is more important for my purposes now that the method you employ may be entirely different. Epistemic strategy is sensitive to matters of

---

[1] A good exposition of the crucial distinction between avoiding falsity and avoiding error is made in Goldman (1986: ch. 1). The distinction, though, goes back to Levi (1967).

non-epistemic importance. (There are connections with epistemological contextualism here, which I take up in the 'Rationality' section below.)

In this case belief-acquisition is tuned by desires. Often the influence is the other way round, and decision procedures are tuned by beliefs. Suppose, for example, that you are walking down the main street of a strange town looking for a restaurant, and you believe that very soon you will come upon the town's only four restaurants, in close proximity. (Your guide book may tell you this.) Then your strategy for making your decision may be one of running through all the possibilities taking in much of the relevant information: you visit each one, read the menu and stick your head inside to sense the atmosphere, delaying a decision until you have done this for all four. Or, on the other hand, you may believe that there are many restaurants, of varying quality, scattered randomly for a long way down the street. Then your strategy may be to satisfice, and, say, to sample the first three restaurants with some care and then choose the first one after that which is at least as good as any of the first three. Decision strategy is sensitive to belief.

In fact most of the time there are influences both ways. The restaurant example illustrates this. As you walk down the street looking into restaurants you are picking up evidence of the distribution of restaurant quality in the town; this affects your intentions for the evening meal. For example you may decide that it is just hopeless to expect a decent Indian meal in a Midwestern American town, but that Thai is a more promising possibility. So you don't cross the road to look into the occasional Indian restaurant, but make efforts to check out the Thai restaurants. Your initial beliefs and desires lead to strategies for revising beliefs and desires—finding out what kind of a town it is, food-wise, and choosing somewhere to eat—which themselves lead, jointly, both to further belief-revision strategies and further decision-strategies—cross this road to check out this place, choose the first Thai place as good as the last two we've seen. This is the way it generally is, though when we reflect on our thinking we often focus only on one side of the picture.[2]

In these examples the modulations of the thinking leading to choices have gone deeper than those leading to beliefs. There is a reason for this. Rational strategy is driven by resource-allocation more than by anything else. Intellectual resources (time and working memory, centrally) are scarce in comparison to the complexity of most intellectual problems, so we must distribute what we have efficiently towards the best attainable outcomes. The study of constrained rationality, as Herbert Simon called it, is well under way in decision theory, but is hardly visible in epistemology.[3] But in fact the same issues arise, and the same responses are

---

[2] Why is decision theory full of restaurant examples? I suspect it is because they summon basic foraging problems: this way to get this food, or that way for that?

[3] I am not going to cite the now enormous and varied literature on bounded rationality. For an accessible exposition with unexpected philosophical connections see Slote (1989) and for advanced work in decision theory see Rubinstein (1988). Foley (1992: ch. 4) is also very stimulating in this connection. It would be wrong to claim that all epistemologists ignore the connections between belief and decision. Isaac Levi (1967; 1997) is a notable exception. Another exception is Bas van Fraassen (1989: ch. 8).

Adam Morton

attractive. (And run into similar obstacles.) When making a decision one can economize by sifting more hastily through a preliminary list of options to get a 'short list' to give more intensive consideration. Or one can satisfice, that is, pick a threshold of acceptability and then choose any option (or the first that arrives) that is above the threshold. The epistemic analogs of both of these are often reasonable ways of proceeding. If you are reasoning by inference to the best explanation of a phenomenon, you do not give equal attention to the pros and cons of all candidates. You quickly focus on a few potentially powerful explanations and compare them carefully. (You want to understand the pattern of the tides. You consider for a moment, but only a moment, the possibilities that schools of fish move in an almost daily pattern that causes the ocean to shift, or that the patterns are random so as to generate an illusion of high and low tides, and then you move quickly onto hypotheses involving the moon and the sun, gravitation and momentum. If none of these work out you may go back to considering the fish.) Or for analogs to satisficing suppose that you have a series of hypotheses of decreasing initial implausibility. You do not know whether any of them will explain all the phenomena in question, and it may take forever to consider them all. So you begin with the most plausible, and reject it if it does not explain 'enough' of the data, moving on to the next. Eventually, with luck, you come to a hypothesis that leaves few enough mysteries and anomalies that you are satisfied with it, and you accept it. The balance of factors could also be the other way round. You could have a large body of hypotheses, all of which explain the data adequately. You run through them as they occur to you, and accept one when its initial plausibility is high enough. Even if it explains everything you are not going to believe something that seems crazy to you, but there comes a point when high explanatory force overcomes implausibility, even though if you wait you or someone else may come up with a simple intuitive explanation that is just as powerful.[4]

The influence of standing desires, and desire-changing strategies, on epistemic strategy in examples such as these, that is to say in nearly all real cases, is clearly not confined to setting the balance between risk of falsity and possibility of informative truth. As the examples above show, the influence is much more pervasive. What we learn on any occasion is shaped in all respects by the action-choosing strategies we have adopted, which are themselves shaped by belief-acquiring strategies. Everything happens at once. This presents a problem of normative regress, though. As long as we consider beliefs to be fixed

[4] This is not to say that the situations with respect to belief and choice are fully symmetrical. Some differences come from the fact that a choice once made and acted on is normally irrevocable, while beliefs can be revised. (If the hypothesis that is both plausible and powerful comes along, you switch to it.) But this does not affect the point I am making here. A subtle difference between the choice and belief situations with respect to thresholds comes from the fact that as part of choosing an act one can choose a decision method. But as part of coming to believe one does not deliberately choose anything. Rather one *believes* in advance that, e.g., a hypothesis with high explanatory power and more than 'enough' initial plausibility is likely to be true. This is an issue that calls for a lot more attention.

when considering desire-development, and vice versa, we can suppose that individual agents can, when the situation calls for reflection, consult some fixed principles which tell them what to choose or what to accept. But if the methods, the procedures, are themselves among the variables then the task for the reflective agent is very different. Should she reflect about which reflective criteria govern her choosing and her learning? If so, what principles govern *those* reflections?[5] It seems clear that an intelligent human agent would very rarely gain by going down this path. (And with hindsight we can see that the problem was there all along in the form of the question: what tells a person when it is an appropriate time to reflect on—apply explicit norms to—her thinking?)

FEEDBACK ROUTES

There is a dogma that when you change your beliefs some of your desires may change, because you now see the consequences of achieving them differently, but that when you change your desires your beliefs should be unaffected. The thoughts in the previous section do not challenge this doctrine because they show two-way connections between *strategies* for changing beliefs and desires, not those changes themselves. Yet there is a feedback from questions of method to first-order questions of what one should believe and what one should choose. I shall describe two feedback routes.

First, a variation on a Humean theme: the potential atypicality of all samples. You are testing a coin to see if it is fair, by tossing it ten times, recording $(H_{eads}-T_{ails})$, tossing it ten times again, and then after you have done this 20 times calculating the total. If it is less than 15 you intend to announce that the coin is fair, and if it is more than 30 or less than -30 you intend to announce that the coin is biased. You have got through 19 of the 20 sets, and the total balance is 11. In none of the previous sets was $|(H-T)|$ more than three. This is pretty strong evidence that the coin is fair, and if your original plan had been to do 19 sets you would have announced just that. But the twentieth set is about to begin and you know that the coin might just come down heads four or more times out of the 10. It might do so even if your inclination to think it fair is right. So you do not conclude that the coin is fair. Your attitude is 'wait and see' until the last set is over.

This example does not turn on the effect of practical on epistemic deliberation. But it does show one way that the consequences of the support that evidence gives to a hypothesis can depend on the strategy in the course of which the evidence was obtained. Very often you should not perform the temporary closing of the file on a topic that we describe as belief (or as concluding or reporting with conviction)

[5] In this connection see the discussion of the 'AEA' pattern in Morton (2000).

until you have completed your investigations.[6] (Bayesians may complain that your degree of belief in the hypothesis should be independent of the investigatory strategy. I'm not sure even of this, since it assumes that your prior probabilities are independent of your strategy, which I'm not convinced of. But, be that as it may, the Bayesian world-view just doesn't have a place for belief or acceptance.) And since the choice of strategy itself usually depends on some larger practical (practical plus epistemic) context, the point at which it is appropriate to form a belief on a topic is very often a result of the practical context, among other things. To return to the example, you might have set 20 sets as your target because you were intending to place a large bet on the coin and needed a certain minimum assurance of its propensities for the risk to be reasonable.

The next feedback route has a paradoxical air. There are many topics on which you have no opinion, though you may have some ideas about the general charac-ter of the evidence. In the course of working out how to satisfy a desire you may acquire a reason to investigate something. And then it is very likely that you will acquire an opinion. Sometimes, indeed, you can tell which way the opinion is likely to lie. Suppose, for example, that you are an agnostic by reason of a complete lack of interest in religious questions. You undertake to give some lectures in the philosophy of religion, though, to help out a colleague, and as a result plan to read and think about arguments for and against the existence of God. Your general impression before really going into the matter was that the arguments against were stronger (the dubious intelligibility of the concept, the problem of evil, and so on.) So you now think that very likely in a month's time you will be an atheist. Does that give you reason to revise your beliefs in the direction of atheism now, before considering the arguments? Intuitively it does not, although it is slightly puzzling why. In other cases the existence of evidence you have not yet seen can itself count as evidence. (A person in whom you have great trust and who is in a position to know assures you that an envelope, which will be unsealed tomorrow, contains overwhelming evidence that X is the murderer. You should feel pretty sure now that X is the murderer.) If you do have reason now to incline to atheism then the decision to help your colleague will have made it rational to change your religious beliefs. Even if it does not, the decision will have given you expectations about what your future beliefs will be, together with expectations that these beliefs will be better founded than your present ones, which comes to something very similar.[7]

These two feedback routes may be connected, in that our reluctance in the atheism case to think that you should change your opinions now may be connected with the fact that you have not yet gone through arguments and

---

[6] One reason for saying 'very often' rather than 'always' is situations in medical experimentation where a partial tally of the evidence suggests that it would be wrong to continue with the experiment as planned.

[7] The issues here are connected with the issues about the reflection or principal principle discussed by Williamson (2000: ch. 10).

evidence in the way you intend to. It is only at some stages that we count our inclinations as beliefs. This cannot be the whole story, though. I suspect that there is a body of principles waiting to be articulated here, governing the effect that engagement in strategies for developing one's beliefs and desires should have on those beliefs and desires.

VIRTUES OF INTELLIGENT ACTIVITY

In matters of both belief and decision people can be responsible, careful, sober, and prudent. They can also be adventurous, stubborn, and brave. These are all characteristics that can lead to good results in some circumstances. Characteristics in the first list are often thought to be valuable in all circumstances, while those in the second are valuable when they appear at the right moment. For this reason it helps to distinguish between character traits and virtues, though they often have the same names. A character trait is a disposition to some way of thinking, acting, or feeling. A virtue is a disposition to exhibit the thought, action, or emotion *when it is appropriate*. So someone may have character marked by intellectual courage, frequently defending unpopular positions, and often going out on limbs even when she knows it may expose her to ridicule or disagreement. But this is not an intellectual virtue unless the positions she defends are not transparently lunatic ones, and her defenses and conjectures often result in interesting truths and profitable decisions. I would argue, in fact, that we must make this distinction even for characteristics from the first list. You can be *too* responsible, if it makes you boring; or too careful, if it makes you miss worthwhile opportunities. A virtue must embody two kinds of tacit knowledge: of when it makes sense to exhibit the trait, and to what extent.

Nearly all the intellectual virtues that we have everyday names for are virtues of intelligent activity generally, and not specifically of belief formation, decision, or some other category of thought. Even epistemologically oriented virtues such as respect for evidence are applicable generally: someone with no respect for evidence will make disastrous decisions. And decision-oriented virtues such as prudence have epistemic relevance: in planning and carrying out a belief-acquisition strategy one has to look forward as carefully as in any other activity. I think there are two closely related reasons for this, the ubiquity of strategy and the centrality of limitation management.

It should be clear by now that strategy is everywhere. Whenever we think we do so as part of a plan, even if sometimes a simple one, in which getting clearer about some things and making some decisions takes one along the way to getting clearer about some targeted facts and making some targeted decisions. But since that is so, the capacities to make and carry out suitable plans are everywhere, and are everywhere essential. So the epistemic virtues, in particular, are pointless unless they coincide with or cooperate with virtues of epistemic strategy. And these virtues are just virtues of strategy in general. Epistemic care, for example, requires that one not overlook slight possibilities of evidence against one's intended conclusion. But this is a particular case of not overlooking slight possibilities in general, particularly slight possibilities of unwelcome outcomes, and this is not epistemic care but prudential care. The pattern is the same.

This is not to say that someone who has the virtue of epistemic care, for example, will have the virtue of prudential care. The discrepancy may be crude, in that someone might rarely be disposed to be careful in prudential matters though they often are in epistemic matters. (Though given the inextricability of the two, a failing in one will lead to problems in the other.) Or it might be subtler, in that someone's dispositions to care in respect to evidence gathering might be more or less appropriate than her dispositions to care in respect to scouting out dire possibilities. But, then, for that matter, someone who often exhibits epistemic care may exhibit it with regard to scientific matters, say, and not religious ones, or may exhibit it as a virtue in one of these and not the others. Virtues are like this: their instantiation as virtues in any person are very scattered. There is a deep problem here, a discrepancy between a simple interpretation of what they might seem to involve and what they could in fact possibly be, and it is not resolved by distinguishing between epistemic and prudential virtues.[8]

There is a reason why most intellectual virtues are virtues of making and carrying out plans. It is that we are so very finite; our working memories are so small in comparison with the complexity of the intellectual projects we can set ourselves. Many stages of most processes involve searches: one has to consider a fact, assess it, then consider further facts suggested by one's assessment, assess them, and so on through a ramifying tree of possibilities. For obvious combinatorial reasons (a binary tree has 2^n branches to depth n) no real agent can search both thoroughly and deeply. But different stages of an enquiry may require one to

— search the consequences of an act or a proposition for advantages or plausibilities in general;
— search the consequences of an act or a proposition for disadvantages or implausibilities in general;
— search the consequences of an act or a proposition for advantages or plausibilities of a particular kind;
— search the consequences of an act or a proposition for disadvantages or implausibilities of a particular kind;
— search the consequences of an act or a proposition to a great depth, looking for advantages/disadvantages/plausibilities/implausibilities generally/of a particular kind;

[8] For the variability of behavior that any realistic concept of a virtue will have to take into account see Harman (1999) and Doris (2002).

— search the consequences of an act or a proposition very thoroughly, looking for advantages/disadvantages/plausibilities/implausibilities generally/of a particular kind.

This is just too hard to do by brute force. We have to content ourselves with doing some aspects of it, with many shortcuts most of which are inconsistent with doing other aspects of it. We have to learn which short cuts pay off, for us, and when.[9]

Intellectual care, for example, has at its heart searching comprehensively, to a shallow depth if need be, carrying out subsidiary searches when necessary to check the relevance of facts as they emerge. Intellectual daring, on the other hand, has at its heart deeper and usually less comprehensive searches, trusting that details will not be missed that invalidate the whole procedure. Both are necessary, and they can very rarely be combined. Each, then, needs to be accompanied with the capacity to employ it when it is needed and not when it is obstructive.

Most intellectual virtues have essential connections to capacities to search in some particular manner, and capacities to know when that kind of search is a good idea. These are the capacities that we make names for, because they are the ones we need names for. They are hard-to-acquire and vary from individual to individual, and they cannot be summoned on a particular occasion unless the ground has been prepared by practice and self-modulation. So we need to name them and become friends with them. And since their important characteristics apply to searches in many kinds of thinking, they are multi-purpose virtues of intelligent activity.

RATIONALITY

One 'virtue' has particular historical importance, and has played a large role in the development of Western culture. That is rationality, and I have scare-quoted its claim to virtue not because rationality does not have many of the characteristics of an all-purpose intellectual virtue, but because part of the point of thinking in terms of intellectual virtues is to avoid begging questions about the relations between the qualities that make for intellectual success. They may not have much in common; they may often act contrary to one another; it may not be possible for one person to cultivate all of them. In standard epistemology the idea of rationality is reflected in the concept of a justified belief. At first this seems simple: a belief is justified if it is acquired in the right way, with no bad reasoning involved. On second thought complications arise. A justified belief may be acquired in an irrational way, as long as the reasons the person continues to hold it, or would defend it, with are good ones. This clearly opens up a large amount of vagueness, to add to the vagueness of good reasons or reasoning. Further thought raises further complications. We count the beliefs a person acquires by honest inference

---

[9] For more on this theme see Morton (2004).

from misleading evidence as justified. But suppose the person could easily have realized that the evidence was misleading, if only she had followed up a line of investigation she was too lazy to pursue. Or suppose a person follows a line of reasoning that is actually incorrect but which is generally taken in her circle to be alright, and whose mistakes are too subtle for her to notice. Are her beliefs going to be justified or not? (This can easily happen with statistical reasoning, which can produce problems that will baffle anyone, however sophisticated and intelligent.)

I think that no contemporary epistemologist takes the idea of a justified belief to be a very clear or useful one, unless it is hedged about with prescriptive definitions and made into a technical term of a well-developed theory.[10] At this point the concerns of this paper open up some new positions addressing traditional issues. I shall state these possibilities, without defending them. The important thing is that there are more possible reactions to the issues than we had thought.

What concepts of rational belief may we deploy without making dangerous assumptions about the psychology of belief and action or fudging the complexities of human thinking? The two below seem to be intelligible, if not always precise.

First, there is the possession of evidence or similar grounds for a belief. A person may have considerations in favor of a claim that she can produce to persuade others. People are rarely very well placed to assess exactly how strong the evidence they possess is, but the strength of the support that it gives to a claim is a relatively objective matter. The conditional probability of the claim given the evidence conjoined with relevant background beliefs is the most precise measure of support. Its precision and objectivity is admittedly qualified by the indefiniteness of what is to count as relevant background belief but, still, in most cases we know how to begin assessing whether given evidence supports a claim strongly, weakly, or not at all.

Second, there is the reasonableness of change of belief. A person has a set of beliefs at one time and another set at a later time. The transition from the one to the other may or may not be in accord with the way a well-constructed human agent would operate in the given situation. There are many aspects of the situation that might be taken into account. The ones that interest me are the belief- and desire-forming strategy that the person is pursuing and the person's whole prior complex of beliefs and desires. If the changes in belief, deletions as well as additions, result from a strategy that is a reasonable one for that person to follow, given everything she believes and wants and her particular capacities, then the change of belief is reasonable. I am not going to give any analysis of the central attribute here: the acceptability of a belief-and-desire-evolving strategy. It obviously has vague edges, but my claim is that it is relatively objective and

[10] As, e.g., Goldman (1986).

unparadoxical, and grounded in human psychology. Given this very substantial assumption, there is a piece of normative human psychology that needs a name: I'll call it directed big state rationality. (Directed because it concerns changes that result from a strategy; big state because it concerns both beliefs and desires.)

There are other ways of trying to understand change of belief. In particular, one could study the reasonableness of changes of belief alone, not in relation to desire. And one could study 'unmotivated' changes of belief, considering for example cases in which a person passes from one complex of beliefs to another as a result of the random play of neurons. These are rivals, and if they give robust and useful ways of understanding belief change then the line I am developing in this paper is less interesting. To sharpen the rivalry I shall state a thesis, an aggressive claim which if true makes the study of strategies for simultaneously changing beliefs and desires central to epistemology.

The big state rationality thesis: the possession of evidence for one's beliefs and their acquisition by directed big state rationality are the only sustainable concepts of rational belief.

According to the whole state transition thesis there is only one concept of rational belief, and only one concept of rational change of belief. Only one kind, that is, that stands up to analysis and handles complex examples without ad hoc requirements, coheres realistically with actual human psychology, and sheds light on the forms of thought that are worth cultivating. Moreover the two are very different. At the heart of evidence there is an abstract relation between propositions, taken as semantical objects, evaluated ultimately in terms of the possible worlds in which the claim-proposition is true which are excluded by the evidence proposition. At the heart of big state rationality are details of very contingent human psychology: what patterns of thought in the pursuit of what projects our brains can follow effectively. The claim is that there is nothing in between.[11]

When we keep these two parts of rationality apart, and don't glance between them, we find that many puzzle cases can be described quite simply. For there is no problem with an irrational acquisition giving a perfectly rational (well-evidenced) result. Consider, for example, cases in which a person adopts a perfectly idiotic belief-forming strategy and comes up with a well-supported belief. The kitchen is on fire and the flames remind someone of the distribution of primes, so that he muses on a conjecture in number theory instead of thinking how to get his children out of an upstairs bedroom. At the end of the story the children are dead, the person is heartbroken, and there is a good proof of a new result. We should have no compunction about calling this person irrational, and describing the thought process that led to the number-theoretical belief as very defective, while allowing that the person's great losses are mitigated by the gain of one small rational belief.

[11] Harman (1986) can be read as claiming something similar. Harman does not stick his neck so far out though.

There are also examples in the opposite direction, in which an irrational belief is acquired by a rational process. Sometimes it is reasonable to acquire a belief although the evidence for it is fairly feeble. Another burning house case. A person realizes that the house is on fire and that his children are upstairs. There are two ways to get to them and out with them. One is up the stairs, but the staircase is already beginning to smolder. The other is to dash out the front door, up the metal fire escape, then in and out through the bedroom window. He decides that the latter gives the best chance, though only if he moves immediately, given the greater distance. Consider his belief, as he begins to run, that the outside route gives a greater chance of getting there and returning with the children. He doesn't have much evidence for it: the stairs were only smoldering rather than flaming, and he hasn't really considered the difficulty of getting two sleepy children through the window onto the fire escape. But to delay while considering the evidence would be to make the situation worse: the right thing is to take the most plausible-seeming possibility and act on it decisively. So his thinking is as it should be, though the belief it leads to is not strongly based.[12]

JUSTIFIED BELIEFS?

According to the view I am suggesting, there are facts about what ways of thinking are best for a person at a time, given her whole situation, and there are facts about the strength of the evidence for some of her beliefs, but there are fewer facts that cross the categories of objective evidence and valuable ways of thinking. In particular, one epistemologist's staple, the concept of a proposition belief in which is justified for a person at a time, begins to seem less and less solid. A number of philosophers have expressed doubts recently about the usefulness and intelligibility of the concept of a justified belief, and of related concepts such as that of what it is epistemically permissible to believe, so I shall concentrate on doubts stemming from the big state rationality thesis, and more generally from connections between getting beliefs and choosing actions.

The idea is that there is a particular relation that holds between a person and a proposition when that person believes that proposition *on the basis of* reasons which provide that person with their best chance of having true beliefs involving propositions *of that kind*. The belief is one that the person would have if she was motivated only by the desire to have true beliefs on the topic in question and was satisfying this desire as effectively as possible. I have italicized two phrases whose vagueness invites further specification. Other philosophers have described the

---

[12] All these cases raise questions about what is to count as belief. My own inclination is not to take the concept of belief too seriously, as I argue in Morton (2002: ch. 3), and to say that beliefs are whatever we act on and tell one another. That suggestion is not essential here: for example the fire escape case can be taken to show just that the result of a bit of good thinking can be an informational state about which the evidence is inadequate.

difficulties filling the gaps represented by these phrases; I shall concentrate on the idea of 'best chance of having true beliefs'.[13]

Here is my central doubt: we have no reason to believe that any person ever believes anything for reasons that are optimal in terms of truth-directedness. All our actual beliefs are shaped so intimately by our practical concerns that it is hard to imagine how we would think if truth were our only concern. Among the things we aim at are good explanations of data, and the truth-conducive properties of inference to the best explanation are not at all clear. So as long as we hold many of our beliefs as parts of inferences to the best explanation they are held for reasons that are not obviously those we would hold if we were interested only in truth. Quite apart from this, the actual patterns of thinking we make use of, to acquire and to defend our beliefs, are determined by our cognitive limitations. On almost any topic, a being with super-human intelligence would have found different reasons for an overlapping set of beliefs. Some of these reasons we would appreciate if they were explained to us and some of them we would find mysterious.

Consider Dretske's (2000) famous zebra example. A person sees a striped equid in the zoo, in an enclosure marked 'zebra', remembers pictures of zebras, and concludes that this animal is a zebra. He does not have what we would normally consider sufficient evidence to rule out the possibility that the animal is a donkey painted to look like a zebra, a possibility that does not cross his mind. Dretske concludes that justification is not closed under logical consequence, since the man is justified in believing that the animal is a zebra but not justified in believing something that follows from it, that it is not a painted donkey. But note how the natural judgement that the zebra belief is an okay one for the man to have is shaped by our conception of normal human information-processing powers. In a community of geniuses the reasons for thinking that it isn't a painted donkey might be obvious, and then the person who has not eliminated that possibility would not have a justified belief. Or vary the story so that the man goes to the zoo with his six-year-old daughter. He reads to her a sign that says in very convoluted language that some of the animals are fakes. The language is convoluted so that parents will understand but children will not be disappointed. The child sees the zebra and thinks 'that's a zebra'. The parent sees the zebra and forgetting the sign also thinks 'that's a zebra'. We would normally take the child to have a justified belief, but the parent not to. Were we now to learn that the child is a genius and at the age of six can read such signs and apply them to apparent zebras, we would retract our approval of her belief.

So in those cases where we do judge some of a person's beliefs as justified (epistemically acceptable) the thought we are expressing is 'this belief has *good enough* reasons, given the constraints on the person.' The most fundamental of the constraints consist in limitations of thinking power, working memory, and the like. A reasonable reaction to these limitations clearly will take into account the

---

[13] This section is a response to an invitation from one of the OUP referees.

non-epistemic demands on the person: what else she has to be attending to in order to keep her life on track. Is there a purely epistemic version of this? Can we reconstruct a concept that we recognize as both useful and roughly familiar along the lines of: this proposition is among those that this person would believe were she interested solely in true beliefs about this topic, and were she devoting her intellectual resources most effectively to that end alone? All I can say is that I need to be convinced that we can.[14]

KNOWLEDGE

The big state rationality thesis concerns the range of considerations that are relevant to what is traditionally thought of as the justification of a belief (though it suggests that the terminology of justified belief is rather confusing: better to talk of rational belief change and of evidence). The same emphasis on the agent's total cognitive state can be applied to issues about knowledge. Go back to the example early in the paper, in the rationality of strategies section, contrasting the amount of evidence you would collect before accepting that a school demonstration or that a batch of vaccine was ready to go. Suppose that in the vaccine case you had settled for the amount of evidence that would have been adequate in the classroom case. Then you would not be judged to have known the composition of the chemical, in spite of the truth of your belief and evidence which would have been strong enough in a different context. Your procedure would not have eliminated some possibilities that in that practical context were relevant.

Though this example does suggest that big state factors discriminate knowledge from non-knowledge, it is of limited impact because they operate through their effect on what it is reasonable for a person to believe. We get more interesting suggestions by playing with some of the cases from earlier in this section. Suppose, for example, that in the fire escape case the person does not have adequate evidence to exclude the possibility that the window into the bedroom may be jammed, or that he cannot get the children through it without injuring them, but that these possibilities are in fact false, and the person's belief that the fire escape route will get him in and the children out is true. Not only true but formed in the best way, given human limitations and the situation the person was in.[15] Then, according to my intuitions, the person knows that fact about the fire escape route.

---

[14] There's a connection here with the debate between evidentialists and pragmatists. Evidentialists say 'believe only what you have adequate evidence for' and pragmatists say 'believe what makes your life go well.' (Well, to a first approximation.) This section asks what 'adequate' might mean. If non-epistemic aims affect what is adequate evidence then we can accept the evidentialist slogan while giving it a pragmatist twist. The classic source is the debate between James (1948) and Clifford (1901). For some recent developments see Adler (2002) and Conee and Feldman (2004).

[15] This is a conclusion that could also be derived from a virtue-epistemological approach to the definition of knowledge, e.g., Zagzebski's (1999). I don't know if many virtue epistemologists would find this a welcome consequence.

Since it would have been irrational to waste time excluding the possibilities that the person didn't waste time excluding, the person's failure to exclude them does not demote his belief from knowledge.[16] On the other hand, in the fire and number theory case the person does, intuitively, know the theorem in question, even though the thought process was all things considered insane. But that does not really tell against the relevance of the whole state to the ascription of knowledge, because the important aspect of the whole state—the person's desire to avoid the fire danger to his children—is not relevant to the exclusion of any possibility in which the number-theoretical conclusion is false.

There are examples like the fire and number theory case, in which the whole state is relevant, though. First, a far-out case. A soldier ought to be on guard duty on the ramparts, and in fact he wants to do his duty and protect the city but his alcoholic tendencies have got the better of him and he is in the tavern far from his post. He wonders where his wife is and figures that she would have returned from the neighbors and will be at home putting the children to bed. The possibility that she has been abducted by aliens does not occur to him, so he considers no evidence for or against it. Now, as it happens, just above his post on the ramparts a flying saucer has just circled, on its way to its mother ship with a cargo of human specimens, not including the soldier's wife. Had he been at his post, as he should have been, he would have seen it, and thought about alien abductions, and then when he wondered about the whereabouts of his wife he would have suspended judgement. The epistemic relevance of alien abductions derives ultimately from his practical obligation to be at his post.

A more normal case. A young biologist is running an experiment on whether a new antibiotic inhibits the growth of a bacillus in a culture. A colleague is running a very similar experiment with a different antibiotic, bacillus, and culture, and his samples are in the same lab as our biologist. One Saturday morning she has come in to the lab to check on her experiment, and has also promised her colleague to check on his. She intends to do both, but instead gets distracted and while looking at her experiment muses about what it would be like to win a Nobel prize at the age of 26. So she doesn't even glance at her colleague's samples, but does inspect her own and realizes that the bacillus is being killed off. She checks various obvious possibilities and comes to the conclusion that it is the antibiotic that is killing the bacillus. She does not even consider the extremely rare and unlikely possibility that the bacillus is being attacked by a particular virus V that normally does not infect that bacillus. But, though she does not consider it, if that virus had been present the symptoms in the affected bacilli would be exactly as she observed. Now as it happens though V is not present in her samples it is present in the simultaneous decimation of the bacilli in those of her colleague, which are much more susceptible to V. Had she done as she intended and looked at

---

[16] This is a sort of converse of David Lewis's (1996: 556) assertion that '[w]hen error would be especially disastrous, few possibilities may be properly ignored.' See also Hawthorne (2004: ch. 2).

her colleague's samples, she would have immediately wondered whether V was present, and then would have been led to check whether it was present in her own samples. But in fact she did nothing to rule out this possibility, because of an irrational distraction from the course she had wanted to follow. The epistemic relevance of the data about the overlooked samples derives from her practical commitment to helping her colleague.

Does the soldier know that his wife is at home? Does the biologist know that the antibiotic is attacking the bacilli? My intuitions suggest that they do not. I expect these examples to be controversial, but what they suggest to me is that when considering knowledge, too, considerations about how a person ought to be thinking turn on the person's big state, their whole complex of beliefs and desires.[17]

KNOWING WHEN TO REFLECT

The big state rationality thesis is a conjecture, which if true connects the enlarged theory of belief and decision that I am looking forward to with traditional epistemology in a particularly simple way. If it is right then epistemology is a simpler and less puzzling subject in the new context. But it is definitely conjectural. To end the paper I shall discuss another aspect of rationality that has played a large role in the history of epistemology: the ability to reflect critically on one's own processes of belief formation.

Few contemporary epistemologists will defend the idea that a rational human agent should exercise constant control of her belief-forming processes, always conscious of them as they occur and always checking them against explicit norms of rationality. But skepticism about the ideal of conscious rational control should not make one deny that there is a special importance to the virtue of knowing when one should reflect, and run-over, check, and reconsider one's thinking. In fact it is particularly significant when belief and choice interact. Reflection can be a naïve business of pausing and asking 'does that seem right?' or it can consist in applying explicit norms of rationality. In either case, it offers as many possibilities of obstruction as of help. Reflection burdens working memory, introduces new sources of error, and generally slows things down. Done at the wrong moment, it can hinder or even sabotage reasoning that would otherwise succeed. So we have to know when to do it. And usually we cannot or should not try to know this by thinking out in a principled way 'this is/is not a moment to pause and take stock,' for two reasons. Explicit thinking of this kind is very expensive in cognitive

---

[17] Both my examples have a moral flavor, which I have tried to keep out of the discussion. But it would be good to explore examples in which whether a person knows something is affected by the possibilities excluded by intellectual strategies they morally ought to be adopting or avoiding. The suggestion here is in accordance with a suggestion that John Hawthorne (2004: 188 n.53) attributes to Jonathan Schaffer.

resources, which are not likely to be available at the very moments that reflection might be called for. (It is when everyone has been called out to fight the fire that it might be most relevant for someone to tell us that it is a false alarm, but at that of all times we cannot spare someone to find out.) And we very rarely have enough knowledge of our own thinking to give us the cues that such principles would engage with. (Even if we could spare someone to check for false alarms, he would be guessing half the time.) If the big state rationality thesis is right, then the barriers to self-knowledge here are even more formidable. It would be asking much too much to demand that one know what strategy one is following, the relevant characteristics of the totality of everything one believes and wants, *and* the limits of one's own particular capacities. So in general one will not know if one's belief is formed by an acceptable process; we're better off considering simply how adequate the evidence is.

These two reasons connect, in that even when we could learn enough about our on-going thinking to apply such meta-principles doing so would draw on the very resources whose scarcity makes reflection often a bad idea.[18] This is so even though there are exceptional cases, where it is easy to tell that reflection is called for. For example, it doesn't cost much to follow the principle 'when you find yourself driven to a transparently implausible conclusion, stop and see if you've done something stupid.' But the conclusion has to be transparently implausible. Usually when a claim is very improbable given one's prior beliefs, or even contradictory, it would take a lot of thinking to make this explicit. So even this mild principle carries the danger that it might lure someone into excessive fussing at the boundaries of what is obvious.

So how do we know when to reflect? Very often we don't, and do it too often, too little, or at the wrong times. But there is a virtue of appropriate reflection, which some people exhibit on some topics. (We don't have a good name for it: perhaps 'rationality' will do, taken as a more subtle thing than simply the capacity to reflect: that capacity plus the sense when to use it.) The cognitive psychology of intellectual virtues is largely unexplored, but however the details work out, it seems to me that it must consist in sensitivities to large libraries of typical cognitive situations built up over a period of time and then recognized as similar to situations as they occur. So one has to be able to build up the library, store it in an accessible way, and recognize relevant similarities with actual events. (The pattern is not unique to intellectual virtues. Chess players build up large mental databases of 'combinations', which they have to recognize in actual token combinations of pieces. Courageous, honest, or generous people will have gone through the Aristotelian process of observing and cataloging the admirable actions of their elders and betters, while slowly learning what it takes to imitate them.)[19] The important point is that the working of the virtue will usually be inaccessible to the

---

[18] In this connection see Kornblith (2002: ch. 2).
[19] For more on this again see Morton (2004).

agent and not tune-able by her on the particular occasion. She cannot simulate it by thinking 'what would a well-constructed agent do in this situation?'[20]

At this point we should ask: what makes it an appropriate time to reflect? One should reflect when it helps to, of course. But helps what? Helps one's reasoning to conform to norms of rationality? Helps one achieve epistemic and practical ends? When it is a matter of reflecting on the thinking that concerns us here, thinking that combines belief and choice, the aim of conforming to rational norms is really not an option. For we don't really have any culturally inherited or apriori accessible norms for this general case. We have norms for assessing the force of evidence and a few rough and ready norms of good epistemic procedure; we have rough norms of means–ends rationality and more precise rules for calculating expected utility. But we do not have anything explicit to guide us in choosing how to allocate our intellectual resources between competing parts of an epistemic/practical project, or how to choose a procedure for choice of belief or action that will fit best with the rest of an epistemic or practical project. So if there are moments that are appropriate and inappropriate to stop and consider one's thinking, they are surely determined by more externalist considerations, in terms of what procedures are in fact likely to produce what kinds of results.[21]

It is interesting that we almost never reflect on how our belief-acquisition and our decision-making fit together, even though their fitting is crucial to almost all of our activities. The virtue of knowing when to reflect has an aspect of benign illusion about it: it directs us at only part of the cognitive situation at any time. It says 'rethink the logic here,' or 'go slowly about the choice of options here,' or 'there must be further consequences'; but rarely more than one of these, and almost never asks us to reflect on our belief-formation and our choice at the same time. That is just as well, as we wouldn't know how to go about such a complicated reflection, but it leaves us with the impression that we are aware of far more of our thinking than we are. In fact, the choice of intellectual strategy, the way that we nudge ourselves into one or another procedure for coming up with choices and beliefs, guided at suitable points by explicit reflection on tiny parts of our thinking, is by and large a mystery to us, both introspectively and in terms of normative lore.[22]

The choice of strategy, then, probably the most crucial element in our intellectual life, is not something that we can evaluate in accordance with any

---

[20] The virtue of appropriate reflection is a higher-order virtue, consisting in the direction of first-order thinking. Its relation to simpler intellectual virtues is analogous to the relation of the virtue—also vital, also nameless—of being able to feel regret at the right moment and in the right amount to simpler moral virtues such as courage and honesty.

[21] But given the length of time it has taken to get at all clear about evidence—from Humean gropings about induction to confirmation theory à la Hempel and Carnap to the Bayesian orthodoxy that I take to be our best current account—one could doubt whether many people have ever made much conscious appeal to correct and explicitly formulated norms of evidential force.

[22] Another aspect of the benign illusion: it tends to direct us to the tractable question 'is this reasoning valid?' rather than the more important and much less tractable question 'are these claims consistent?'

standard norms. But some strategies are clearly successful and some disastrous. And, discriminating more finely, some are clearly more successful than others. There are many indeterminate cases, too. Consider a person who values truth above everything and who adopts an epistemic policy which gives beliefs that allow her to achieve many of her less abstract desires and live happily, but at the cost of a large number of false beliefs. Is the policy Right because it gets her a good measure of what she wants, or Wrong because it does not achieve the good that she would herself have judged it by? I am not sure there are answers to such questions. But this fine-grained indeterminacy should not obscure the fact that there are systematic factors which make some strategies successful and others not.

These factors are extremely complicated. They would involve far too much searching for individuals to think them through instance by instance. So they are externalist factors; they are not to be applied in reflective regulation of one's own thinking. But they are externalist factors with a twist: they determine the internalistic criteria that we do apply reflectively. For when it is appropriate to reflect and we reflect successfully we apply standards of reasoning that are appropriate to part of our reasoning given the unreflected-on nature of the rest of it. The standards are only appropriate because they fit into a larger pattern, which itself is valuable simply because it works.

REFERENCES

Adler, J. (2002). *Belief's Own Ethics*. Cambridge, Mass.: MIT Press.

Clifford, W. (1901). 'The Ethics of Belief', in *Lectures and Essays*, vol. 2. London: Macmillan, 163–205.

Conee, E., and Feldman, R. (2004). *Evidentialism: Essays in Epistemology*. Oxford: Clarendon Press.

Doris, J. (2002). *Lack of Character: Personality and Moral Behavior*. Cambridge: Cambridge University Press.

Dretske, F. (2000). 'Epistemic Operators', in *Perception, Knowledge and Belief: Selected Essays*. Cambridge: Cambridge University Press, 30–47.

Foley, R. (1992). *Working Without a Net*. New York: Oxford University Press.

Goldman, A. (1986). *Epistemology and Cognition*. Cambridge, Mass.: Harvard University Press.

Harman, G. (1986). *Change in View*. Cambridge, Mass.: MIT Press.

—— (1999). 'Moral Philosophy Meets Social Psychology: Virtue Ethics and the Fundamental Attribution Error'. *Proceedings of the Aristotelian Society*, 99: 315–31.

Hawthorne, J. (2004). *Knowledge and Lotteries*. Oxford: Clarendon Press.

James, W. (1948). 'The Will to Believe', in *Essays in Pragmatism*. New York: Haffner, 88–109.

Kornblith, H. (2002). *Knowledge and Its Place in Nature*. Oxford: Clarendon Press.

Levi, I. (1967). *Gambling with Truth*. New York: Knopf.

—— (1997). *The Covenant of Reason: Rationality and the Commitments of Thought*. Cambridge: Cambridge University Press.

Lewis, D. (1996). 'Elusive Knowledge'. *Australasian Journal of Philosophy*, 74: 549–67.

Morton, A. (2000). 'Saving Epistemology From the Epistemologists: Recent Work in the Theory of Knowledge'. *British Journal for the Philosophy of Science*, 51: 685–704.

—— (2002). *The Importance of Being Understood: Folk Psychology as Ethics*. London: Routledge.

—— (2004). 'Epistemic Virtues, Metavirtues, and Computational Complexity'. *Noûs*, 38: 481–502.

Rubinstein, A. (1988). *Modelling Bounded Rationality*. Cambridge, Mass.: MIT Press.

Slote, M. (1989). *Beyond Optimizing: A Study of Rational Choice*. Cambridge, Mass.: Harvard University Press.

van Fraassen, B. C. (1989). *Laws and Symmetry*. Oxford: Clarendon Press.

Williamson, T. (2000). *Knowledge and its Limits*. Oxford: Clarendon Press.

Zagzebski, L. (1999). 'What Is Knowledge?', in J. Greco and E. Sosa (eds.), *The Blackwell Guide to Epistemology*. Malden, Mass.: Blackwell, 92–116.

8

Ideal Agents and Ideal Observers in Epistemology

Linda Zagzebski

I. INTRODUCTION

Epistemology is an intrinsically normative discipline. Knowledge, justification, certainty, understanding, rationality, and intellectual virtue are all objects of investigation because epistemologists think each of them is good in one of the ways of being good—the desirable, the admirable, or both. Epistemology is also normative in the narrow sense of the normative since it focuses attention on how we *ought* to form and maintain beliefs. Epistemology needs value theory to provide the wider theory of the good and the ought of which the epistemic good and ought are forms.[1] In this paper I will argue that the epistemological analogue of an Ideal Observer Theory or an Ideal Agent Theory can be used to anchor the normative concepts of epistemology and can resolve important disputes over foundationalism, contextualism, and the problem of the alignment of rationality and truth.

Overlooking the normative aspect of epistemological theories can make it more difficult to resolve disputes over these theories. The debates between foundationalism and coherentism, and between contextualism and invariantism, are cases in point. The dispute over foundationalism and coherentism (and now Klein's infinitism)[2] is a dispute about the way we ought to structure our systems of belief. What can be misleading about these theories is that they are not theories about the epistemic life in the way a foundationalist ethical theory is a theory about the ethical life. In ethics, foundationalism is a theory that starts with some foundational proposition about a good life or a good motive or a good state of affairs or the categorical imperative, and it then explains the moral life by a system of propositions that are in some way based upon the foundational one.

---

[1] I am using 'normative' in the broad sense that includes the good as well as the right, and what I mean by value theory is a theory of both normative and evaluative properties.

[2] Peter Klein (1999) first proposed the theory he calls infinitism.

In epistemology, however, foundationalism is not a theory that says some feature of the epistemic life is foundational and which then sets out a system of propositions about our epistemic lives that are based upon the proposition at the foundation. Similarly, coherentism is not a set of propositions about the epistemic life that are mutually supporting. Instead, foundationalism and coherentism are theories that say our epistemic lives are theories. A good thinker's beliefs have a theoretical structure, the structure endorsed by the theory. The epistemological theory itself is neither foundationalist nor coherentist. It is the theory that says a foundationalist or coherentist system of beliefs is the one we ought to have, or is one that a rational or intellectually virtuous person would have. That theory is normative.

Epistemologists usually think they can determine the right way to structure a belief system by using a few epistemic principles allegedly known a priori, but the intractability of the dispute over foundationalism, coherentism, and now infinitism suggests that more is required to resolve it. The first step to resolving this dispute, I propose, is to clarify the theory's normative basis. It is instructive to notice that foundationalism, coherentism, and infinitism all propose an idealized picture of the epistemic life that probably does not describe the mind of any actual human being. Why is reference to an idealized mind used to answer the question of how human beings ought to structure their belief systems? The answer, I think, is that these theories obliquely refer to a normative theory that makes reference to an idealized mind central. I do not mean to suggest that the participants in this dispute intend to do that, but focusing on an idealized mind helps to resolve the substantive dispute over foundationalism and its alternatives.

Another popular epistemological theory whose normative basis needs to be unpacked is contextualism. The contextualist asserts that what counts as knowledge that p in some context depends upon the relevance or salience of the alternatives to p in that context. In David Lewis's version of contextualism, S knows p just in case S's evidence eliminates every possibility in which not-p 'except for those possibilities that we are properly ignoring' (1996: 554). Note the term 'properly'. What separates this theory from a traditional rigorous infallibilism is the fact that it sorts out the possibilities in which not-p into those that are properly ignored and those that are not properly ignored, given one's epistemic situation, and that division is normative. But Lewis continually refers to what 'we' can ignore, what is relevant to 'us' in certain situations, and so on. His norms are determined from the point of view of rational *persons*, in particular, us. The fact that the evaluative state of knowing is given from the perspective of rational persons who find themselves in certain circumstances, rather than by criteria of rationality detached from its embodiment in persons, is a meta-epistemological position with important implications.

Tying epistemic evaluation to the judgement of persons is central to another form of contextualism according to which standards for knowledge are stronger the more the attributor or subject[3] cares that the belief is true. The idea here is that when more is at stake if the belief is false, the subject must satisfy higher standards for ruling out the possibility that the belief is false, but the fact that, and the degree to which, something is at stake is determined from the perspective of human persons who have cares and values other than the epistemic.[4] But the theory is plausible only if the perspective is constrained by an ideal perspective. Consider first the subject-based version of this theory according to which the more the subject cares if a belief p is false, the higher the standards for knowing p. It would be very implausible to say that a subject knows less than everyone else simply because she cares more about everything than everybody else. Likewise, it would be implausible to say she knows more than everybody else simply because she cares less. Qualities such as normality, rationality, and perhaps virtue ought to limit the permissible variations in what the subject cares about that are relevant to the attribution of knowledge to her.

Similar points apply to attributor-based contextualism. Does it really affect the issue of whether some subject has knowledge that the attributor cares about abnormal matters or cares to an abnormal degree? Do we want to say that a subject gains a lot of knowledge as soon as the attributor becomes depressed and ceases to care about anything? To avoid such implausible consequences attributor-based contextualism has to say something about the attributor and must address the issue of idiosyncratic carings and what is important *simpliciter*. This leads the contextualist into the issue of the properties of the attributor.

The invariantist opponent of contextualism denies that the question of whether S knows p depends upon the context in which the issue of whether S knows p arises. That may mean that the invariantist would accept the judgement of an ideal observer of S, and she maintains that that judgement would not vary with context. If so, the approach I will propose in this paper can settle the dispute between the contextualist and the invariantist.

The normative aspect of the debates over foundationalism/coherentism and contextualism/invariantism point us in the direction of giving conditions for knowledge and perhaps other evaluative epistemic states by reference to the perspective of a person who possesses some ideal epistemic quality, at least rationality, and perhaps something stronger, like intellectual virtue. In previous work I have endorsed an approach to the foundations of ethics I call exemplarism. I believe this approach is as useful in epistemology as in moral theory. It has the potential to not only resolve some new and old disputes, but to broaden the range of issues of interest to epistemologists in the future. In the following sections I will describe the method and the way it can be used to resolve the disputes over foundationalism and its alternatives and over contextualism and its alternatives. I will then turn to a problem that I find one of the most difficult in epistemology,

---

[3] It is common among contextualists to use the word 'subject' for the bearer of beliefs and knowledge, although I prefer the term 'agent', as will become apparent in this paper.

[4] See, e.g., Keith DeRose (1992).

the problem of how rationality aligns with truth. Exemplarism can help illumin-ate this problem and the related problem of irresolvable disagreement in belief.

II. EXEMPLARISM

Above I suggested that the foundationalist (coherentist, infinitist) grounds her claim that we ought to structure our beliefs in a certain way by implicit reference to a person whose mind has an ideal epistemic structure. Similarly, the contextual-ist says that we may properly ignore certain alternatives in which our belief would be false, and whether we should or not depends upon features of either the putative knower or the person making the attribution of knowledge. The subject or attributor need not be ideal, but there are constraints on her cares and concerns and the way she determines relevance which need to be explored. The issue I want to raise now is how the epistemic theorist makes the move from the type of reasons usually offered in support of one of these theories to the conclusion that something is what we ought to do or is a good way to behave epistemically. How does the implicit reference to persons, ideal or otherwise, underwrite the epistemologist's move to a particular judgement of what ought to be the case or what is or is not proper? In some of these disputes there is an implicit use of an ideal observer theory or an ideal agent theory analogous to those used in ethics. In others a theory of that kind may not be implicitly used, but I wish to argue that doing so can help resolve these disputes.

I promote an ideal agent theory I call exemplarism. Before describing the theory, I want to make it clear that I do not think that every particular moral judgement rests on a theory. On the contrary, I grant that some judgements of what we ought or ought not do are more central in our idea of the normative than any theory. Examples of judgements that probably have this feature in ethics include the judgement that it is always wrong to punish an innocent person or the judgement that the intentional killing of a human being is prima facie unjustified. It seems to me that any acceptable ethical theory must be consistent with these judgements since the judgement enjoys a more central place in our thinking about morality than any theory. If that is right, it is also plausible that the epistemologist is entitled to offer such judgements as well. An example would be the judgement that one ought not to have inconsistent beliefs, or to be more cautious, that inconsistent beliefs are prima facie epistemically wrong. I think that some epistemologists treat the judgement that every belief ought to be justified by a belief that is itself justified as having this status. Presumably they think our confidence in the judgement is greater than our confidence in any theory of epistemic wrongness. But moral philosophers cannot get very far with judgements such as those mentioned above, and I doubt that epistemologists can either. In fact, the judgement that every belief ought to be justified by a belief that is itself justified generates the regress that produces the dispute over foundationalism and coherentism. It is unlikely that the judgements that enjoy primacy over normative theory in epistemology are sufficient to resolve the disputes among coherentists, foundationalists, and infinitists, nor among contextualists and invariantists, even when supplemented by additional a priori principles and intuitions about particular cases.

In describing moral exemplarism I begin with the intuition that among the judgements that have priority over theory are judgements about the identity of paradigmatically good persons. Some of these exemplars are well known and historically important, such as Jesus Christ and the Buddha. Many others are known only to a small circle of family and acquaintances, and it is generally the latter that serve as models for our own behavior because our experience of them is much more direct and their behavior is easier to imitate than the more historically important exemplars. Exemplars stand out from the rest of the community for their good sense, good counsel, wide knowledge and experience, and emotional attunement to the world. I am not suggesting that these qualities are criteria for being a paradigmatically good person. On the contrary, I believe that there is something about exemplars that attracts us, and it is only when we look at them more carefully to determine what is attractive about them that we identify these qualities and many others. My position is that we may be mistaken about some of these exemplars, but we cannot be mistaken about very many because the identity of exemplars of goodness is not merely contingently related to our general moral judgements and the construction of a moral theory. What we mean by a good person is *a person like that*.

Judgements about the identity of paradigmatically good persons can be used as the basis for constructing a moral theory. I have previously argued that we can model a theory of this kind on the theory of direct reference, which became well known by Kripke and Putnam as a way of defining natural kind terms such as 'gold' and 'water'.[5] For example, gold is, roughly, whatever is the same element as *that*, water is whatever is the same liquid as *that*, a human is whatever is a member of the same species as *that*, and so on. In each case the demonstrative term 'that' refers to an entity to which the person doing the defining refers directly, in the simplest case, by pointing. One of the main reasons for proposing definitions like this was that Kripke and Putnam believed that often we do not know the nature of the thing we are defining, and yet we know how to construct a definition that links up with its nature. This proposal had the interesting consequence that competent speakers of the language can use terms to successfully refer to the right things without going through a descriptive meaning.[6] It is not necessary that speakers associate descriptions with natural kind terms and it is even possible

[5] This theory originated with Saul Kripke (1980) and Hilary Putnam (1975). The next few pages are adapted from my (2004: 40–50).

[6] Initial discussion focused on natural kind terms and proper names, but later the theory was applied to a broader class of terms. The extent of the class of terms which can refer directly is not important for my purposes.

that they succeed in referring to water and gold when they associate the wrong descriptions with natural kind terms.[7] What is required instead (on some versions of the theory) is that they be related by a chain of communication to actual instances of water and gold. It is not even necessary that every speaker be able to identify water and gold reliably themselves as long as some speakers in the community can do so and the other speakers rely on the judgement of the experts.

Another consequence of this theory is that there are necessary truths that can only be known a posteriori. If a natural kind is defined as whatever shares the same nature as some indexically identified object, then under the assumption that the chemical constitution of water is essential to it, the discovery that water is H_2O is a discovery of the nature or essence of water. It is necessary that water is H_2O, but Kripke claimed that that truth is a posteriori because it takes empirical observation to discover it.

Arguably Aristotle defined *phronesis*, or practical wisdom, in a similar way. He does not appear to be confident that he can give a full account of it, yet he seems to think that we can pick out persons who are phronetic in advance of investigating the nature of *phronesis*. The *phronimos* can be defined, roughly, as a person *like that*, where we make a demonstrative reference to a paradigmatically good person. Just as competent speakers of English can successfully refer to water or gold and make assertions about it whether or not they know any chemistry, so can competent speakers successfully talk about practically wise persons. They can do this even when they can neither describe the properties in virtue of which somebody is a *phronimos* or even reliably identify the *phronimoi* in their community. But, like 'water', '*phronesis*' (or the English 'practical wisdom') is a term that the speakers in a community associate with paradigm instances. The *phronimos* is a person *like that*, just as water is a substance *like that*.

Our judgement of the identity of exemplars is revisable, as is our judgement that some liquid is water or some metal is gold. Some items in the initial set of exemplars may be dropped as we proceed with our investigation of the underlying nature of the items in the set. Just as there is fool's gold, there may be persons who initially appear to be practically wise, but turn out not to be. But unlike water and gold, there is no single underlying simple property in virtue of which somebody is a *phronimos*. I suspect that what makes a person practically wise is their psychological structure, just as what makes some liquid water is its chemical structure, but obviously psychological structure is considerably more complex than chemical structure, and we no doubt accept a great deal of variation among practically wise persons, whereas we accept very little variation among instances of water.

An exemplarist moral theory can be constructed by anchoring all moral concepts in exemplars, direct reference to which gets the theory going. Good

---

[7] On one version of the theory natural kind terms have no meaning; they are purely denotative (like Mill's theory of proper names). On another version of the theory natural kind terms have a meaning, but meanings are not in the head. That is, they are not something a speaker grasps and through which he finds the referent. See Putnam (1975).

persons are persons like that, just as gold is stuff like that. The function of an exemplar is to fix the reference of the term 'good person' or 'practically wise person' without the use of concepts. I have previously argued that good motives, virtues, right and virtuous acts, and good outcomes can be defined by reference to the motives and traits of exemplars, what they would or might do in circumstances of a certain kind, and the states of affairs they aim to produce. But the way in which I develop my version of exemplarism in ethics is not important for the purposes of epistemology. What I want to stress are the various uses of a theory of this kind. If all the concepts in a formal ethical theory are rooted in a person, then narratives and descriptions of that person are significant because it is an open question what it is about the person that makes him or her good. It may even be possible for observations of exemplary persons to yield necessary a posteriori truths about the good or the right parallel to the alleged necessary a posteriori truth that water is H_2O. But whether or not such judgements yield necessary truths, judgements about the right way to act are derivative from the identification of exemplars, and I suggest that judgements about the right way to believe are similarly derivative.

It is not necessary for the application of exemplarism to epistemology that epistemic and moral exemplars be the same persons. Perhaps exemplars in the epistemic domain are easier to identify than moral exemplars, and it can be argued that there are persons with paradigmatically good intellects who are moral horrors. This raises serious issues on the relationship between moral and intellectual virtues and vices, which I prefer to avoid for the methodology I am promoting in this paper. If Aristotle is right about practical wisdom, it is an intellectual virtue that is both necessary and sufficient for possessing the moral virtues and is the basis for the unity of the virtues. But there are other intellectual virtues besides *phronesis* in the Aristotelian schema of virtues that leave open the possibility that exemplars of theoretical wisdom may not be the same persons as the exemplars of practical wisdom. If that is the case, most of what I am proposing here can be appropriately modified, although my own view is that moral and intellectual exemplars are the same persons.

III. USING EPISTEMIC EXEMPLARS TO RESOLVE EPISTEMOLOGICAL DISPUTES

If a theory is a system of connected propositions intended to describe or explain some area of human life or thought, then foundationalism, coherentism, and infinitism are theories according to which a rational system of belief is a theory whose components are beliefs connected by the relation of justification. All three theories agree on that. They take this position largely because they think that the principle that every belief must be justified by a belief that is itself justified makes foundationalism, coherentism, and perhaps infinitism the only alternatives to skepticism.[8] (Infinitism is an attempt to reinterpret the infinite regress in a non-skeptical and benign way.) What is in dispute, then, is the structure of the theory, not the fact that a rational belief system is a theory with one of the three structures. Some 25 years ago, Ernest Sosa (1980) proposed that to resolve this dispute we need to look at something deeper than epistemic structure to find that which confers epistemic value on beliefs—a virtue. Sosa proposed, roughly, that an intellectual virtue is a reliable disposition to form true beliefs, and so his version of virtue epistemology was a form of reliabilism.

The proposal to focus on virtue was rich and important, but it is not at all obvious how it resolves the foundationalism/coherentism dispute since that dispute arises out of a shared commitment to a principle whose plausibility is not necessarily connected to the truth-conduciveness of justification. Of course, it needs to be admitted that whenever a dispute reaches an impasse it is not likely to be resolved without changing something in the way both sides look at the issue. The problem is that subsequent literature on foundationalism and coherentism indicates that the participants in this dispute were usually unwilling to accept Sosa's position that what makes a belief good is its tie to a disposition to get truth and to avoid falsehood. They did not think of the principle that every belief must be justified by a belief that is itself justified as wholly subservient to the aim of getting truth. While it may not have been completely clear why they thought the grasp of justificatory or evidential connections between beliefs is a good thing, it *was* clear that they thought it is a good thing for reasons that are not exhausted by the fact that truth is more likely to be transferred from one belief to another when such connections are grasped by the agent. My own view is that both coherentism and foundationalism have an advantage over the reliabilist alternative that has not been sufficiently stressed, and that is that both theories advocate a structure that arguably produces understanding, a neglected epistemic value that is not reducible to truth. For this, and perhaps other reasons, foundationalist and coherentist belief structures are admirable. They reflect well upon an agent who has either one. Neither structure guarantees truth, and it can be argued that neither structure even makes it likely that the system is true on the whole, but surely the structure itself is an admirable one.[9]

What is in dispute between the foundationalist and coherentist, then, cannot be resolved by moving to the level of intellectual virtue understood in the reliabilist way. There are too many assumptions in that suggestion that are not likely to be accepted by either side. But the controversy is much easier to resolve if

---

[8] In some forms of foundationalism the foundational beliefs are not self-justified, but are justified by a mental state other than a belief, e.g., a perceptual state.

[9] I am treating reliabilism as an externalist theory in competition with foundationalism and coherentism, both of which have been traditionally treated as internalist theories. Reliabilism can be interpreted as a form of foundationalism in which the foundation consists of facts rather than beliefs regarding the reliability of the relevant belief-forming mechanism. In the sense in which reliabilism can be foundationalist it is not an alternative to skepticism arising from the regress of justification in the internalist sense.

all sides can agree on exemplars of intellectual virtue. To use this method it is not necessary to identify and agree upon the virtues in advance, nor is it necessary to think of virtues as truth-conducive dispositions. It is not necessary to have an account of virtue at all. If I am right that some persons stand out for their admirable intellects, they are the ones we should investigate to determine an admirable way to behave cognitively. Intellectual exemplars may have the belief structure favored by foundationalists, the structure favored by coherentists, some combination of the two, or perhaps something else entirely. It is also possible that the structure shifts from time to time. If so, this is not something we would discover by attempting to derive the structure from the *concept* of a virtue, but rather by looking at how virtuous persons actually behave. This approach not only has the advantage of making it unnecessary to explain what makes a trait a virtue in advance of the investigation, but it also leaves open the possibility that the exemplars take into consideration other principles than the principle most salient to the debate over foundationalism: the principle that every belief must be justified by a belief that is itself justified.

It is also possible, even likely, that the relation between epistemic principles and the beliefs of the exemplars is parallel to the relation between moral principles and the acts of the exemplars. Neither their acts nor their beliefs may be entirely principle-governed. The usual way to explain this in ethics is not to say that morally good persons flout principles on occasion, but to say that the moral principles ethicists use to explain good behavior are not sufficiently precise and nuanced to adequately govern every possible human act. Possibly the principles can be refined in a way that permits universal applicability, but the point is that morally good persons act rightly in advance of the formulation of such principles, and they often do not act 'on principle' even when the principle has been formulated and is a good theoretical tool to explain their behavior.

I think the same point applies to epistemic behavior. The principle that every belief ought to be justified by a belief that is itself justified may function the same way a principle such as 'Promote the good' or 'Act out of good motives' functions in a moral theory. It is not at all clear that the principle holds absolutely, much less that the principle should dominate the basic structure of a rational system of belief. And even if it does enjoy the primacy given to it by some epistemologists, I propose that we do not know that a priori.

In section II I mentioned that an important consequence of the theory of direct reference is that it is not necessary to associate the right descriptions with the referent of a natural kind term in order to refer to it successfully. If I am right that the term 'good person' and its variants, 'epistemically good person' or 'intellectually admirable person', also refer directly, it cannot be settled in advance that the principle 'Believe only what is justified by a belief that is itself justified' is a principle they follow in all of their epistemic behavior, much less that it is the principle underlying the belief structure they have. We investigate moral exemplars to find out whether they follow a principle such as 'Promote good states of affairs,' and if so, whether it underlies and explains all of their acts, and similarly, we may investigate epistemic exemplars to find out whether they follow the principle 'Believe only what is justified by a belief that is itself justified,' and if so, whether it underlies the structure of their belief system. I propose, then, that we should not use the principle to identify the exemplars. We use the exemplars to identify the principle. If foundationalists and coherentists are right, then the exemplars operate on that principle and an investigation of their belief structure will determine who is right: the foundationalists, the coherentists, the infinitists, or some combination of the three. On the other hand, reliabilists may be right that epistemic exemplars do not use such a principle. If so, investigation should reveal whether reliabilists are also right that the epistemic behavior of exemplars is best described by the reliability of their belief-forming processes. I suspect that it is not. There really is something epistemically admirable that the foundationally structured or the coherent mind has and the merely reliable one lacks, but that is not my point here. If we can agree on the epistemic exemplars, we should be able to resolve not only the dispute over foundationalism, but also whether alternatives such as reliabilism are any better. It seems to me that since both foundationalists and coherentists already implicitly refer to an idealized mind, they would do well to use actual instances of ideal epistemic agents for their point of reference rather than to attempt to describe the ideal mind a priori.

A consequence of direct reference theory mentioned above is the importance of observation. Clearly, we cannot observe a person's belief structure the way we can observe the chemical constitution of water, and it is difficult to know how to design empirical studies that would reveal the ways in which a person's beliefs are structured, but I think that we should not overlook the importance of narratives. Narratives have received considerable attention in recent ethics because of the increasingly common belief among moral philosophers that the moral life is more complicated than consequentialist and deontological ethics require. Virtue ethics has the advantage of richness, but even virtue concepts can easily be thinned in an attempt to make them fit more smoothly into a theoretical structure. I do not want to declare in advance what we will find when we investigate epistemic exemplars, but I suspect that the ways in which they go about forming, maintaining, and regulating beliefs will be fairly complicated and will be best explained by a rich description of their dispositions involving such virtues as open-mindedness, intellectual fairness, humility, carefulness, thoroughness, a subtle balance of trust and autonomy, a subtle balance of flexibility and perseverance, and many others. Rather than trying to give a conceptual account of each virtue and attempting to derive appropriate behavior from them, appropriate behavior is best discovered by the more direct route of looking at the way it is actually done by the most intellectually admirable persons. The formulation of norms of believing, the identification of epistemic ends, and the description of epistemic structures would all be projects left until after sufficient data on exemplars are collected. As with the method of exemplarism in ethics, we may need to revise our list of exemplars after we formulate hypotheses on epistemically exemplary behavior, but it cannot turn out that all or even most of the persons on our initial list of exemplars are not exemplary since what we mean by good epistemic behavior is determined by what (most of) those persons are like.

The method of exemplarism makes it an open question whether features of epistemic exemplars other than the purely cognitive are relevant to norms of good believing. What exemplary persons value, what they aim at, how their emotions affect their beliefs, how they relate to other persons in their community and to persons outside their community, are all matters that affect the way we should understand good epistemic behavior. The exemplar may demand a greater degree of justification for her belief in contexts in which it is very important to her that the belief be true. This (probable) feature of the way exemplars manage their beliefs can help us resolve the dispute over contextualism. According to one version of contextualism the degree of justification of a belief in some context varies with the importance of the truth of the belief to the subject or to the attributor. The contextualist maintains that whether the subject has knowledge is also context variant, but let us leave that issue aside for the moment.

If we examine the way the epistemic exemplar treats her own beliefs, I think we will find that she is more epistemically conscientious in believing when something of value morally or to her personally is involved. Consider one of each type of case. The first is famous because of its use by W. K. Clifford (1901) in his essay, 'The Ethics of Belief'. A ship owner sends his ship full of emigrants to sea, believing without evidence that the ship is seaworthy. When the ship sinks and the passengers drown, he is morally blameworthy for their deaths because the belief upon which his act was based was epistemically unjustified. Clifford's point is that the ship owner is morally blameworthy for the belief, not just the act, since he would not have been morally blameworthy for the deaths had the belief been epistemically justified, and he is morally blameworthy for the belief even if, by luck, the ship does not sink. I think Clifford is right about that.

But Clifford draws a surprising conclusion. He claims that it is always morally wrong to believe anything upon insufficient evidence. But surely the moral blameworthiness of the ship owner is directly tied to the degree of the moral importance of the truth of the belief. Where much is at stake morally, a higher level of epistemic justification is required. If the ship was not going to sea but the ship owner could claim a tax deduction if he could attest that the ship was seaworthy, he would satisfy his moral duty with less evidence, and hence a lower degree of justification. An even lower degree of justification would be sufficient if he and an acquaintance were in a bar bragging to each other about their respective ships and there was virtually no chance that either of them would act on the other's claim.[10]

---

[10] I discuss this case, and the relationship between contextualism and what we care about, in (2005).

But on what basis does it seem reasonable to say that there are these varying degrees of justification required of the ship owner? Is it because the ship owner himself cares more about having a true belief when the ship he owns is sent to sea full of emigrants than when he merely wants a guy in a bar to believe him? Surely that is not what makes the difference. We are told nothing in the story about what the ship owner himself cares about and I don't think we are inclined to say we need to find out what he cares about before making the judgement that he needs differing degrees of evidence in these three cases. On the contrary, the ship owner appears not to care very much about the lives of the people on his ship. Nor is it reasonable to say that the degree of evidence required of the ship owner depends upon the values of the person attributing epistemic status to the ship owner. We do not think we need to find out who the attributor is before making the judgement. Of course, we can say that the attributor is us and *we* attribute importance to truth in these situations in the way I have described above, and because we assign importance in that way, we say the ship owner *ought* to have more evidence in the emigrant situation, less in the tax deduction situation, and even less in the bar situation. But it is relevant to notice that we take for granted that we agree, and we think that because we take for granted that we, the philosophers who think about these things, are close enough to being epistemically exemplary that we can trust ourselves to judge how the ship owner ought to behave in these cases. After all, these cases are not that difficult. They are hardly in the category of the genuine quandary. If we tie the truth of the judgement of what the ship owner should do in forming his beliefs to what an epistemic exemplar would do in the same circumstances, and if the exemplar would behave differently in the three circumstances due to the differing degrees of the importance of having a true belief in the three situations, we get a plausible explanation for the attraction to a form of contextualism.

The second type of case is one in which something the exemplar cares about personally is at stake, but it is not an issue of moral importance. If she has always wanted to visit the Uffizi and is unsure whether it will be open on the only day she is planning to be in Florence, an epistemic exemplar will demand higher standards of justification for her belief that it will be open that day than she would if she will be there a week. But she will not expect someone else who will be there a day to satisfy the same standards as herself if that person cares very little about Italian art and is only planning to go because the guide book says he should.

What this shows, I think, is that when the issue is not knowledge, but the degree of justification needed by an epistemic agent for some belief, reference to an epistemic exemplar can adjudicate the dispute between the invariantist and the kind of contextualist who thinks that what someone cares about affects the level of justification required. If the exemplar's judgement is unaffected by what she or anyone else cares about, the invariantist wins. If the exemplar's judgement is affected by what she cares about or by what the subject cares about, then some form of contextualism follows. I suspect that the exemplar is affected by both types of carings. There are things everyone should care about, whether they do so or not, and we put morality in that category. The exemplar cares about morality herself and she judges the degree of justification the ship owner should have based on the degree of moral importance of the belief, whether or not the ship owner cares about it himself. But the exemplar probably also makes some judgements about the level of justification needed for a belief based on what the subject cares about. How important it is to see the art in the Uffizi would probably be in that category. I suspect, then, that *some* judgements of what an epistemic agent ought to do in forming beliefs are subject-based, but we know that because the exemplar refers to what the subject cares about herself.

So far I have been addressing contextualism about justification, but exemplarism can also be used to resolve the issue of whether knowledge is context-variant. Perhaps the invariantist and contextualist can agree on referring to an epistemic exemplar in an Ideal Observer theory of meta-epistemology. The proposal would be, roughly, that S knows p in circumstances C just in case an ideal observer of S (an exemplar) would attribute knowledge of p to S in C. How the exemplar varies the attribution according to the circumstances would be an open question, and it also would be open whether her attribution varies with such things as what the subject cares about and what is important morally. Further, it would be an open question whether David Lewis is right that knowledge of p requires the elimination of all relevant alternatives to p, where what counts as a relevant alternative varies with the circumstances.[11]

Contextualism combined with exemplarism is a variation that avoids the problems with both subject-based and attributor-based contextualism mentioned above. It is implausible to say that a subject can gain knowledge simply by ceasing to care, and it is implausible to say that a person who cares abnormally about the way the world would be if each belief she has is false knows practically nothing. The contextualist claim is plausible only within a certain range of carings, and even then the range should be constrained by carings that everyone ought to have whether they do so or not, for example, those demanded by morality. The exemplarist approach permits these constraints.

Ideal Observer theories in meta-ethics have a long and distinguished history and debate about the features of the Ideal Observer and what he cares about, if anything, is a feature of the literature on that theory. My preferred Ideal Agent theory can also be used for some of the same purposes as an Ideal Observer theory, and I believe it has some advantages, but my purpose in this paper is not to argue for that, but to suggest that both theories can be usefully adopted by epistemologists to resolve a host of seemingly intractable problems. In the next section I want to turn to an issue that I think is even harder to resolve than the issues we have been discussing.

---

[11] In (2005) I argued that the degree of the demand to be epistemically conscientious and the degree of the conscientiousness demanded varies with context, but I am not persuaded that knowledge is context-variant in the same way.

IV. THE ALIGNMENT PROBLEM

In earlier work I have called attention to the problem that knowledge is a more valuable state than mere true belief and a satisfactory account of knowledge must be compatible with this feature of it. I call this the value problem. In this section I want to discuss another value problem, the problem of the relationship between two fundamental values connected with knowledge: rationality and truth. The problem is that epistemic rationality serves two roles in our discourse. We think of it as that epistemic property that makes us most likely to obtain truth, yet epistemic rationality is also a descriptive property applied to a human power and the behavior to which it leads, for example, getting and weighing relevant evidence, open-mindedly considering defeaters for one's beliefs, fairly appraising opponents' arguments, having coherent beliefs, having well-developed powers of inference, and so on. We expect rationality in both of its roles to line up. We think we know what behavior is rational, at least in general, and we think that that behavior puts us in the best position to get truth. We can describe that behavior independently of its propensity to give us truth and virtually all of us are willing to call such behavior good. But if rationality were not a power that led to behavior that put us in the best position to get truth, it is hard to see why we would value it so highly. It is not necessary that behavior such as thoroughly and open-mindedly acquiring and weighing evidence perfectly lines up with the truth, of course, but if there is not a fairly close alignment between rationality in the descriptive sense and truth-conduciveness, the value of rationality would be in jeopardy, and since the goodness of rationality is intrinsically connected to the concept, the concept of rationality itself would be endangered.

It is curious that aside from discussions of radical skepticism, epistemologists generally focus their attention on the best cases for the alignment of rationality and truth—ordinary perceptual and scientific beliefs, whereas moral philosophers focus a lot of attention on the worst cases for the alignment of rationality and truth—irresolvable moral disagreement. But the cases that alarm moral philosophers are a problem for epistemology, not just for ethics and other fields in which irresolvable disagreement is pervasive, such as religion and philosophy. In some domains rationality and truth seem to pull apart. And even in those domains in which it is easier to get agreement, there is still an alignment problem, only it is more subtle. We have no way to tell whether truth is aligned with rationality without using rational procedures, the same procedures whose alignment with truth we are questioning. This is not a matter driven by the threat of global skepticism. It is a straightforward problem of the human predicament.

I see no way to avoid Putnam's point that we cannot get outside of whatever is available to our own consciousness to determine truth, and so we cannot tell whether truth is aligned with rationality or with anything else. However, within the various epistemic practices we have developed, there are numerous checks for internal coherence and coherence with other established epistemic practices. A very important, and I think central, check on epistemic behavior by individuals is the behavior of epistemic exemplars. We would not call someone an exemplar if we did not think she aligns good behavior with the successful achievement of ends. Epistemic exemplars align good epistemic behavior with the successful achievement of true belief and other epistemic ends such as understanding. The test of what counts as both good epistemic behavior and truth is the behavior of the exemplars. We assume, because we have no real choice, that truth is generally aligned with what 'we' think when we are using the norms 'we' endorse when we are reflective and have the time to listen to others who can show us our various mistakes. But 'we' endorse the judgement of some of us whom we recognize as better than most of us are individually.

This model simplifies a much more complicated situation, of course. In many cases it is not necessary to refer to an exemplar in order to learn good epistemic behavior and to confirm success; it is sufficient that we can refer to others who are epistemically superior to ourselves. As we become epistemically more virtuous we will gradually alter our epistemic assessment of those around us, including, in some cases, the identity of exemplars. But even then we have no ultimate point of reference against which to judge good epistemic behavior and the success of the resulting beliefs of such behavior except by reference to exemplars. Rationality even in the highest degree may not perfectly align with truth, but our best guide to truth is convergence of belief among exemplars.

The problem of irresolvable disagreement is a problem for the obvious reason that there are disagreements that *are* irresolvable. But that is not to say that every apparently irresolvable disagreement is irresolvable or that progress cannot be made in resolving even the most intractable disagreements. My position is that there is a trans-cultural kind of rationality, not in the much maligned procedural sense of reason, but in the sense that there are ideally rational qualities of mind that transcend all cultures and which we discover when we investigate the qualities of mind we admire in exemplars—attentiveness, open-mindedness, fairness to opponents, vast knowledge, good memory, good judgement, good counsel, and so on. We may also discover that the most admirable minds are the minds of persons who have certain non-cognitive traits. I surmise that an exemplar is emotionally stable, not insecure or vain, does not feel the need to call attention to herself, and has many other virtues that permit her to be much more trustworthy epistemically than others whose emotional defects interfere with what would otherwise be admirable intellects. The outcome of close dialogue among such persons is our best hope of finding out the truth about the most disputed issues. I assume that there is less divergence in the beliefs of exemplars who have engaged in such dialogue than between ordinary persons in different cultures who do not engage in dialogue. If so, and if the beliefs of the exemplars sometimes conflict, there is still a gap between truth and rationality in even the highest degree, but the gap is much narrower than the much touted problem of diversity of belief would suggest. And it is a gap with which we will have to live since it is the gap between the truth in some domain and the human ability to find it.

I have said very little about the issue of choosing between an Ideal Observer theory and an Ideal Agent theory such as the exemplarist theory I have outlined in this paper. Determining epistemic norms from the point of view I would have if I became an exemplar is not the same as determining epistemic norms from the point of view of an ideal observer. An issue that can affect the choice between the two kinds of theory is the issue of whether there are truths that are determinable only from a non-shareable, first-person perspective. If there are, it would be unsurprising if the question of what an agent should believe and how conscientious she should be in acquiring and maintaining the belief would also be to some extent determinable only from her own perspective. What counts as a virtuous or a justified belief in some cases may require an idealized form of her own qualities, not the qualities of an ideal observer who lacks the distinctiveness of her first person viewpoint.

In discussing contextualism we looked at what the subject cares about as a factor that may alter the degree of epistemic conscientiousness rationally required of her. If what an agent cares about includes emotional responses to events that perhaps nobody else can appreciate, an exemplarist Ideal Agent theory may be better suited to determine the degree of epistemic justifiedness or conscientiousness required of her than an Ideal Observer theory. The Ideal Agent theory may also have some advantages in resolving the dispute over foundationalism. I suspect that the assumption that there is a single ideal structure of mind that each individual ought to have is false. Not only is it possible that there is more than one good way to structure one's belief system, but it is also possible that idiosyncratic features of a person affect the structure ideal for that person. Even more likely is the possibility that one's role in an epistemic community determines the way one ought to structure one's beliefs. The community as a whole may have beliefs that have a different ideal structure than that of the individuals in the community, and the ideal structure of individuals may vary. I think, therefore, that an exemplarist Ideal Agent theory is preferable to an Ideal Observer theory, but my primary purpose in this paper is to call attention to the usefulness of both kinds of theory for the needs of epistemology, not to defend the Ideal Agent theory.

V. CONCLUSION

In this paper I have looked at a series of deeply divisive issues in epistemology: the dispute over foundationalism, coherentism, and infinitism, and the dispute between adherents of these theories and reliabilism; the dispute over contextualism and invariantism; the problem of the alignment of rationality with truth; and the problem of the clash of first-person and third-person perspectives. All of these disputes are about something normative: the right way to structure a belief system, the right way to form beliefs in different contexts, why rationality is a good thing, and the meta-theoretical problem of the perspective that gives us the right answer to our set of questions. I have argued that exemplarism is an approach that has a good chance of resolving these issues, if anything can. The debates over foundationalism and contextualism already implicitly refer to an exemplar as either agent or judge, and I suggest that the models of the Ideal Observer Theory or the Ideal Agent Theory can be usefully adopted by epistemologists in resolving a host of issues involving normative judgements about epistemic agents.

REFERENCES

Clifford, W. K. (1901). 'The Ethics of Belief', in *Lectures and Essays*, vol. 2. London: Macmillan, 163–205.

DeRose, K. (1992). 'Contextualism and Knowledge Attributions'. *Philosophy and Phenomenological Research*, 52: 913–29.

Klein, P. (1999). 'Human Knowledge and the Infinite Regress of Reasons', in J. Tomberlin (ed.), *Philosophical Perspectives, 13: Epistemology*. Oxford: Blackwell, 297–325.

Kripke, S. (1980). *Naming and Necessity*. Oxford: Blackwell.

Lewis, D. (1996). 'Elusive Knowledge'. *Australasian Journal of Philosophy*, 74: 549–67.

Putnam, H. (1975). 'The Meaning of "Meaning"', in *Mind, Language and Reality: Philosophical Papers*, vol. 2. Cambridge: Cambridge University Press, 215–71.

Sosa, E. (1980). 'The Raft and the Pyramid'. *Midwest Studies in Philosophy*, 5: 3–25.

Zagzebski, L. (2004). *Divine Motivation Theory*. Cambridge: Cambridge University Press.

—— (2005). 'Epistemic Value and the Primacy of What We Care About'. *Philosophical Papers*, 33: 353–77.

9

On the Gettier Problem problem

William G. Lycan

It took about ten years for people to get the idea that there was something wrong with the Gettier Problem. By the early 1970s, a number of analyses had been offered to accommodate Gettier's (1963) counter examples to the traditional 'JTB' view: Michael Clark's (1963) simple no-false-lemmas proposal, various 'indefeasibility' analyses beginning with Lehrer (1965) and Lehrer and Paxson (1969), and Goldman's (1967) original causal theory, among others. Those analyses had run into further counterexamples; revision after revision had been offered, only to meet further and more elaborate counterexamples. Not only was there no end in sight; there was not even a sense of beginning to converge.

In itself, that was hardly an unusual situation in philosophy. We might expect the optimism of the most enthusiastic practitioners to have been attended by merely the normal degree of professional pessimism. But, no: the Gettier Problem was not doing so well as that; it had begun to get some bad press.

I. THE GETTIER PROBLEM PROBLEM

Some epistemologists wrote pointedly larger and more general works, being careful to play down the Gettier Problem and address it only unemphatically, in subordinate clauses (even though they did not want us to miss the solutions they offered).[1] Informally, the Gettier Problem became a leading focus, if not the focus, of disenchantment with the definition-and-counterexample method of analytic philosophy. In some cases the disenchantment spilled over into scorn; there were slighting references to 'the "*S* knows that *p*" crowd'. That attitude combined expansively with the complaint commonly made, that among analytic philosophers the adversarial method had gotten out of hand and that people had begun flinging elaborate counterexamples only to be clever and to score points, with no

---

[1] Armstrong (1973: 152–3) is an example. He adds, 'Gettier's paper has been commented upon, with a view to excluding his counter-example by judiciously chosen extra conditions, in a truly alarming and ever-increasing series of papers.'

thought for the larger picture or for positive understanding. (Another popular sneer of the period was, 'Why don't you go publish a little note in *Analysis*?') Above all, it was suggested that the Gettier project was unfruitful, idle, pointless, almost antiphilosophical.[2]

One feature of the postGettier analyses thought to show their fecklessness was their ungainly, sometimes meandering complexity. For example:

S knows that *h* iff (i) *h* is true, (ii) *S* is justified [by some evidence *e*] in believing *h* . . ., (iii) *S* believes that *h* on the basis of his justification and . . . (ivg) . . . there is an evidence-restricted alternative Fs* to *S*'s epistemic framework Fs such that (i) '*S* is justified in believing that *h*' is epistemically derivable from the other members of the evidence component of Fs* and (ii) there is some subset of members of the evidence component of Fs* such that (a) the members of this subset are also members of the evidence component of Fs and (b) '*S* is justified in believing that *h*' is epistemically derivable from the members of this subset. [Where Fs* is an 'evidence-restricted alternative' to Fs iff (i) For every true proposition *q* such that '*S* is justified in believing not-*q*' is a member of the evidence component of Fs, '*S* is justified in believing *q*' is a member of the evidence component of Fs*, (ii) for some subset C of members of Fs such that C is maximally consistent epistemically with the members generated in (i), every member of C is a member of Fs*, and (iii) no other propositions are members of Fs* except those that are implied epistemically by the members generated in (i) and (ii).][3]

Faced with such a monster, we may be unable to think of a further counter-example, but that inability is as well or better explained by the very convoluteness of the analysis than by its correctness.

Yet no similar opprobrium attached to other, ostensibly similar chisholming projects, for example, the Gricean analysis of speaker-meaning, the analysis of

---

[2] It should be noted that Professor Gettier himself has taken no interest in the literature that bears his name. At least, he says he never has, and I have no reason to doubt his word.

[3] Swain (1974: 16, 22, 25), an indefeasibility theory. And here is a comparably advanced version of the causal theory (Swain 1972: 292; 1978: 110–11, 115–16):

S has nonbasic knowledge that *p* iff (i) *p* is true; (ii) *S* believes that *p*; (iii) *S*'s justification renders *p* evident for *S*; . . . (iv*) [w]here '*e*' designates the portion of *S*'s total evidence *E* that is immediately relevant to the justification of *p*, *either* (A) there is a *nondefective* causal chain from *P* to *BSe*; or (B) there is some event or state of affairs *Q* such that (i) there is a *nondefective* causal chain from *Q* to *BSe*; and (ii) there is a *nondefective* causal chain from *Q* to *P*; or (C) there is some event or state of affairs *H* such that (i) there is a *nondefective* causal chain from *H* to *BSe*; and (ii) *H* is a *nondefective* pseudo-overdeterminant of *P*. [Where a causal chain *X* → *Y* is 'defective' with respect to *S*'s justification for *p* based on evidence *e* iff: Either (I) (a) there is some event or state of affairs *U* in *X* → *Y* such that *S* would be justified in believing that *U* did not occur and (b) it is essential to *S*'s justifiably believing that *p* on the basis of the evidence *e* that *S* would be justified in believing that *U* did not occur; or (II) there is some significant alternative *C** to *X* → *Y* with respect to *S* justifiably believing that *p* on the basis of *e*. [Where *C** is a 'significant alternative' to *X* → *Y* with respect to *S* justifiably believing that *p* on the basis of *e* if (a) it is objectively likely that *C** should have occurred rather than *X* → *Y*; and (b) if *C** had occurred instead of *X* → *Y*, then there would have been an event or state of affairs *U* in *C** such that *S* would not be justified in believing that *p* if *S* were justified in believing that *U* occurred.]

Notice that, running out of energy, I have spared us the unpacking (ibid.: 118) of 'defectiveness' for 'pseudo-overdeterminants', employed in (iv*)(C)(ii).

social convention inaugurated by David Lewis, the Kripkean causal-historical theory of linguistic referring, the search for criteria of personal identity through time, or the counterfactual theory of causality. Why not? Perhaps the difference was an historical accident of timing or of personality. Or perhaps it was just that those enterprises have never led to the breathtaking complexities that 'S knows that P' did.[4] It is well to remind ourselves that no effort of analytic philosophy to provide strictly necessary and sufficient conditions for a philosophically interesting concept has ever succeeded. And there should be a lesson in that. Yet the Gettier project still seems to have outstripped all others in the extent of its failure; why did the other analytic projects never reach the extremes of futile complexity that the Gettier industry did? More deeply, is there something wrong with the Gettier project? Does it rest on some false presupposition?

What I shall call the 'Gettier Problem problem' is that of explaining what is distinctively wrong with the Gettier project. There have been a number of attempts over the years. My purpose in this paper is to survey and evaluate those. I shall argue that there is nothing wrong with the project properly conceived, and that work on it should proceed, though on a basis slightly different from the original one.

II. UNINTERESTING SOLUTIONS

Originally the Gettier Problem was cast as the search for the 'fourth condition' of knowing, a condition to be added to 'J', 'T', and 'B', to block Gettier's counter-examples to the sufficiency of 'JTB'. The search took place during the sunset years of

---

[4] The most complex competitor I can recall is Stephen Schiffer's (1972: 75–6) analysis of speaker-meaning:

S meant that *p* by uttering *x* iff *S* uttered *x* intending thereby to realize a certain state of affairs *E* which is (intended by *S* to be) such that the obtainment of *E* is sufficient to secure that

- (1a) if anyone who has a certain property *F* knows that *E* obtains, then that person will know that *S* knows that *E* obtains;
- (1b) if anyone who is *F* knows that *E* obtains, then that person will know that *S* knows that (1a); and so on;
- (2a) if anyone who is *F* knows that *E* obtains, then that person will know (or believe)—and know that *S* knows (or believes)—that *E* is conclusive (very good or good) evidence that *S* uttered *x* with the primary intention
  - (1') that there be some *ρ* such that *S*'s utterance of *x* causes in anyone who is F the activated belief that *p*/ *ρ*(*t*);
  and intending
  - (2') satisfaction of (1') to be achieved, at least in part, by virtue of that person's [i.e., the person(s) satisfying (1')] belief that *x* is related in a certain way *R* to the belief that *p*;
  - (3') to realize *E*;
- (2b) if anyone who is *F* knows that *E* obtains, then that person will know that *S* knows that (2a); and so on.

Notice that speaker-meaning is here analyzed in terms of knowing.

'conceptual analysis', the activity of taking a philosophically interesting notion and trying to find a set of conceptually necessary and sufficient conditions for the notion's being exemplified. Outrageous and fantastical counterexample scenarios were allowed, of course, because a mere conceptual possibility would be enough to refute a claim of conceptual necessity or sufficiency.

That feature alone would have made some philosophers scorn the Gettier project, because of healthy Quinean skepticism about 'conceptual truth' and analyticity.[5] If the very idea of a conceptual truth is infirm, then to seek conceptual truths about knowing is obviously misguided. (And Gettier practitioners did typically style themselves as investigating 'the concept of' knowing, even into the 1970s.) But even if one is a Quinean skeptic, there are three reasons why that is no satisfactory solution to the Gettier Problem problem. First, the Quinean complaint applies across the board; it does not reveal anything wrong with the Gettier project that is not wrong with any other 'strictly conceptual' quest such as that of trying to analyze causality or linguistic referring, or for that matter trying to define 'doctor' or 'bachelor' or 'doe'. Second, one cannot complain, as against, for example, the personal identity literature, that the hypothetical cases are all fantastical or wildly science-fictional and ordinary concepts just do not bear that close scrutiny. The counterexamples that figure in the Gettier literature, though usually unlikely, are just as usually not fairy-tale or science-fictional or otherwise *merely* conceptual, but nomologically possible. Some are actual.[6] Third, by the same token, it is entirely possible by any standard to have JTB without knowing; people actually do that. So for all that any Quinean has shown, it is not only reasonable but very interesting to ask what must be added to mere JTB in order to constitute a case of knowing. Analyticity is not required.

I pause in this section to review a few other uninteresting solutions to the Gettier Problem problem, though in slightly ascending order of interestingness.

Denying 'J'. Early on, it was occasionally suggested that Gettier's examples were not counterexamples, because they did not in fact satisfy 'J'; what they showed is rather that no sheer *amount* of conventional evidence suffices for complete justification. Though the luckless S's evidence was strong enough ordinarily to count as knowledge-affording, it was not evidence of the right sort or structure, and so was not fully justifying (Pailthorp 1969).

This is uninteresting because it is verbal. What the examples showed is that no amount or strength of evidence short of entailing evidence would do, unless that justification were *also* not defective in Gettier's characteristic way; it does have to have the right structure in addition to its strength. There are two distinct

---

[5] Particularly Quine (1963; 1966). Lycan (1994a: chs. 11, 12) defends a strong version of the skeptical doctrine, though not quite so strong a one as Quine's own.

[6] I am the grateful owner of a wristwatch that once, to his delight, actually gettiered Marshall Swain. Swain very graciously made me a present of the watch upon the occasion of my leaving the Ohio State University in 1982.

factors, strength and structure. Even if we choose to withhold the verdict 'J'
until the second factor has been established, that does not tell us how to
establish it.

The TB analysis. Sartwell (1991; 1992) notoriously argued that knowledge is
merely true belief, i.e., that every true belief counts as a piece of knowledge.[7]
If Sartwell is right, then Gettier's cases cannot be counterexamples, because
there can be no counterexamples to 'JTB'. Not even ordinary 'J' is required for
knowing.

This is uninteresting (as a solution to the Problem problem) because Sartwell's
position is so radical that if one actually accepts it, the rest of one's theory of
knowledge will have little if anything to do with traditional epistemology. Also
and in particular, one will lose the distinction aforementioned, between two ways
in which justification can be found wanting (insufficient strength, and Gettier
defect); for in what respect is a Gettier victim's justification found *wanting*, if not
in that it fails to constitute knowledge?[8]

Skepticism. The Gettier Problem presupposes that ordinary 'J' is fallible, in that
a person can have an *epistemically* justified but false belief. (Recall that according
to the usage of the time, 'epistemic' justification is justification that would normally be strong enough to afford knowledge, so long as the subject is not gettiered in
some way.) This means that (indeed) ordinary 'J' is enough for knowledge when
the subject is not gettiered or the like. But any skeptic will tell us that that presupposition is false. Epistemic justification requires the truth of the justified belief;
otherwise the conceded evil-demon possibilities and other skeptical scenarios
would preclude knowledge. If there is no empirical knowledge at all, we should
hardly be surprised that Gettier victims lack it.

This is less uninteresting than the TB diagnosis, because skepticism is believed
by some epistemologists and taken very seriously (to say the least) by many more.
But it is still comparatively uninteresting. *Of course* the Gettier Problem arises in
the first instance only for those of us who are not skeptics.

Also, as in the case of TB, we lose the distinction between failing to know
because our justification is not strong enough and failing to know because we have
been gettiered. The Problem does arise for a skeptic in the second instance: Any
skeptic should admit that knowing is at least a regulative ideal, and that some
cognitive conditions come far closer than others to satisfying it. A subject who has
what anyone would consider overwhelmingly strong evidence should be counted
as just-about-knowing, or as-good-as-knowing, or knowing-for-all-practical-
purposes (compare 'flat', for those who hold that nothing is absolutely flat: Unger
1971; 1984) even if the skeptic is right and no one ever strictly knows. But
this holds only so long as the subject is not gettiered. A Gettier victim does *not*

---

[7] A number of authors have argued that *there is a sense of* 'know' in which TB suffices for knowing
(Hintikka 1962: 18–19; Powers 1978; Goldman 1999: 23–5; Hetherington 2001). But Sartwell's
radical claim is that there is no other, more demanding sense. (Lycan 1994*b* argues directly against
Sartwell.)   [8] But on this, see Hetherington (2001).

just-about-know or as-good-as know; a Gettier victim *simply does not* know.[9] That difference remains to be explained, even for a skeptic.

Nomic reliability. Dretske (1971) and Armstrong (1973) argue that one knows only if, in the circumstances, one *could not* have the reason one has for one's belief (Dretske) or be holding the belief itself (Armstrong) unless the belief were true. This is not to say that one's evidence must be entailing. Rather, it is about the natural relation one bears to the relevant chunk of one's environment: The relation between one's having that reason or holding the belief is nomic. One cannot be mistaken; by law of nature, the only way in which one could now have that reason or hold the belief is for the belief to be true. If that nomic requirement is satisfied, one cannot be gettiered, because in any Gettier case there is an element of luck or fluke in *S*'s being right. This explanation is like the skeptic's in that it pre-empts Gettier by denying the knower a kind of fallibility that Gettier requires, but it does not entail skepticism, and neither Dretske nor Armstrong is a skeptic.

This is by far the least uninteresting of the comparatively uninteresting solutions, because it was independently motivated and also because it (demonstrably) opened up a positive research program. Reliabilism dominated the field for years, both as a theory of knowing and as a theory of justification more generally. But as a solution to the Gettier Problem problem, it is still comparatively uninteresting, for two related reasons. First, though it does not entail skepticism, it militates for great stinginess in knowledge ascription; no one would suppose that the nomic requirement is met in any but the most felicitous of circumstances (Lycan 1984). How often does it happen that even if my eyes and brain are working normally and atmospheric conditions are good, it would be *nomically impossible* for me to be in my current perceptual-cum-cognitive state and still be fooled?—much less the other homey sorts of things we take ourselves to know, such as our own names, what we ate an hour or two ago, who chairs our department, etc. If nomic Reliabilism is true, we know hardly anything.

Second, it is now generally conceded by Reliabilists themselves that the Dretske–Armstrong nomic formulation was too strong in more specific ways (for example, Pappas and Swain 1973). Subsequent versions have variously weakened that formulation (for example, Goldman 1976). The weakenings burden their respective authors with the need to block Gettier cases, and so the Gettier Problem returns for them.

III. INTERLUDE: A SIMPLE ANALYSIS

Before I proceed to the more interesting and viable suggestions that have been offered as solutions to the Gettier Problem problem, I should confess that I have my own favorite solution to the original Problem. (All right, I am *announcing* that

---

[9] *Pace* Hetherington (1999; 2001) and Weatherson (2003); see Section V below.

I have one, and with at least a bit of pride.) For a reason that will emerge, I can guarantee that my analysis will convince almost no one; and on inductive grounds I can predict with complete confidence that someone will find a clear counter-example. But here it is.

Start with Clark's no-false-lemmas proposal, which was immediately suggested by Gettier's own two cases: *S*'s belief must not rest upon any false grounds; in particular, *S*'s reasoning must not pass through any false step. This was of course instantly counterexampled. (Space does not allow detailed description of all the cases; I shall assume some familiarity with them.)

Against the sufficiency of 'no-false-lemmas':

Noninferential Nogot (Lehrer 1965; 1970). Mr Nogot in *S*'s office has given *S* evidence that he, Nogot, owns a Ford. By a single probabilistic inference, *S* moves directly (without passing through 'Nogot owns a Ford') to the conclusion that someone in *S*'s office owns a Ford. (As in any such example, Mr Nogot does not own a Ford, but *S*'s belief happens to be true because Mr Havit owns one.)

Cautious Nogot (Lehrer 1974; sometimes called 'Clever Reasoner'). This is like the previous example, except that here *S*, not caring at all who it might be that owns the Ford[10] and also being cautious in matters doxastic, deliberately refrains from forming the belief that Nogot owns it.

Testimony Nogot (Saunders and Champawat 1964). *S*'s evidence is all hearsay, but very reliable hearsay. *S* is told overwhelming evidence that Nogot owns a Ford. *S*'s grounds are all true: *S* was (indeed) told all those things, and by a highly reliable informant.

Existential Nogot (Feldman 1974). *S* does not acquire the evidence itself, but only the existential generalization of it: 'There is someone in the office of whom it's true that...'. *S* has no idea who that person, the protagonist of the evidence, is. But from that existential generalization, *S* justifiably infers the generalization 'Someone in the office owns a Ford.'

Stopped Clock (Scheffler 1965, following Russell 1948). *S* looks at a clock and forms a true belief as to the time of day. *S* has every reason to believe that the clock is working well, but in fact it has stopped.

Sheep in the Field (Chisholm 1966). Looking into a field, *S* sees an animal only a few yards off that looks, sounds, smells, etc., exactly like a sheep, and *S* noninferentially forms the perceptual belief that there is a sheep in the field. Actually the animal is of a different species but has been artfully disguised. Yet there is a real sheep in the field—way off in a remote corner of the field, completely hidden behind thick hedges.

Sure-Fire Match (Skyrms 1967). *S* strikes a dry Sure-Fire match and is epistemically justified in thinking it will light. Actually the match has an incredibly rare impurity and could not possibly be lit by friction, but it lights anyway because of a freakish burst of Q-radiation from the sky.

---

[10] Actually in this example, Lehrer upgrades the vehicle to a Ferrari.

And there is the obvious sort of counterexample to the necessity of 'no-false-lemmas' (Saunders and Champawat 1964; Lehrer 1965). *Nondefective Chain*: If *S* has at least one epistemically justifying and non-Gettier-defective line of justification, then *S* knows even if *S* has other justifying grounds that contain Gettier gaps. For example (Lehrer), suppose *S* has overwhelming evidence that Nogot owns a Ford and also overwhelming evidence that Havit owns one. *S* then knows that someone in the office owns a Ford, because *S* knows that Havit does and performs existential generalization; it does not matter that one of *S*'s grounds (*S*'s belief that Nogot owns a Ford) is false. (It does not matter if *S* has fifty or a thousand other gettiered justifications.)

Further: *Togethersmith* (Rozeboom 1967). On a Sunday afternoon, *S* ('Mrs Jones') sees the Togethersmith family car leaving the driveway, and *S* knows that every Sunday afternoon all the Togethersmiths go for a drive in the country. Because *S* believes that all the Togethersmiths are in the car today as well, *S* concludes that Mrs Togethersmith is not at home, and *S* is right. But it is false that all the Togethersmiths are in the car today; one of the children is attending a friend's birthday party.

What the counterexamples to the sufficiency of 'no-false-lemmas' have in common, of course, is that in them *S* does not engage in a process of reasoning that passes through the relevant false step ('Nogot owns a Ford,' 'That clock is working well,' etc.). Gilbert Harman (1973) argues that the no-false-lemmas strategy should be maintained in the face of such examples, indeed should be aufgehoben into a methodology for investigating the structure of epistemic justification (indeed, the nature of inference itself). He makes a preliminary case for his principle P: 'Reasoning that essentially involves false conclusions, intermediate or final, cannot give one knowledge' (47). Then, rather than entertain putative counterexamples to P, he retains P and looks to see what epistemological consequences ensue. A first one is that justification does not proceed by purely probabilistic rules of acceptance, since such rules do not rely on intermediate conclusions at all (120–4). Further appeals to P encourage Harman to posit non-conscious mediating inferences where we might otherwise see none. For example, he says, a gettiered subject makes tacit inferences concerning causal connections and other explanatory relations, and the falsity of those tacit grounds explains, via P, why the subject fails to know despite being epistemically justified.[11] Harman uses P in this leveraging way to motivate his general idea that all inference is or involves 'inference to the best explanatory statement' (ch. 8).

Now, as we saw, our counterexamples to sufficiency are cases in which there does not seem to be reasoning that passes through a false step. Harman's strategy would be to hypothesize that there is such reasoning nonetheless. I take a different line: What seems more obvious and less potentially controversial is that in each of

---

[11] In this way he neatly accounts for Goldman's (1967) otherwise incongruous need to require that *S* 'reconstruct' the main links in the relevant causal chain from fact to belief.

the counterexample cases, S *tacitly believes* or assumes something false. This is a weaker notion than that of an unconscious inference that occurrently passes through a false step, for it does not require any occurrent assumption or inference, even an unconscious one. For example, in Noninferential Nogot, we can concede to Lehrer that S does not engage in a reasoning process that passes through 'Nogot owns a Ford,' but clearly S does tacitly assume that Nogot owns a Ford, else why on earth would S form the belief that someone in the office owns one?

Similar remarks hold for the other counterexamples to sufficiency. Perhaps Testimony Nogot and Existential Nogot are less obvious than the rest, but each is fairly obvious: in Testimony Nogot, S falsely assumes that *the person S's informant is talking about* owns a Ford; in Existential Nogot, S falsely assumes that *the protagonist of the evidence* owns one. I propose, then, that (for now) the no-false-lemmas analysis be replaced by the weaker no-false-assumptions theory.

What went wrong? That is, if I am right, why was this simple adjustment to Clark's proposal not made or even considered? What happened was that theorists tacitly bypassed the notion of tacit assumption and, in effect, tried to analyze it in turn. The nearly instantaneous result was the indefeasibility literature, which began with the useful notion of a defeater, a proposition which if added to S's epistemically justifying evidence would render the expanded evidence set no longer epistemically justifying. That literature had no success (*pace* Swain 1974, quoted above); but I say its failures showed, not that the no-false-assumption analysis of knowing was wrong, but that the notion of tacit assumption is itself hard to characterize (in turn) by reference to a defeater. (Indeed, that difficulty was predictable, because (a) it was almost irresistible to start the further analysis with a subjunctive of some kind,[12] and (b) any time any analysis of anything contains a subjunctive, irrelevant counterexamples will ensue. (b) is worth a paper of its own.) In fact, the notion of tacit belief is hard to characterize in any terms at all, never mind subjunctives (Lycan 1986). It was the further 'defeater' analyses of assumption that were wrong, not the no-false-assumption analysis of knowing.

(Should it be protested that I should not analyze 'know' in terms of a notion whose own analysis is so vexed, one would have to make the same complaint against many theorists, in particular against anyone who analyzes anything in terms of causality.)

But the counterexamples to necessity are effective, even against the weakened no-false-assumptions analysis. The mere presence of a false assumption does not blight knowledge.

---

[12] Lehrer's (1965) (iv c) is a leading example: 'If S is completely justified in believing any false statement *p* which entails (but is not entailed by) *h*, then S would be completely justified in believing *h* even if S were to suppose that *p* is false' (174). This was readily counterexampled by Harman (1966) and Shope (1978). Rozeboom's (1967) principle (A) is probably closest to my no-false-assumptions formula, though it still injects a quasi-subjunctive element: 'If person X believes *p*—justifiably—only because he believes *q*, while he justifiably believes *q* on the basis of evidence *e*, then *q* as well as *p* must be the case if X's belief in *p* is to qualify as "knowledge" ' (281–2).

Harman (1973: 47) provides the obvious fix: What is required is only that a justification must not *essentially* rest on a false assumption; any false assumption on which it does rest must be dispensable. As before (the reply is prefigured in the description of Nondefective Chain itself), if S has even one nongettiered epistemic justification, it does not matter if *S* has other justifications containing false assumptions. So we move from no-false-assumptions to no-essential-false-assumptions.

The same applies, though not quite so directly, to Togethersmith. *S* does assume that all the Togethersmiths are out in the car, and that assumption is false. But it is not essential to *S*'s justification. As Rozeboom himself insists, it is irrelevant that the one child is not in the car. *S* also tacitly assumes that Mrs Togethersmith is in the car, and has just as good inductive evidence for that assumption as *S* has for the belief that all the Togethersmiths are in it.

But now (the expert reader will have been shouting for some time) two further putative counterexamples to sufficiency loom, each very well known: Harman's (1973) unpossessed-defeater sort of case, and the Ginet–Goldman barn case (Goldman 1976).

The assassination: Jill reads a true newspaper account of a political assassination. The reporter is known to be entirely trustworthy, and he was himself an eyewitness. Nor is Jill gettiered. But the victim's associates, wishing to forestall panic, have issued a television announcement saying (falsely) that the assassination attempt failed and that the intended victim is alive. Nearly everyone has heard the television announcement and believes it. However, by a fluke, Jill misses it and continues (epistemically justified and nongettiered) to believe that the victim is dead.

(Harman's other two very similar examples are those of Tom Grabit's mother's false but widely accepted testimony, and Donald in Italy and his faked letters from California.)

Fake Barn Country: Henry is looking at a (real) barn, and has impeccable visual and other evidence that it is a barn. He is not gettiered; his justification is sound in every way. However, in the neighborhood there are a number of fake, papier-mâché barns, any of which would have fooled Henry into thinking it was a barn.

It is claimed that Jill and Henry do not know.[13] What distinguishes these cases from the preceding counterexamples to sufficiency is that, in them, there are no identifiable false tacit assumptions. In no reasonable sense is Jill tacitly assuming that no one has issued a television announcement that the assassination attempt failed; nor is Henry assuming that there are no papier-mâché barn replicas in the neighborhood. (Or if there is such a sense, it is a very loose one and not that same clear one in which our previous Gettier victims were making their specific

---

[13] '[I]t is highly implausible that Jill should know simply because she lacks evidence everyone else has' (Harman 1973: 144).

tacit assumptions.) The no-essential-false-assumptions theory does not rule out these examples.

My reply is that, on quite independent grounds, I reject the received intuitions; I do not share them and I also think they are mistaken. I maintain that Jill and Henry do know, despite the chance elements that peripherally invade their situations. I have argued that at length in Lycan (1977), and not on behalf of the present analysis. Readers who do share the unpossessed-defeater and barn intuitions and who have not read my arguments cannot be expected to agree, but I stand by the no-essential-false-assumptions analysis. A bit more argument against Harman and Ginet–Goldman will be enlisted from Hetherington (1999), in Section V below.

IV. FAMILY RESEMBLANCES

One cannot help noticing that the Gettier project is a Socratic search for a set of necessary and sufficient conditions for knowing. In the 1960s that would have been even harder not to notice, because under the influence of Wittgenstein, the Socratic assumption had come under siege: it was nearly anathema to suppose that an interesting concept could be defined by a crisp set of necessary and sufficient conditions. Accordingly, it was thought in some quarters that that is what was wrong with the Gettier project; the '*S* knows that *p*' crowd had not read their Wittgenstein, and did not understand that 'know' is a family-resemblance term (for example, Saunders and Champawat 1964).

Given the aforementioned nonsuccess of later chisholming projects, the Wittgensteinians' negative judgement is hard to fault. Perhaps no philosophically interesting concept admits of explication by strictly necessary and sufficient conditions. However, that does not explain why the Gettier project was held to be worse off than the other Socratic quests of the day. Also, the Wittgensteinians' positive judgement is a substantive commitment and in need of defense: Is 'know' a family-resemblance concept?—i.e., does it in fact have that structure?

Actually there are two or more different structures that have been called 'family-resemblance' structures. The most distinctive one is that in which a concept 'X' is defined by a paradigm case: There is a list of features, each of which would be possessed by a paradigm case of an X; if a thing has every feature on the list, the thing is an X by any standard, a *real* X, an X and a half, an X on wheels. To be an X per se, however, is just to have 'enough' of the features on the list. (Perhaps the features are weighted in combinations, but not so thoroughly as to constitute a traditional analysis.) We cannot be much more precise than just to say 'enough'. There will be pretty-much-Xs, sort-of-Xs, borderline Xs, things that are Xish but not really Xs. Call this the 'Paradigm' structure.

'Know' does not have the Paradigm structure. I suppose there is a paradigm for inferential empirical knowledge. (Though according to Plato or Descartes, no case of inferential empirical knowledge would be very close to the paradigm of Knowledge itself.) If *S* has overwhelming amounts of evidence for believing that *p*, has not the slightest reason to doubt that *p*, and is not gettiered or beset by fluke in any way at all, then (barring global skepticism) *S* surely knows that *p*. But suppose *S* meets the first of those two conditions but not the third, i.e., *S* is a classic Gettier victim. Then (as before) *S* does not pretty-much-know that *p*; *S* is not a good though imperfect example of a knower. *S* simply and flatly does not know. It is not that *S* fails to have 'enough' of the paradigm features of knowing. It is that *S* is gettiered and so disqualified, period.[14]

Wittgenstein's own 'family resemblance' metaphor does not support the Paradigm interpretation, even though his central examples, such as 'game', do exhibit the Paradigm structure.[15] '[W]e see a complicated network of similarities overlapping and criss-crossing; sometimes overall similarities, sometimes similarities of detail. . . . I can think of no better expression to characterize these similarities than "family resemblances"; for the various resemblances between members of a family: build, features, colour of eyes, gait, temperament, etc. etc. overlap and criss-cross in the same way' (1953: §§66, 67). On this model, there is no one paradigm, because some of the traits in question may be mutually incompatible and nothing could have them all. There might be sub-paradigms, but there need not be those either. As before, though, to fall under the concept to a degree is to have 'enough' of the traits in some acceptable combination. Call this the 'Criss-Crossing' structure.

But 'know' does not have the Criss-Crossing structure either, for the same reason as before. It is not that poor gettiered *S* fails to have 'enough' of the family features; it is that *S* is disqualified. Also, there is no very visible 'family' composed of people who have one or two or three of the traits: believing that *p*, its being true that *p*, having evidence that *p*, not being gettiered. Rather, there is more of an epistemological hierarchy: believing that *p*, believing truly that *p*, justifiedly and truly believing that *p*, epistemically-justifiedly and truly believing that *p*, epistemically-justifiedly and truly believing that *p* and not being gettiered (though one wonders where on this scale to put epistemically-justifiedly and falsely believing that *p*, and it is not obvious whether justifiably and truly but not epistemically-justifiedly believing that *p* but not being gettiered should be ranked higher or lower than epistemically-justifiedly believing that *p* and being gettiered).

Even if 'know' does not have any family-resemblance structure, there is a more basic complaint that has sometimes been made: that 'JTB' is flawed to begin with, before we get to the question of its sufficiency. In particular, it is said, knowledge is not a kind of believing, indeed is not a psychological state at all

---

[14] A similar point is made by Weatherson (2003: 19). But again *pace* Hetherington (2001).

[15] This point was called to my attention by Dorit Bar-On, who offered the resemblances between members of her own extended family as an example. There may be yet other structures that come under the heading of 'family resemblance'; e.g., Craig (1990: 15) speaks of a 'prototypical case', and seems to mean by that something about statistical frequency.

(Austin 1961; Vendler 1972). Indeed, knowing does not even *entail* believing (Radford 1966).

But this is no solution to the Problem problem. The traditional claim that is needed to set up the Problem is only the sufficiency thesis: that if *S* does believe that *p* truly and with epistemic justification, then *S* knows. The falsity of that thesis is interesting and important and raises the Gettier question, whether or not knowing entails believing. There are people who have JTB and accordingly know; but, surprisingly, there are people who have JTB and do not know. What distinguishes the former from the latter?

V. MORE RECENT COMPLAINTS ABOUT THE GETTIER PROBLEM

Insolubility. Craig (1990) and Zagzebski (1994) suggest an argument for the claim that the Gettier Problem is insoluble: So long as a particular fourth condition added to the original three still leaves a logical possibility that a belief might meet all four conditions and still be false, there will always be room for further Gettierish flukes and hence there will be counterexamples; *S* could be super-gettiered, even if *S* is not gettiered in the customary way. But if the fourth condition shuts off that possibility, it will rule out lots of ordinary instances of knowing and hence be too strong. Thus, the Gettier Problem is insoluble and for a predictable reason, and that is what is wrong with it.

Neither Craig nor Zagzebski actually accepts this argument; indeed Zagzebski (1999) rejects the second horn of the dilemma, and goes on to offer her own solution to the Problem. Fogelin (1994) and Merricks (1995) too accept the first horn but not the second, drawing the moral that whatever 'epistemic justification' is, it must guarantee the truth of the belief: either *S* has evidence that entails that *p*, or *S* could not possibly be believing that *p* on the basis of that evidence in the circumstances unless *p*.[16]

Each horn is somewhat plausible. If there is no guarantee of truth, then it does seem that a Gettierish fluke would always be available, though we have not seen an algorithm for generating one. The second horn is supported by the same problem that afflicted its particular instance, the Dretske–Armstrong nomic reliability theory: that perfectly ordinary cases of knowledge do not seem to meet the guarantee-of-truth requirement.

But, whatever the merits of the Craig–Zagzebski argument, it would not be a very interesting solution to the Gettier Problem problem, because if sound it shows that some version of skepticism is true. It says that to be knowledge, a belief must meet the guarantee condition, and that hardly any beliefs meet the guarantee

---

[16] I believe Almeder (1974) was the first to take this line, though Rozeboom (1967) says something similar.

condition.[17] That is an interesting argument for skepticism, all the more so for being instigated by the Gettier Problem itself, but for our present purposes it still proves too much.

Unanalyzability. There is an ambitious anti-Gettier claim, seemingly unanswerable if true: that 'know' is unanalyzable. Even if knowledge has necessary conditions such as truth and belief, of course it does not follow that 'know' is analyzable in terms of those. Williamson (2000) argues at length that 'know' should be taken as primitive. If he is right, then of course any project which bills itself as 'analyzing knowledge' is doomed to failure. And that is what the Gettier project did bill itself as doing.

However, even if 'know' is unanalyzable and has no set of conceptually necessary and sufficient conditions, the claim needed to set up the Problem is (again) only the sufficiency thesis: that epistemically justified true belief suffices for knowledge. The falsity of that thesis still needs explaining, because, as before, there are real people who have JTB but still do not know, and that raises the question of what distinguishes the knower from the Gettier victim. (We need not commit the subtraction fallacy, of supposing that because JTB does not suffice for knowing there is some crisp condition C such that JTB + C = K. The task is only to explain why the victim does not know.) The Gettier project can rage on unabated.

Rejecting the Ur-intuition. Hetherington (1999; 2001) maintains that a Gettier victim does know, though in a somewhat inferior or 'less-then-ideal' way: s/he knows very 'failably'.

'Failability' is a generalization of *fallible* knowing, and means roughly that although S knows, there is a single element of luck, in virtue of which S might not have known or even nearly failed to know. More precisely: Either there is a possible world in which S believes that p and is justified by the same good evidence, but it is not true that p, or there is one in which S correctly believes that p but is not justified by the same evidence in doing so, or there is one in which although S would be both correct in believing that p and justified by the evidence, S does not hold that belief (1999: 567). (Thus, one has *in*failable knowledge iff '[i]n each world where one exists and where one has two of the elements of knowing that p, one also has the third element': 568.) Note that failability is a matter of degree; some knowledge will admit *more and/or closer* epistemic-failure worlds than does other knowledge.

Having identified *fallible* knowing with the first of the three foregoing disjuncts, Hetherington argues that it is arbitrary to single out that disjunct in preference to the other two, and so his generalization from fallibility to failability is natural and nontendentious. There is at least a presumption, then, that knowledge can be failable in either of the other two ways as well.

Fallible knowing is of course presupposed by the Gettier Problem; hence so is failable knowing. Now Hetherington suggests that a Gettier case is one in which,

---

[17] Adler (1981) argues for skepticism in this way, and also in effect defends the first horn of the dilemma.

although *S* does know, *S* knows only *very* failably; 'the epistemic subject almost fails to have his well-justified true belief' (573). A classic Gettier example falls under the first disjunct; there are scads of very nearby worlds in which *S* believes (on the very same very strong evidence grounded in Mr Nogot) that someone in the office owns a Ford, but in which neither Havit nor anyone else owns one. A Harman unpossessed-defeater case falls under the third disjunct, for there are lots of nearby worlds in which the assassination does occur and Jill has her same evidence for it, but in which (because she did there hear the government denials) she has abandoned her belief.

Obviously, if the Gettier victim knows, her/his knowledge is not just failable but very failable. But why should we forsake all received judgement and concede that s/he does know? Rather than giving a positive reason, Hetherington spends the rest of his article suggesting diagnoses of our failure to fall in with his view. The mainstream epistemologist has made a tacit fallacious inference: from the fact that 'there must be a difference in the quality of the instances of knowing in, respectively, a normal situation where there is failable knowledge that *p*, and a Gettier situation where there is failable knowledge that *p*' (575); or from 'how easy it is to imagine changes to the circumstances within a Gettier case, changes which would have led to the case's epistemic subject not having the well-justified true belief he actually has' (579); or from the subject's true belief owing anything at all to luck (581); or from the subject's epistemically justified belief being not robust, a 'near thing' (581–2); or from the fact that 'the more failable . . . [a piece of knowledge] is, the less confident we might be that it is knowledge' (585); or, when we are already sniffing around knowledge's 'lower boundary', from the fact that knowledge has a lower boundary (586).

I suspect that few of my fellow mainstreamers will recognize themselves in these diagnoses, and even fewer will be persuaded to adopt Hetherington's maverick verdict on Gettier cases generally. But, although my most diligent introspection reveals none of the fallacious inferences on my own part either, I am more sympathetic to Hetherington's view than most will be. He very usefully distinguishes between 'helpful' Gettier cases and 'dangerous' ones: A helpful case is one in which the Gettierish 'strange occurrence' or fluke saves JTB itself, as when Havit owns a Ford even though Nogot does not. A dangerous case is one in which the 'strange occurrence' prevents knowledge despite existing normal JTB, as in Harman's unpossessed-defeater examples and the Ginet–Goldman barn case.

As I declared in Section III, I reject the majority view that the victims in unpossessed-defeater cases and the barn case lack knowledge. And now Hetherington has shown that those examples have something distinctive in common, viz., being 'dangerous' as opposed to 'helpful'.[18] Moreover, I think his interpretation of

[18] A similar distinction was made by Fogelin (1994). Notice, incidentally, that the 'dangerous' cases are not really Gettier cases at all, except in the generic sense of being (alleged) counterexamples to 'JTB', precisely because they do not have the characteristic false-assumption structure; it would be

them is pretty much right: that although their protagonists' knowledge is failable and some luck is involved in a peripheral way, it is knowledge nonetheless. True, Jill and Henry nearly failed to know; it does not follow that they fail to know. With Hetherington, I maintain that they do know.

(But in my view the same cannot be said about the classic, 'helpful' cases. I could not possibly jolly myself into agreeing that S knows that someone in the office owns a Ford, when S's only reason for believing that is that S thinks Nogot owns one. I find it hard to imagine that anyone would credit S with knowing that there is a sheep in Chisholm's field when the sheep that quite coincidentally makes S's belief true is off in a distant corner of the field, hidden from view by hedges. (However, this may only show the poverty of my imaginative powers; see below.))

Weatherson (2003) also urges, though on grounds very different from Hetherington's, that gettiered people do know. His idea is a very general one about philosophers' 'intuitions': that intuitions about cases should be trumped, as they are often considered overruled in ethical theory, by a good (otherwise) coherent and systematic theory that says otherwise. Though an analysis must respect a majority of intuitions, it may disregard one when that one forces us into 'unnatural' complications and draws the analysandum away from comparatively natural properties in the world. (No one who has read the indefeasibility analysis quoted in Section I above could deny that the Gettier intuition has been known to do such forcing and drawing.)

Weatherson's paper is complex and rich, and I cannot do it justice here. I accept his 'main claim . . . that even once we have accepted that the JTB theory seems to say the wrong thing about Gettier cases, we should still keep an open mind to the question of whether it is true' (10).[19] I shall merely state four reasons why, though I agree that the seeming does not entail the falsity of 'JTB', I continue to join in the majority view.

First, though Swain's indefeasibility analysis is hideously 'unnatural', of course I chose it as an extreme case. Not every proffered analysis is so complex or so disjunctive. Just to take a random example, my own no-essential-false-assumptions analysis is not so unnatural. It is rather neat, I think.

Second, I do not believe that JTB is a conspicuously *more* natural kind than nongettiered JTB. If anything, I would say a Gettier victim has more in common with a not fully justified believer than with a knower.[20] (Also, those of us who think that 'know' inherits normativity from its relation to justification would not expect knowledge to be a particularly natural kind.)

---

inaccurate to say that either Jill or Henry had been gettiered. (Obviously I do not mean that remark as an argument either for my claim that their protagonists know or for my proposed analysis.)

[19] After all, I myself reject the widely embraced Harman and Ginet–Goldman examples. But notice that this is different: I reject those intuitions because I do not share them in the first place. Weatherson is urging that even when we firmly share the original Gettier intuition, we should set it aside and not allow it to guide our belief.

[20] Weatherson (2003: 27–8) attributes a similar point to Peter Klein in conversation.

Third, I believe intuitions have enough authority that if we want to reject one, we ought to explain it away. I think Weatherson agrees, and of course he is well aware that this happens often in philosophy. Why, then, is there so widespread instant agreement that Gettier victims do not know? As noted above, Hetherington put in some work on this, however plausible or implausible we think his explanations are; but unless I have missed it, Weatherson does not offer anything comparable.

Finally, Weatherson's argument does not single out the Gettier Problem, even though the Problem is his stalking horse. Similar points could be made about all the other analytic projects mentioned in Section I. So Weatherson has not solved the Problem problem, so far as that requires exhibiting some special defect in the Gettier Problem that distinguishes it from analytic projects generally.

Actual diversity of intuitions. Weinberg, Stich, and Nichols (2001) present data they have collected, according to which the intuitions of subjects from different ethnic groups vary statistically. In particular, 60% of subjects originally from the Indian subcontinent, presented with a Gettier example, judged that its protagonist does 'really know' as opposed to 'only believe'. For that matter, nearly 25% of the European-descended American subjects made the same antiGettier judgement. This raises two issues: First, is there cultural relativity in the concept of knowing? Second, even within the class of, say, educated European-descended Americans, is the Gettier intuition reliable? If the answer to either question, especially the second, is 'no', then the Gettier project is parochial at best, and is not an augustly Socratic inquiry into the nature of Knowledge Itself.

I have several doubts about the experimental procedures described by the authors, and I would not take their results at face value. But they do not claim too much for them. And to make things interesting, let us ignore such doubts, and suppose that the survey results are impeccably produced and robustly replicated: 60% of an Asian ethnic group and 25% of European-descended American undergraduates firmly reject Gettier and insist, clearheadedly and understanding the terms and the issue, that a Gettier 'victim' does know.

In that eventuality, I submit, we have a conceptual difference. In the speech of the 60% and the 25%, 'know' really does mean justified true belief, period. We would have to regard that speech as a dialect that differs from our own. It would be interesting to go on to ask those subjects whether they see any important difference between the two kinds of 'knowers', ordinary ones and Gettier victims. Perhaps they would stigmatize the Gettier victims in some way for which there is no simple convenient expression. Or, less likely, they would see no important difference, and simply have no stronger conception of successful cognition.

This sort of dialect difference is less rare than one might think. It can lurk unsuspected for decades or whole lifetimes, because it is slight and the sort of hypothetical case that would bring it out is unusual. Here is an example from my own experience. Sartre bemoans the fact that we have no simple expression for the following situation:

A believes that not-*p*, but for selfish reasons wants *B* to believe that *p*. In a persuasive manner, *A* tells *B* that *p*: '*p*, *B*; trust me, old friend, would I ever lie to you?' Now in fact, *A* is mistaken, and it is true that *p*. *A* has tried to lie to *B*, and *A*'s character is that of a liar. But what *A* said was true, so it cannot be called a lie.

On many occasions I have mentioned this in my undergraduate classes, and every time, about 40% of the students balk at Sartre's judgement, and say they have no difficulty in calling *A* a liar. When I protest that a lie cannot be true, they say, 'Sure it can'; all that matters to them is the intent to deceive. On the basis of induction, I predict that 40% of my readers will likewise have rejected Sartre's complaint.

There is no substantive issue here. Neither I nor the 40% are right to the exclusion of the other. It is simply a dialect difference—one that I did not discover until I was in my 40s.[21]

If another culture has a word that we have been translating as 'know' but turns out not to share the Gettier intuition, then their word should not strictly be translated as 'know' (though there may be no convenient competing expression of English). And if it is really true that 25% of ordinary English speakers simply do not share the intuition, there is a dialect difference.

Weinberg, Stich, and Nichols may urge that such an outcome would diminish the importance of the Gettier project. Gettier practitioners would then be pursuing only the minutiae of a concept possessed by some speakers of English. I reply: So be it. The concept has proved to be an important one among English-speaking philosophers, regardless of how more widespread it may be. If another culture or another dialect group simply does not have that concept, then of course the Gettier Problem does not arise for them.

Now, I take very seriously the cynical suggestion that the Gettier concept is a philosophers' artifact and does not represent anything possessed by ordinary people. No professional philosopher is qualified to make any pronouncement about the ordinary concept of anything, period, though few of us can resist making such pronouncements. I believe that some philosophically important and contentious concepts are such artifacts. My leading example would be Putnam's (1975) externalist natural-kind concepts. When I teach 'The Meaning of "Meaning" ' to novices, they invariably resist. At best I can get them to concede that *there is a sense* in which XYZ on Twin Earth is not water.[22] But there is a sharp

---

[21] In fact, I suspect that such hidden dialect differences occur not infrequently in philosophy, though this is not the time or place to argue that. For a hypothesis to this effect within epistemology, and a nice theoretical framework that helps to explain the phenomenon, see Battaly (2001).

[22] Indeed, there was a good deal of resistance to Putnam's own original presentations in the mid-1970s. But, as Rob Cummins would say, the people who disputed Putnam's 'intuition' were not invited to the next conference. Of course, I am inclined to think that Harman's unpossessed-defeater examples and (especially) the Ginet–Goldman barn case are artifacts of this sort. For the record, I do not share the lottery intuition either; I believe that if the chances are 10,000,000 to 1 against and

contrast here: I have never had the slightest trouble convincing novices by Gettier example that 'JTB' is insufficient for knowing. And I do not think that is because of my being the instructor or my natural authority, let alone force of personality or great professional stature.

VI. PROGNOSIS?

Fodor et al. (1980) have argued convincingly that no interesting concept can be analyzed in the traditional Socratic way, by a nice set of individually necessary and jointly sufficient conditions. At least on inductive grounds, we should not expect a solution to the Gettier Problem having that form. But it remains to be shown what we should expect, instead.

And as I have argued, none of the going solutions to the Problem problem succeeds. *So far as has been shown*, there is nothing particularly wrong with the Gettier Problem, and people who work on it do not (for that reason) deserve the sneers that are sometimes sent their way.

I am happy with my simple no-essential-false-assumptions analysis. What about you?[23]

REFERENCES

Adler, J. (1981). 'Skepticism and Universalizability'. *Journal of Philosophy*, 78: 143–56.
Almeder, R. (1974). 'Truth and Evidence'. *Philosophical Quarterly*, 24: 365–8.
Armstrong, D. M. (1973). *Belief, Truth, and Knowledge*. Cambridge: Cambridge University Press.
Austin, J. L. (1961). 'Other Minds', in *Philosophical Papers*. Oxford: Clarendon Press, 44–84.
Battaly, H. (2001). 'Thin Concepts to the Rescue', in A. Fairweather and L. Zagzebski (eds.), *Virtue Epistemology: Essays on Epistemic Virtue and Responsibility*. New York: Oxford University Press, 98–116.
Chisholm, R. M. (1966). *Theory of Knowledge*. Englewood Cliffs, NJ: Prentice-Hall.
Clark, M. (1963). 'Knowledge and Grounds: A Comment on Mr. Gettier's Paper'. *Analysis*, 24: 46–8.
Craig, E. (1990). *Knowledge and the State of Nature: An Essay in Conceptual Synthesis*. Oxford: Clarendon Press.
Dretske, F. (1971). 'Conclusive Reasons'. *Australasian Journal of Philosophy*, 49: 1–22.
Feldman, R. (1974). 'An Alleged Defect in Gettier Counter-Examples'. *Australasian Journal of Philosophy*, 52: 68–9.

nothing vital hangs on it, you do know you will not win, and so much the worse for various forms of 'rule-out' epistemology.

[23] Many thanks to Ram Neta for extensive and very helpful discussion. I am grateful also to Kati Farkas for correcting a serious error.

Fodor, J. A., Garrett, M., Walker, E., and Parkes, C. (1980). 'Against Definitions'. *Cognition*, 8: 263–367.

Fogelin, R. (1994). *Pyrrhonian Reflections on Knowledge and Justification*. New York: Oxford University Press.

Gettier, E. (1963). 'Is Justified True Belief Knowledge?' *Analysis*, 23: 121–3.

Goldman, A. I. (1967). 'A Causal Theory of Knowing'. *Journal of Philosophy*, 64: 357–72.

—— (1976). 'Discrimination and Perceptual Knowledge'. *Journal of Philosophy*, 73: 771–91.

—— (1999). *Knowledge in a Social World*. Oxford: Clarendon Press.

Harman, G. (1966). 'Lehrer on Knowledge'. *Journal of Philosophy*, 63: 241–7.

—— (1973). *Thought*. Princeton: Princeton University Press.

Hetherington, S. (1999). 'Knowing Failably'. *Journal of Philosophy*, 96: 565–87.

—— (2001). *Good Knowledge, Bad Knowledge: On Two Dogmas of Epistemology*. Oxford: Clarendon Press.

Hintikka, K. J. J. (1962). *Knowledge and Belief: An Introduction to the Logic of the Two Notions*. Ithaca: Cornell University Press.

Lehrer, K. (1965). 'Knowledge, Truth and Evidence'. *Analysis*, 25: 168–75.

—— (1970). 'The Fourth Condition of Knowledge: A Defense'. *Review of Metaphysics*, 24: 122–8.

—— (1974). *Knowledge*. Oxford: Clarendon Press.

—— and Paxson, T. (1969). 'Knowledge: Undefeated Justified True Belief '. *Journal of Philosophy*, 66: 225–37.

Lycan, W. G. (1977). 'Evidence One Does Not Possess'. *Australasian Journal of Philosophy*, 55: 114–26.

—— (1984). 'Armstrong's Theory of Knowing', in R. J. Bogdan (ed.), *Profiles: D.M. Armstrong*. Dordrecht: D. Reidel, 139–60.

—— (1986). 'Tacit Belief', in R. J. Bogdan (ed.), *Belief: Form, Content, and Function*. Oxford: Clarendon Press, 61–82.

—— (1994a). *Modality and Meaning*. Dordrecht: Kluwer.

—— (1994b). 'Sartwell's Minimalist Analysis of Knowing'. *Philosophical Studies*, 73: 1–3.

Merricks, T. (1995). 'Warrant Entails Truth'. *Philosophy and Phenomenological Research*, 55: 841–55.

Pailthorp, C. (1969). 'Knowledge as Justified True Belief'. *Review of Metaphysics*, 23: 25–47.

Pappas, G., and Swain, M. (1973). 'Some Conclusive Reasons against "Conclusive Reasons"'. *Australasian Journal of Philosophy*, 51: 72–6.

Powers, L. (1978). 'Knowledge by Deduction'. *Philosophical Review*, 87: 337–71.

Putnam, H. (1975). 'The Meaning of "Meaning" ', in K. Gunderson (ed.), *Language, Mind and Knowledge: Minnesota Studies in the Philosophy of Science 7*. Minneapolis: University of Minnesota Press, 215–71.

Quine, W. V. (1936). 'Truth by Convention', in O. H. Lee (ed.), *Philosophical Essays for A.N. Whitehead*. New York: Longmans; reprinted in Quine (1966: 90–124).

—— (1963). 'Carnap and Logical Truth', in P. A. Schilpp (ed.), *The Philosophy of Rudolf Carnap*. LaSalle: Open Court; reprinted in Quine (1966: 385–406).

—— (1966). *The Ways of Paradox and Other Essays*. New York: Random House.

Radford, C. (1966). 'Knowledge—By Examples'. *Analysis*, 27: 1–11.

Rozeboom, W. W. (1967). 'Why I Know So Much More than You Do'. *American Philosophical Quarterly*, 4: 281–90.

Russell, B. (1948). *Human Knowledge: Its Scope and Limits*. London: Allen & Unwin.

Sartwell, C. (1991). 'Knowledge is Merely True Belief'. *American Philosophical Quarterly*, 28: 157–65.

—— (1992). 'Why Knowledge is Merely True Belief'. *Journal of Philosophy*, 89: 167–80.

Saunders, J. T., and Champawat, N. (1964). 'Mr. Clark's Definition of "Knowledge"'. *Analysis*, 25: 8–9.

Scheffler, I. (1965). *Conditions of Knowledge: An Introduction to Epistemology and Education*. Chicago: Scott, Foresman.

Schiffer, S. (1972). *Meaning*. Oxford: Clarendon Press.

Shope, R. (1978). 'The Conditional Fallacy in Contemporary Philosophy'. *Journal of Philosophy*, 75: 397–413.

Skyrms, B. (1967). 'The Explication of "X knows that p"'. *Journal of Philosophy*, 64: 373–89.

Swain, M. (1972). 'Knowledge, Causality, and Justification'. *Journal of Philosophy*, 69: 291–300.

—— (1974). 'Epistemic Defeasibility'. *American Philosophical Quarterly*, 11: 15–25.

—— (1978). 'Some Revisions of "Knowledge, Causality, and Justification"', in G. Pappas and M. Swain (eds.), *Essays on Knowledge and Justification*. Ithaca: Cornell University Press, 109–19.

Unger, P. (1971). 'A Defense of Skepticism'. *Philosophical Review*, 80: 198–218.

—— (1984). *Philosophical Relativity*. Oxford: Blackwell.

Vendler, Z. (1972). *Res Cogitans: An Essay in Rational Psychology*. Ithaca: Cornell University Press.

Weatherson, B. (2003). 'What Good are Counterexamples?' *Philosophical Studies*, 115: 1–31.

Weinberg, J. M., Stich, S. P., and Nichols, S. (2001). 'Normativity and Epistemic Intuitions'. *Philosophical Topics*, 29: 429–60.

Williamson, T. (2000). *Knowledge and its Limits*. Oxford: Clarendon Press.

Wittgenstein, L. (1953). *Philosophical Investigations*. Oxford: Blackwell.

Zagzebski, L. (1994). 'The Inescapability of Gettier Problems'. *Philosophical Quarterly*, 44: 65–73.

—— (1999). 'What is Knowledge?', in J. Greco and E. Sosa (eds.), *The Blackwell Guide to Epistemology*. Oxford: Blackwell, 92–116.

10

Epistemic Finitude and the Framework of Inference

A. C. Grayling

1

Sit at an outdoor café table in a busy city square and watch people crossing streets, buying newspapers, locating and entering buildings, catching buses, checking the time, tying shoelaces, meeting acquaintances. Watch them for an hour, or for that matter five minutes, because it takes scarcely any time to reacquaint oneself, if reacquaintance were necessary, with a very familiar but signal fact, namely, that ordinarily competent human beings manifest a high level of success in navigating their environment, dealing with what they encounter in it, making appropriate judgements about it, rapidly correcting mistakes if such occur, and generally giving every evidence of acting with a large measure of rationality on the basis of largely true beliefs, or at least powerfully successful theories, about their spatio-temporal environment and how to deal with it. Epistemic mistakes in everyday life can be harshly punished, even by death (as, for example, might happen upon misjudging when to cross the road), so epistemic practicality is a serious and consequential matter, and so therefore are the assumptions, beliefs, perceptual interpretations, and inferential practices in which it consists.

Such anecdotal reflections permit us to assume something philosophically interesting: the availability of an account of the everyday conceptual scheme upon which epistemic practice is based. Such an account will in particular sketch how we transcend the limitations of our epistemic capacities, by specifying conceptual commitments determining a set of permissible views, of a particular and austerely practical character, about what the world is like, not just an ontology (an inventory of what there is) but an ontological theory (a theory that tells us—to adapt a Tractarian phrase—what can be, and usually is, the case).[1]

---

[1] I shall throughout use 'epistemic' to qualify what concerns knowing, and 'epistemological' to qualify what concerns our theories about knowing. Some writers treat these expressions as synonyms.

One of the chief questions that would need reply in this project is: what kinds of epistemologically significant relations obtain between the commitments and the particular beliefs they license? The commitments will behave as if they were foundational beliefs of a type to be specified, and the particular beliefs are just that: individual beliefs about ordinary things, for example, about the way large heavy mobile objects like buses and lorries behave, and how they might interact with one if one were crossing a road in front of them. This is a request to describe the framework of inference constituted by the commitments' having a foundational role, a request designed to elicit fulfilment of promises contained in the idea of such a framework, namely, that it constitutes a way of fitting together solutions to an assortment of epistemological problems, primarily those of justification and ampliative inference.

An answer cannot be neutral with respect to the nature of the commitments themselves, so it is necessary to state them more precisely. It is likely that arguments in defence of choices here are harder to give than arguments about the character of connections between such commitments and the mundane beliefs they license, but the interest lies mainly with aspects of the latter question, and therefore one can be summary in sketching what the commitments are like.[2]

First, however, it is appropriate to locate more precisely the concern being addressed; so far it has been characterised in general terms only, as being about the scheme that enables ordinary epistemic practice to function in its usually successful ways. An economical means of precisifying the task is to note that a characteristic shortcoming of foundationalist theories in epistemology is their failure to give a satisfactory explanation of the relation between basis and superstructure in the epistemic edifice. Across a range of proposals embracing Kant's categories, Russell's postulates, Ayer's basic propositions, various phenomenological 'givens', and even Wittgenstein's 'scaffolding' metaphor in *On Certainty*, there is little persuasive detail about the mechanisms, logical or otherwise, by which these very different candidates for the role of conceptual support play their part.[3] In a sketch of the transcendental strategy for responding to scepticism I have argued that a promising view of this relationship is suggested by the 'covering law' model, the idea being that an assertion about some particular matter is legitimate when its being inferable from a description of its grounds is a result of that inference's being licensed by one or more covering generalised expressions of our conceptual commitments for that region of interest.[4] This intuition I still think right; the task is to make it out in detail. Here I reflect on some preliminaries for doing so.

The idea is to work from a recognition that the conceptual framework we are seeking to describe has the primary role of overcoming the limitations of any individual's necessarily finite epistemic powers, which, unaided by such a

---

[2] The question of the commitments is dealt with at length in Grayling (1985: esp. chs. 1, 4 *passim*) and Grayling (2003).

[3] Some of the sources of these views are to be found in Kant (1781), Russell (1948), Ayer (1954), and Wittgenstein (1969).   [4] See Grayling (1985) and esp. (2003).

framework, would be restricted to operating with immediate experience and such memories as survived the absence of any organising principles to make them useful in interpreting occurrent experience. And the suggestion to be explored is a maximally uncontroversial one: that the framework which makes ordinary epistemic practice possible consists in a folk historico-geographical theory, a folk physics and biology, and a folk psychology, that between them (and simultaneously) locates epistemic subjects in a physical context that obeys folk physical and biological laws, and in a social context that obeys folk psychological laws, thereby situating them in a comprehensive narrative whose themes are an informative mixture of both, and in which the subject is his own point of reference and typically the central actor.

The two tasks confronting someone interested in describing the general features of such a framework are, first, identification of the structural concepts (the basic or foundational concepts) in the scheme, and secondly, description of the way these relate to the repertoire of particular empirical beliefs deployed in ordinary epistemic practice. The desideratum is to give a conservative account of both features together, 'conservative' because it aims to accomplish the second task by using only standard logical notions, and the first by invoking the familiar idea that the folk theories in question tell us that the world of perceptual experience contains causally-interactive particulars (and events involving them) in space and which, whether perceived or not, persist through stretches of time. Because the relations between the elements of this ontology are causal, the physical realm they constitute is nomological, which gives epistemic subjects a high degree of confidence in its perceived regularities. Moreover, some of the elements of this ontology are persons and other sentient beings, with all that this implies for the applicability of the folk psychology that supervenes on some of the physical and biological aspects of the domain.

Expressed with this degree of generality, the account remains neutral with respect to more detailed metaphysical questions, for example, as to whether there are things other than spatio-temporal items, whether these latter should properly be construed as particulars or events, and what among either is ontologically ultimate.

In common with the main tradition of thought in this vein I restrict attention to experientially mediated knowledge of the spatio-temporal realm, and proceed as follows. In Section 2 I sketch, and make some comments about, the background proposal which succeeding sections will premise. In the later sections I look at some aspects of the relations, especially inferential ones, which might obtain in such an epistemic framework. I stress that the enterprise is merely exploratory.

2

The rich truism from which, as noted, the investigation begins is that the powers of individual epistemic subjects are finite. For a careful account of what this implies, some distinctions of nomenclature are required. The rich truism expresses what I call 'the finitary predicament' to distinguish it from certain other superficially similar epistemic predicaments, as follows (Grayling 2003).

One way of illustrating the finitary predicament is to reflect on how things would be for someone who was a lifelong solitary (and thus not the inheritor, via the acquisition of language and other social media, of a world-view). What might he need to construct a world-view with nothing other than the resources of a native cognitive endowment of sense organs, memory, and intelligence? Ayer (1973: ch. V) offered an 'analytic reconstruction' of what would have to be additionally attributed to such a subject if his experience is to resemble ours. His interesting project is however derailed at the very outset by a problem with its setting up; for even at this juncture one must take care not to confuse, as arguably Ayer did, the importantly different notions of an epistemically *solipsistic* predicament, which is what a true solitary such as Ayer envisages would suffer, and the *finitary* predicament, which is suffered even by members of a community sharing a language and other epistemic resources.[5]

First, note that if (improbably) the notion of a solipsistic predicament is intelligible, it is so as an instance of the finitary predicament, for although what makes it *solipsism* is the isolation of the subject, the problem he faces is precisely the limitation of his cognitive resources, viz., his epistemic finitude. But in any case the idea of a 'solipsistic predicament' does not survive scrutiny, for it rests on the notion of a subjective perspective whose owner is said to recognise it as *his* perspective without having the means to place it among alternative perspectives, since by definition none exist. This is questionable, for the good reason that it seems hard if not impossible to make sense of the idea of a self—or, more minimally, even just of a subject of experiences whose experiences are in some sense taken by it to be its own—independently of the existence of other selves recognised as such (or: of other experiential perspectives in some way recognised as such from a given perspective), which implies that for anything to be a self or a minimally self-aware subject of experience is to be a member of a community of such things.[6]

Noting that the idea of a 'solipsistic predicament' does not bear too close examination does nothing, however, to remove the epistemological challenge of epistemic finitude. The fundamental consideration here is that, even granted that an epistemic subject belongs to a community of epistemic subjects capable of communicating and pooling epistemic resources, he, and even the community as a whole, remains constrained by the finitary limitations in question. And this reveals the existence of a large gap in need of filling: that between the world-view an individual epistemic subject might be conceived as capable of constructing from his native resources, and the conceptual framework which human beings in

---

[5] I had an opportunity to discuss this with Ayer while his pupil at Oxford in the 1970s, and took it that if he had rewritten the account of his epistemic solitary he would as a result have observed this distinction.

[6] Cf. Strawson's (1959) argument about self-ascription of states of consciousness.

fact possess and which makes ordinary everyday epistemic practice largely so successful.[7]

Recognition of the existence and character of this gap is what has forced the abandonment of the Cartesian perspective in epistemology. The Cartesian perspective has it that we are to begin with the data of individual private consciousness and work outwards to knowledge of, or at very least justified belief in, an 'external' world. Privileged access to the incorrigible data of our own consciousnesses is supposed to make us confident about what they convey to us; and what they convey to us is, together with a guarantee attaching to responsible use of our epistemic capacities, a reliable story about a realm independent of but responsible for the data themselves. (Descartes's (1641 *passim*) guarantee was the *goodness* of a deity; whereas an evil deity might wish us to fall into error, a good one would not.)

Notoriously, however, the familiar sceptical challenges that Descartes took to provide a route to a point of fundamental epistemic certainty, themselves subvert the project of moving from the data of consciousness to their supposed independent sources. It is precisely the debate about these challenges that has been fatal to Cartesian epistemology, whose starting point was accepted by every Western epistemologist from Descartes himself to Russell and Ayer. In particular, the empiricist project of justifying knowledge-claims by nominating the data of private experience as a fundamental content-conferring constraint on concepts, and a condition of their use, has been one of the main targets in the rejection of the Cartesian starting-point for knowledge.[8]

But it is important to note that there are still lessons to be learned from examining the gap that Cartesian epistemologists opened by means of their assumptions, and then sought so heroically to close. The lessons arise from trying to answer the question: how, given epistemic finitude, do we come to have and use a shared common-sense conceptual scheme? What status does that scheme have, given its radical underdetermination by the evidence that individual subscribers to it can acquire in the course of activities bearing upon the verification or falsification of what constitutes it?

One ready and obvious answer is that a shared conceptual scheme which no individual could have generated unaided, is a community product that turns crucially upon the fact of language. Language plays the major role in enabling individuals to divide and apportion epistemic tasks, to process the results, to record them, and to apply them. This is not to deny that there can be shared conceptual schemes without language; numerous species of languageless animals behave in ways that strongly suggest they possess indispensable shared conceptual

---

[7] To avoid difficulties with relativist challenges over the notion of a conceptual scheme, I restrict attention here to the most basic cognitive levels of any scheme, and refer to the cognitive/cultural relativism distinction and arguments against the possibility of the former, in Grayling (1985: ch. 3 *passim*).

[8] More recently, most attention has been focussed on the private language argument and rule-following considerations, which push in the same direction.

schemes, no doubt hard-wired, fulfilling precisely the function here attributed to them. But there is no reason to suppose that conceptual schemes not mediated by language have complexity above a certain level. Think of Wittgenstein's point: we can say that a dog expects his master home, but not, if his master is Lord Mayor of London, that he expects the Lord Mayor of London home. This is why it is uncontroversial that the evolved scheme we (humans) possess would be impossible without language.[9]

It is useful to clarify matters by noting another way of discussing the finitary predicament, which is to focus especially on the deficiency or incompleteness of any subject's information relative to his practical needs in navigating the world, and his consequent need of ways to flesh out and interpret his always partial occurrent data. From the viewpoint of this kind of characterisation it is natural to begin by considering the dilemma posed by our practical need for techniques of ampliative inference and their imperfection in the light of deductive standards. But this way of discussing matters could be misleading, for the real problem at hand is not so much the deficiency of any individual's state of information about the world as, at a quite different level, its surprising completeness. At the level of detail, of particular matters, individual knowledge is indeed radically deficient. Yet at the same time, as we see, each normal epistemic subject also possesses and applies the rich background of the conceptual framework, in the presence of which his ordinary discourse and practice proceeds. So, once again, we see that it is this overarching picture, and its relation to the minutiae of ordinary epistemic practice, that invites closest attention.

3

To recapitulate so far: we are taking individual (and collective) epistemic finitude seriously, and recognising that the fact of it makes questions about the global theories constituting a background conceptual framework intensely interesting. Those questions are not about how epistemic subjects come to have such a framework—the answer to that has already been suggested—but rather about the work that the conceptual framework does. Recognising this second question as the right one is something Kant has taught us to do, by pointing out that the crucial matter is not the source of our concepts, but the role they play.

One immediately obvious feature of the framework is that it is realist in character; it assumes the independence of the objects of experience from acts of cognising them (perceiving, thinking about, or referring to them). At this point it is necessary to make a halt, and notice a crucial fact. Realism, despite appearances

[9] We are always at risk of reading our own conceptual categories into animal behaviour. But if we did not, how would ethology get started? It at least requires us to attribute needs, desires, pleasures and fears, capacity to learn, etc. The point surely is: the difference between language-using and languageless creatures is a biological one anyway.

and much misleading debate, is an *epistemological* commitment. It is a thesis asserting the independence of the objects of knowledge or belief from the means of acquiring that knowledge or belief. It is not a metaphysical thesis about the things or the domain that the knowledge or belief in question is about. A debate between realists and anti-realists about a given domain of discourse is not a debate about what the domain contains, but about the relation of cognition to what it contains.[10] Thus, more precisely put, realism asserts that relations between acts or states of mind and what they are about, are external or contingent relations. For this claim I offer a full argument elsewhere (Grayling 1997: 299–320).

For present purposes we can recognise, as fundamental to understanding the way in which thought and talk operate, that the framework rests upon assumptions of the kind identified earlier, assumptions about the world being a nomological spatio-temporal realm of causally interactive particulars or events. Commitments in these respects naturally show why ordinary discourse invites realist construals of reference and truth, for a view of this kind is naturally allied to familiar views about reference and truth in much recent discussion in this arena, to the effect that reference works on a naming paradigm by causal links, and that truth consists in fit between what we think or say and what we are thinking and speaking about.

Whatever difficulties infect an account of the ontology and semantics associated with this realist picture, it is at least clear that it well meets the demands made on it by experience. But that is a matter independent of debates about whether the realist commitments of the scheme are *literally true*, or whether they are *assumptions* of the scheme, even if undischargeable ones, and this is a question on which a great deal turns. For present purposes it can be ignored, because we need only note that the commitments are here being taken irenically on the weaker construal as assumptions of the scheme.[11]

4

For a first approximation to what the conceptual framework of ordinary epistemic practice looks like, we need to focus upon its central function, which is to serve as an inferential scheme, more accurately still, an inference-licensing scheme. Typically, empirical judgements are represented as inductively based on evidence regarded as relevant, and as being defeasible to the degree that the evidence is

[10] An inventory: between thought and its objects, perception and its targets, knowledge and what is known, acts of referring and referents; call them 'mind-world' relations, although they are all different if intimately connected.

[11] Whether they are taken as literally true or merely as assumptions, the scheme's justificatory character remains. It becomes a matter for the second task, identified earlier, to settle this question of 'literal truth', that is, how these first-order facts about the scheme are to be interpreted in the light of the sceptical problem which gives that second task its content. Many complex issues arise here: see Grayling (1992).

partial. But we noted that the framework consists of a set of assumptions about the nature of the domain ranged over by experience, to the effect that the world is as described by the general features of the folk theories described earlier. See these assumptions as suppressed general background premises conjoined to the statements reporting particular evidence for a given empirical judgement, and the logical picture alters dramatically: the form of reasoning being employed is then seen as an enthymematic deduction on the covering-law model.

Put schematically, the suggestion is that particular judgements are inferred from appropriate evidence, reported by *evidential premises*, in the presence of usually suppressed premises of greater degrees of generality, *background premises*, one or some of which are about the kinds of things in question, and one or some of which are general standing premises about the world. This form of reasoning is deductive: the conjunction of evidential and background premises entails the judgement.

Empirical judgements are of course defeasible. This appears to conflict with the claim that inferences to them are deductive in form. The answer is that, first, background premises have to include clauses about normal conditions (*ceteris paribus* clauses), and second, evidential premises are only as good as the evidence they report—and the usual finitary constraints apply. So we can be wrong in our judgements, and often enough are. ('Being wrong' is a defeasible matter too.) But equally, we can measure the degree of confidence to be placed in a judgement by taking into account the relevant defeating possibilities inherent in the evidence that evidential premises report, and the stability of the normal conditions required by background premises. This is how the view retains what is persuasive about conceptions of probability: to assign a probability is to offer a measure of confidence in the light of the possibility that defeaters operate. Note, though, the highly significant corollary: that the view solves the problem of induction by obviating it.

Light is cast on the idea of an inferential scheme by recalling Aristotelian classification. There is only heuristic value in noting the connection because Aristotelian classification by genus and species is too neat even where it is most plausible, namely, in biology; and anyway discussion of it is too often distracted into discussion of definition, in which guise it invites too many objections. Some are tellingly summarised by Locke (1690): not every term can be precisely explained by two other terms giving genus and differentia; and some words cannot be lexically defined, on pain among other things of regress and failure to constrain their meanings by reference to extralinguistic considerations. Nevertheless it has some suggestive features (made yet clearer in later logic: see the Kneales (1962) on medieval theories of assumption, topics, and place propositions). A notable example is the close resemblance between the Tree of Porphyry and the inferential structure required by the game of Twenty Questions, in which skilled questioners can home in on an individual thing in fewer than twenty steps, exploiting the classificatory conventions that govern our picture of the world, and the cognitive strategies that they imply as relevant to identification of its constituents. What is captured by consideration of the Tree of Porphyry and the Twenty Questions game is the way reasoning and judging about matters of fact proceed according to the deductive inferential structure outlined: premises of greater generality are conjoined with premises of lesser generality, including particular ones, in any number of steps within practical constraints, to yield, in a highly reliable way even in the face of defeasibility considerations, judgements about matters of fact.

5

These thoughts are of course merely schematic, and do no more than indicate the direction a research programme might follow. But its implications are clear. It meets the central request of epistemology—the request for an account of justification—by explaining how the background conceptual framework provides it. Justification proceeds from reports of relevant evidence in a given case to invocation of the background assumptions constituting the scheme. 'This', we would say to a persistent sceptic who began by challenging some particular empirical claim and who had not been satisfied by demonstration that normal defeaters did not apply in the case, 'is how (we think) the world is.' The sceptic might (and indeed should) thereupon raise his sights to the question of the scheme itself, and enquire what our justification is for employing it; but that is a different and further matter. (There are those, among them Carnap and Wittgenstein in their different ways, who take it that such higher-level sceptical challenges are contentless.) In this form, the problem posed by the sceptical challenge is the problem of relativism.

Solving the problem of justification in epistemology was traditionally taken to be best done by defeating the defeaters that familiar sceptical arguments opposed to knowledge claims. The failure of efforts to do this on a blow-by-blow basis suggests that the better tack is to offer a positive theory of justification, one that shows how justification is secured. In the spirit of satisfying the *endoxa*, as Aristotle required, such a theory that respects the ordinary everyday experience of epistemic success obviously has major advantages. The idea mooted here does just this. It postulates ultimate justification by reference to the assumptions of the background scheme, serving as foundational premises from which, together with other premises, judgements of lesser generality are deduced. The theory is conditional upon there being an answer to the higher-order question of the justification we have for accepting the scheme itself, of course, which is a task for another place; but it can be said that something like a transcendental deduction of the scheme's assumptions, together with an argument that any alternative scheme can only be a variant of this one (the modality of 'can' is seriously intended), would fully meet such higher-order scepticism.[12]

---

[12] I offer just such an argument in (1985). See esp. ch. 4.

Much else might be said about the strategy outlined here, but I shall mention just one consideration. In earlier debates about empirical knowledge—for a highly illustrative if not indeed classic instance, the debate between Austin and Ayer about perceptual judgements—it was pointed out that judging matters of fact does not take the form of inferences from conjunctions of evidential and background premises (thus Austin: 'when I see a pig I do not say: it smells like a pig and looks like a pig, therefore it is a pig; I just say, lo! a pig').[13] Judgements, most particularly perceptual ones, are standardly immediate, consisting in the exercise of well-rehearsed, experience-based recognitional capacities. Now, as a description of the phenomenology of making an empirical judgement, this is obviously correct; but the Austinian criticism involves a confusion of psychological and logical facts about the structure of judgement making. It is true that as a matter of psychological fact a judger does not usually go step by step through a process of inference; but if challenged to justify his judgement he would have to state his grounds and, if further pressed, the background assumptions that license them as grounds. In the full story of what went into the making of the judgement, the work done by the conceptual framework would be transparent, enabling us to track the inferential route to the judgement itself.

6

The central claim here is that the problem of justification can be redescribed as the problem of epistemic finitude, so that by marking how epistemic finitude is successfully overcome in everyday epistemic practice, and asking what is required to explain this happy fact, we can hypothesise the possession and employment of a realistic conceptual scheme which serves as a framework that makes experience coherent, by serving as a framework of inference, deductive in form, in which the general assumptions underwrite workaday epistemic judgements. We thereby also see where the principal philosophical task in this region of debate lies: namely, in justifying the scheme itself, which comes to the same thing as refuting scepticism in its most interesting and substantial form, namely, relativism. But to repeat, this is a different problem, which only comes properly into focus when epistemology's traditional problem of justification has been resolved: and in the end it is the more important of the two.[14]

---

[13] Austin (1962: 104–7, 112–19, ch. XI *passim*); Ayer (1967 *passim*).

[14] Once again it is important to stress that the kind of relativism here connoted is cognitive relativism, not cultural relativism (see footnote 7). On Davidsonian lines one might recall that the latter unexceptionable kind of relativism is only possible on condition of the falsity of the former; for if cognitive relativism were true, there would be cases where we could not even recognise another conceptual scheme's existence, and a fortiori could not grasp, still less appreciate, its different practices and values.

REFERENCES

Austin, J. L. (1962). *Sense and Sensibilia*. Oxford: Clarendon Press.

Ayer, A. J. (1954). *Philosophical Essays*. London: Macmillan.

—— (1967). 'Has Austin Refuted the Sense-Datum Theory?' *Synthese*, 18: 117–40.

—— (1973). *The Central Questions of Philosophy*. London: Weidenfeld & Nicolson.

Descartes, R. (1641). *Meditations on First Philosophy*.

Grayling, A. C. (1985). *The Refutation of Scepticism*. London: Duckworth.

—— (1992). 'Epistemology and Realism'. *Proceedings of the Aristotelian Society*, 92: 47–65.

—— (1997). *Introduction to Philosophical Logic* (3rd edn.). Oxford: Blackwell.

—— (2003). 'Scepticism and Justification', in S. Luper (ed.), *The Skeptics: Contemporary Essays*. Aldershot: Ashgate, 29–44.

Kant, I. (1781). *Critique of Pure Reason*.

Kneale, W. and M. (1962). *The Development of Logic*. Oxford: Clarendon Press.

Locke, J. (1690). *An Essay Concerning Human Understanding*.

Russell, B. (1948). *Human Knowledge: Its Scope and Limits*. London: Allen & Unwin.

Strawson, P. F. (1959). *Individuals: An Essay in Descriptive Metaphysics*. London: Methuen.

Wittgenstein, L. (1969). *On Certainty*. Oxford: Blackwell.

11

If You Know, You Can't Be Wrong[*]

Mark Kaplan

I

As I write this, I am looking out on a beautiful little Venetian garden. There are trees, a rosebush, vines, begonias, and a couple of small palms. The sun is shining and traffic on the Grand Canal is occasionally visible through the trees. How do I know any of this, you ask? How do I know, in particular (say), that there is a rosebush in the garden? My answer is that I see it. I know it in the way I know everything else about the world around me. By experience: by seeing, smelling, feeling, hearing, tasting things. In this case, it is by seeing the rosebush that I know it is in the garden.

But there is a line of reasoning to the effect that my answer to your question—my rendering of what it is for me to know the world around me by experience—must be mistaken. The line of reasoning is this. True enough: insofar as I know what is in my Venetian garden, I know it by experience. But my description of the experience via which I know what is in my Venetian garden, 'I see it', cannot be correct. After all, I am sometimes subject to illusions and other sorts of perceptual errors. This being so, it behooves me to admit that, for any seeing of x I have to my credit, I might have had the very same experience yet have failed to have seen x. (Likewise for cases of hearing x, smelling x, tasting x, and so on.) So, in describing my experience as I did—I said 'I see it'—I misdescribed my experience. 'I see it', is true only if the thing in question is there and I am related to it in the manner required for perception to occur. But, given my recent admission, I could be having exactly the same experience even if those conditions were not met. Correctly described, my experience is neutral as to whether I am seeing the items I claim to know to be in my garden or not.

But (or so this line of reasoning continues) this gives rise to a skeptical problem. Once I have admitted that all my experience is neutral as to whether or not I am

* I have benefited enormously from conversation and (in some cases) correspondence with the following four people, none of whom should be (or, I expect, would care to be) held responsible for what has resulted: Adam Leite, John McDowell, Charles Travis, and Joan Weiner.

seeing what I take myself to be seeing, I have admitted that it is entirely compatible with my having the experience I have when I take myself to be seeing x, that I am mistaken. That is, even as I explain to you how I know that my Venetian garden contains a rosebush, by appeal to my (now) seeing-a-rosebush-neutral experience, I must allow that I could be mistaken and not be seeing a rosebush at all, that there could, in fact, be no rosebush in the garden at all. But this I cannot coherently do. Once I have made this latter concession that I could be wrong about there being a rosebush in the garden I can no longer claim to know that there is a rosebush in the garden. I cannot say, 'I know, but I may be wrong.'[1]

The disjunctivist view of experience is tailor-made to block this line of reasoning. For the disjunctivist view denies that the phenomena of illusion and perceptual error force me to admit that, for any seeing of x I have to my credit, I could have had the very same experience yet have failed to have seen x. The disjunctivist maintains that the fact that an experience constitutes a seeing of x is part of what makes it the experience it is. It wouldn't be the same experience were it not a seeing of x. It is true (as the phenomena of illusion and perceptual error show) that there are circumstances in which I fail to discriminate between a case of seeing x and a case which is not a seeing of x. But all that means is that there are circumstances in which I fail to detect which sort of experience I am having: one that is a seeing of x or one that is not. And that I sometimes make such mistakes does not in any way force me to think of experiences as things that are to be individuated without regard to whether they are seeings or not, any more than the fact that I sometimes mistake a Bellini for a Carpaccio forces me to think of paintings as things that are to be individuated without regard to who painted them.[2]

---

[1] It is important to notice that this argument is not meant to show that I don't know that there is a rosebush in the garden. It is only meant to force me to concede that *I have no business claiming to know* that there is a rosebush in the garden. There are plenty of conceptions of knowledge (Robert Nozick's tracking conception (1981: 167–247), to pick one particularly well-known example) on which my making this concession is (provided I continue to believe there is a rosebush in the garden) entirely compatible with its being true that I know that there is a rosebush in the garden.

Why, then, does the argument have any interest? Because the thought that (say) Nozick makes available to me, the thought that, the argument notwithstanding, I may well know that there is a rosebush in the garden, is not of itself much of a comfort. I want to claim (as I have, indeed, claimed) that I *do know* that there is a rosebush in the garden. And it is precisely my entitlement to make that claim that the argument means to attack.

My wanting to claim that I know this particular thing is not in any way eccentric. After all, none of us is particularly concerned with the question, 'Do I have knowledge?' We are concerned with the question, 'What do I know and what don't I know?' We want to treat (we think we ought to treat) the things we know differently, in our inquiries and decision making, from the way we treat the things we don't know. (See Kaplan (2006) for an account of how we treat differently the propositions we regard ourselves as knowing from the way we treat those we regard ourselves as not knowing.) To do that, we need to be able to distinguish what we know from what we don't. So, any argument that would have us conclude that we cannot do this, because we cannot legitimately claim to know much of anything, is (at least to that extent) an argument of interest.

[2] See Snowdon (2005) for expression of a version of disjunctivism much like this. One can also find there references to the disjunctivist literature, and a brief guide to the distinct doctrines which bear the disjunctivist label.

It seems to me that the disjunctivist response to this version of the argument from illusion is fine as far as it goes. That is, it seems to me that there is no good reason to resist the disjunctivist way of individuating experiences. (Indeed, if some of the advocates of disjunctivism are right, the case for disjunctivism is much stronger than this: the conception of experience that the disjunctivist's would supplant is problematic in other ways, if not simply incoherent.)[3] And, on the disjunctivist way of individuating experiences, the argument simply does not go through.

All the same, it seems to me that the disjunctivist response does not go all that far. For it is easy to see how one can recast this argument from illusion without appealing to the way of individuating experiences that the disjunctivist contests.

Suppose that we agree to individuate experiences as the disjunctivist would have us do. It would still seem that I have to admit that, for any circumstance in which I credit myself with a seeing of x (the one under discussion included), there is another imaginable circumstance, indistinguishable by me from the first, in which I likewise credit myself with a seeing of x, but have failed to see x. After all, the cases in which I have been taken in by illusions, the cases in which I have been guilty of perceptual error, are cases in which some such imaginable circumstance has, in fact, obtained. But once I admit this much (the argument will continue), I have admitted that, in many (if not all) of the cases in which I take myself to be seeing x, I could be mistaken. That is, even as I place before you my explanation of how I know that my Venetian garden contains a rosebush—my original (and by disjunctivist lights, perfectly appropriate) explanation was: 'I see it'—I must allow that I could be mistaken that there is a rosebush in the garden. But this I cannot coherently do. Once I have conceded that I could be wrong about there being a rosebush in the garden, I can no longer claim to know that there's a rosebush in the garden. I cannot say, 'I know, but I could be wrong.'[4]

And once one sees that what lies at the heart of the skeptical challenge is not a thesis about the proper way of individuating experiences, once one sees that the argument from illusion is easily stated without any appeal to the nature of experiences, one sees that the argument is available for deployment against far more

---

[3] See, e.g., McDowell (1994) and Travis (2004).

[4] It might be thought that I have the following reply available: 'I hate to repeat myself, but, as I already said, by way of explaining how I know there is a rosebush in the garden, I do see it. And if I see it I *can't* be wrong. So I have no reason to withdraw my claim to know that there is a rosebush in the garden.' But this reply is not available. My saying I see it, my being supremely confident that I am seeing it, my stamping my foot as I say I see it, none of that makes it the case that I actually do see it. After all, there have been circumstances in which, with respect to an object, I have been every bit as confident that I was seeing that object as I am now that I am seeing the rosebush, every bit as convinced as I am now that the set up was favorable for seeing the object as I am now that the set up is favorable for seeing the rosebush, yet I was mistaken: no such object of the sort I thought I was seeing was actually there. Indeed, there are imaginable circumstances, indistinguishable by me from this one, in which I would be claiming to see a rosebush, every bit as confident of that claim as I am now, yet there is no rosebush in the garden. This much conceded (or so the argument will proceed), it is hard to see how I can deny that I could be wrong that I am seeing a rosebush, wrong that there is a rosebush there to be seen. But this much conceded, how can I continue to claim to know one is there?

than just claims to perceptual knowledge. It is available equally for deployment against claims to knowledge by non-deductive inference, to cases in which I explain how I know something by appeal to evidence that does not necessitate the truth of the thing I am claiming to know.

These cases are legion. I know I will still be in Venice tomorrow. How do I know? I've made an appointment to see someone tomorrow at 4:00 pm. I know that my wife is right now at a language class. How do I know? She told me that this is where she would be. I know that George Bush is president of the United States. How do I know? I read about his doings in today's paper, and I've since heard no news of his resignation or demise. In each of these cases, I explain how I know the thing in question by appeal to something whose truth is compatible with the false-hood of my claim to knowledge. Indeed, it has sometimes happened in cases just like these that the thing to which I have appealed has been true while the proposi-tion I have claimed to know has been false. So (the argument will go) in each of these cases, I must admit, even as I explain how I know the proposition in ques-tion, even as I assert the truth of the proposition(s) to which I appeal to explain how I know the proposition in question, I could be mistaken: the proposition I claim to know might be false. But (again) this is something I cannot coherently do. Once I have conceded that I could be mistaken, I can no longer claim to know the proposition I claimed to know. I cannot say, 'I know, but I could be wrong.'

My claim that the disjunctivist response to (what I will henceforth refer to simply as) the argument from illusion does not go far enough comes, then, to this. The anxiety the argument from illusion expresses is an anxiety about the possibility of our sustaining our claims to knowledge in the face of the fallibility of those claims. It is an anxiety born of the following two thoughts: (i) there are few (if any) circumstances in which we claim knowledge, yet cannot imagine how that claim to knowledge could be in error and the proposition we are claiming to know false (indeed we are sometimes victims of error in circumstances in which we think our knowledge claims very secure); yet (ii) we cannot in any circumstance coherently say, of some proposition P, 'I know that P but I could be wrong.' The crux of the argument from illusion is that these two thoughts jointly mean that there are few (if any) circumstances in which we can legitimately claim to know propositions about the world around us. And, for all the good work done by the disjunctivist response to the original argument from illusion,[5] this last allegation is one that the disjunctivist response simply does not touch.

What I want to do in the remainder of this essay is address (what I have iden-tified as) the real anxiety of which the argument from illusion is born. I want to explain how we can credit the two thoughts rehearsed above, yet still regard ourselves as knowing the things we ordinarily take ourselves to know: what it is we see, where we will be tomorrow, where our loved ones are right now, who

[5] And it would certainly be unjust to criticize disjunctivism on the grounds that, while it provides a perfectly good response to one skeptical argument, it does not provide a perfectly good response to *all* skeptical arguments.

is president of the United States. I take only partial credit for what follows. In my view, the essential outline of how to think about these matters correctly was provided almost sixty years ago in the pages of J. L. Austin's essay, 'Other Minds'.[6] There is some filling in required, which I mean to supply. But if what follows carries conviction, the credit will redound mostly to Austin, not to me.

In laying out, and filling in a bit, Austin's way of thinking about these matters, I mean not only to be explaining how Austin thought about these matters, but also to be following Austin's method of approaching epistemology. Austin was, of course, the leading exponent of the 'ordinary language philosophy' movement that dominated Anglo-American philosophy for a significant part of the middle of the last century. His view was that the way to test a philosophical argument about the nature and extent of, say, knowledge, was to assess how faithful that argument is to our ordinary practices: to the things we ordinarily say and do (and are happy to say and do). So I want to begin by testing the argument from illusion, and its variant stable mates, in this Austinian way.

Let me emphasize that I do not mean here to follow Austin blindly. There would be little point in that. I am fully aware that many, if not most, of the readers of this essay will be coming to it with grave misgivings as to the propriety of Austin's approach to epistemology. One of my major burdens (taken up in Section III) will be to say why these misgivings are misplaced. My conviction is that the way forward in epistemology is to go back and learn properly some of the lessons that Austin was trying to teach us.

II

Austin's thoughts on the matter at hand are neatly encapsulated in the following passage:

'When you know you can't be wrong' is perfectly good sense. You are prohibited from saying 'I know it is so, but I may be wrong', just as you are prohibited from saying 'I promise I will, but I may fail'. If you are aware you may be mistaken, you ought not say you know, just as, if you are aware you may break your word, you have no business to promise. But of course, being aware that you may be mistaken doesn't mean merely being aware that you are a fallible human being: it means that you have some concrete reason to suppose that you may be mistaken in this case. Just as 'but I may fail' does not mean merely 'but I am a weak human being' (in which case it would be no more exciting than adding 'D.V.'): it means that there is some concrete reason for me to suppose that I shall break my word. It is naturally always possible ('humanly' possible) that I may be mistaken or may break my word, but that by itself is no bar against using the expressions 'I know' and 'I promise' as we do in fact use them. (98)

---

[6] In Austin (1979: 76–116). All parenthetical page numbers in the text refer to pages in Austin (1979).

Austin may appear to be getting off to a shaky start. His reason for thinking that 'If you know you can't be wrong' makes perfectly good sense appears to be just this: you may not say, 'I know it is so but I may be wrong.' It is, of itself, an unconvincing reason. You are also prohibited from saying, 'I believe it is so, but it isn't.' But that is no reason whatsoever to think that if you believe that P then P is true. Indeed, the analogy Austin draws between 'I know but I may be wrong,' and 'I promise I will, but I may fail,' only serves to highlight the difficulty. The fact that you may not say, 'I promise I will, but I may fail,' provides no reason whatsoever to think that you can never promise to do something in circumstances in which, in fact, it is true you may fail—less still to think that you never fail to do what you've promised. And, as we know full well, sometimes you do fail to do what you've promised.[7]

Also Austin is less than forthcoming as to what exactly is the connection between 'I know that P' and 'I may be wrong that P.' That he thinks that you shouldn't say both is clear. But *why* shouldn't you? Is it because, to say 'but I might be wrong' after saying 'I know' would deprive the latter of its illocutionary force? Austin held (99–101) that when I say 'I know,' I invite you to take my word for it. Or is it because it's simply not true that you know so long as it is true that you might be wrong? Or, might there be some other reason?

Fortunately, Austin's lapses here are of no dialectical importance. The argument from illusion and its stable mates assume that once I have conceded that I might be wrong that P, I cannot properly claim to know that P. Austin does not wish to contest that assumption. Exactly *why* he does not wish to contest it is, thus, of small moment. Moreover, it is worth noting that the impermissibility of my saying, 'I know but I may be wrong,' is, in fact, *not* a matter of my not being able properly to say of myself something that someone else may well properly be able to say of me (as is the case with, 'I believe that P, but P is false,' and 'I promise to do X, but I may fail to do it'). *No one* can properly say of me that I know that P, but I might be wrong.

What *is* important is why Austin thinks that this assumption that he does not wish to contest, that once you concede that you might be wrong, you cannot properly claim to know, hasn't the skeptical consequence that the argument from illusion and its mates would have us think it has. It is because (he maintains) the contrary thought rests on a mistake: the mistake of thinking that, when we agree that, once I have conceded that I might be wrong that P I cannot legitimately claim to know that P, we mean by 'I might be wrong' something whose truth can be established simply by noting that I am humanly fallible.

Austin offers us a very clear reason for thinking it is, indeed, a mistake. Here the analogy he draws with, 'I promise I will, but I may fail,' *is* helpful. I ought not promise if I am aware that I may fail to fulfill the promise. But if all it took, to be aware that I may fail, is that I be aware that I am human, and so endowed with

---

[7] And Austin's response to the charge that there is this disanalogy, a charge he anticipated in 'Other Minds' (101–3), is (at least to my mind) less than satisfactory.

the weaknesses humans have, then the question as to whether I may fail (and so should not make the promise) would never be at all exciting. But it *is* sometimes exciting. One considers carefully whether one may fail before one promises; it is sometimes a difficult matter to decide, a matter over which, in cases in which important things are at stake, one may even agonize. If the mere fact that I am a human (and so have the weaknesses inherent in being human) settled the matter, there would be no difficulty: it would be clear in every case that I may fail. No one would ever, because no one in good conscience *could* ever, promise to do anything, and no promise would ever be accepted. The fact that I find the matter of whether I may fail not always clear—the fact that, fully aware of our human fallibility, we do in good conscience make and accept promises—shows that, in agreeing that I shouldn't promise if I am aware that I may fail, we do not mean by 'I may fail' something whose truth can be established by the mere fact that I have the weaknesses inherent in being human.

The point carries over to the impermissibility of saying that I know once I have conceded that I may be wrong. Were it the case that, in holding it impermissible, we meant by 'I may be wrong' something whose truth can be established simply by noting that I am humanly fallible, the question as to whether I may be wrong would never be exciting. But it *is* sometimes exciting. It can be difficult and even, in cases in which important things are at stake, agonizing to decide whether I may be wrong that P, and so cannot claim to know (as perhaps I did) that P. If the fact that I am humanly fallible were sufficient to decide the matter, there would never be a difficulty: there is no question but that I am humanly fallible. Nor would there be any question as to whether, when (for example) asked breathlessly on the street if I know where the nearest hospital is, I can answer in the affirmative. The obvious answer would be that, of course, I cannot. How could I possibly know where the nearest hospital is when I am a fallible human being and so might be wrong? The fact that this seems an outrageous way to think about the matter—the fact that we comfortably make and accept claims to knowledge, even as we recognize that we are all humanly fallible—would seem to show that, in admitting that I cannot legitimately claim to know once I have conceded that I may be wrong, we do not mean by 'I may be wrong' something whose truth can be established simply by noting that I am humanly fallible.

What more does it take? Austin's answer is that it requires 'a concrete reason to suppose that [I] may be mistaken in this case'. But what exactly is a concrete reason? In particular, what is it about the fact that I am a fallible human being that keeps it from being a concrete reason for thinking I may be mistaken in this case?

Austin never explicitly says. But I think it is possible to see, from what he does explicitly say about knowledge attribution in ordinary life, how he could answer these questions. Let us change venue (from Venice to somewhere in England) and target (from knowledge of flora to knowledge of fauna). I look out the window and say, 'You'll never guess what I am looking at in the garden: a goldfinch!' It is legitimate for you to ask me, 'How do you know it's a goldfinch?' Why is it legitimate? Because claiming to know carries with it a certain justificatory obligation. As Austin puts it,

> Whenever I say I know, I am always liable to be taken to claim that, in a certain sense appropriate to the kind of statement (and to present intents and purposes), I am able to *prove* it. In the present, very common, type of case, 'proving' seems to mean stating what are the features of the current case which are enough to constitute it one which is correctly describable in the way we have described it, and not in any other way relevantly variant. Generally speaking, cases where I can 'prove' are cases where we use the 'because' formula: cases where we 'know but can't prove' are cases in which we take refuge in the 'from' or 'by' formula. (85–6)

Now, it may at first appear that, in the last sentence, about cases in which we 'know but can't prove', Austin is taking back what he says in the first sentence. But I think this worry is easily addressed. Think of being able to prove that I know a statement as being able to offer an adequate answer to the question, 'How do you know it?' Austin is simply reminding us that, in ordinary life, saying how one knows a proposition does not always require very much. To 'How do you know it's a Pakistani rug?' it might do to say 'By the way it feels,' or 'From its feel' (see 84–5). In some cases (like 'How do you know this is a theorem?'), 'It's just obvious' may do. (And that won't look very much like what one ordinarily thinks of as a proof: it won't have clear premises.)[8] Context influences what needs saying, what constitutes saying enough to say how one knows.

So, suppose my answer to your, 'How do you know it's a goldfinch?' is, 'From its red head.' It may be entirely legitimate for you to say that I haven't done enough, that this doesn't prove it's a goldfinch. It may be entirely legitimate to say 'To be a goldfinch, besides having a red head it must also have the characteristic eye-markings': or 'How do you know it isn't a woodpecker? Woodpeckers have red heads too.' (84)

But, while here you can legitimately claim I haven't done enough, there are limits to how much you can legitimately demand that I do before you will count it as enough.

> Enough is enough: it doesn't mean everything. Enough means enough to show that (within reason, and for the present intents and purposes) it 'can't' be anything else, there is no room for an alternative, competing, description of it. It does not mean, for example, enough to show it isn't a *stuffed* goldfinch. (84)

That is not to say that it is *never* in order to demand that a person do enough to show it isn't a stuffed goldfinch. We can surely imagine circumstances (we are in an aviary that has both stuffed birds and live ones) in which that demand would be very much in order. But Austin's thought is that we have an idea (rough to be sure) of what is normally enough to establish the propriety of a knowledge claim of a particular sort

---

[8] This worry about calling something a proof that doesn't have premises harkens back, I think, to Moore.

(where both the content of the claim and the circumstances in which it is made contribute to determining that the claim is of that sort). And, doing enough never requires doing everything one could imagine doing. Indeed, only in special cases, cases in which there is a special reason to suppose something is amiss, can we legitimately demand that more be done than normally counts as enough. As Austin puts it (writing now about claims to knowledge of other minds): 'These special cases where doubts arise and require resolving, are contrasted with the normal cases which hold the field unless there is some special suggestion that deceit &c., is involved.' (113)

This last, I think, pins down Austin's view. A person may not legitimately claim to know that P unless she can prove (within reason and for present intents and purposes) that P. What this requires is that she be able to meet every legitimate challenge to her claim to know that P. Context influences what counts as a legitimate challenge. But this much of a general sort can be said. Even though we recognize that, if Q is true, the person does not know that P, it may yet not be legitimate (before we will credit her claim to know that P) to demand that she be able to explain how she knows that Q is not true. (Hence Austin's goldfinch example. In order to know it is a goldfinch in the tree, I don't need to be able to prove it's not a stuffed goldfinch. This despite the fact that we all recognize that, if the bird really *is* stuffed, then I do not know it's a goldfinch.) That is to say, we are prepared to make and grant knowledge claims even as we recognize that not everything that could conceivably have been done to prove the claim true *has* been done.

We have rough standards (standards that define what Austin calls the 'normal cases') for what it takes to sustain a claim to knowledge of a certain sort (where, again, both content and context decide what sort it is) and, provided those standards are met, we are prepared to credit the claim. It is not legitimate to demand that more be done unless there is some special reason to suppose that something is amiss. And what makes a reason special? At least this much is required: that it *not* be a reason of whose presence we are perfectly well aware as we happily, perfectly appropriately, and without fuss, make and grant claims to knowledge of the sort currently being made and/or evaluated.

This much said, it is clear why my being a fallible human being does not count as a concrete reason to suspect that I am mistaken in the case in which I claim to see the rosebush in my little Venetian garden. We make and credit knowledge claims of this sort, and do so happily and appropriately, all the while aware that the claimants are fallible human beings. We would consider the challenge, 'How do you know it is a rosebush? After all, you are a fallible human being and so could be wrong!' perfectly outrageous. We would consider it just as outrageous as we would my saying, to someone in apparent need, that I do not know where the nearest hospital is—where my saying so is born solely of the thought that I am a fallible human being, and so could be wrong that the hospital is but three blocks away, on the corner of Rogers and 1st.

So, I can admit my human fallibility, admit that it is humanly possible that I am mistaken in this case, without having to admit that I may, therefore, be wrong that there is a rosebush in the garden, and so cannot claim to know it at all. When it comes to deciding whether I might be wrong, for the purposes of deciding whether I know a given claim, the mere fact that I am humanly fallible simply does not settle the matter. Absent any legitimate reason to suppose that I have failed to do what ordinarily counts as enough to prove that I know what I claim to, it would take a special reason to suppose I am mistaken in this case to make it appropriate to say that I might be wrong. And the mere fact that I am humanly fallible is not such a reason.

III

I know that the foregoing is going to strike many readers as less than satisfying. I know this because I know that many philosophers are singularly unmoved by exercises in ordinary language philosophy, as the exercise above is. What I want to do is try to express why it is I think so many philosophers will find the foregoing wanting, and try to say why I think their misgivings are ill-placed.

Objection. The foregoing is unsatisfying because it simply assumes the propriety of our ordinary practice of knowledge attribution; it does nothing to say why one should think that the practice is actually worthy of our endorsement.

Response. True, nothing has been said here that provides any reason to suppose our ordinary practices are worthy of our endorsement. But, then, that is not the burden of the exercise. The argument from illusion is meant to convince us that there is something deeply problematic about our ordinary practices, the practices we endorse. It is meant to convince us that perfectly mundane facts, the admission of which our ordinary practices require of us (the admission that we are humanly fallible, the admission that if we know we cannot be wrong), require us to draw conclusions that, if true, undermine our ordinary practice's pretension to propriety. Austin has undertaken to show that the argument does not succeed, that, properly understood, the mundane facts which we must admit do nothing to undermine the propriety of the ordinary practices to which we are committed. Insofar as Austin is successful in this, he has met the only challenge the argument from illusion and its stable mates have thrown our way.

Objection. To follow Austin's method of dealing with the argument from illusion and its mates requires us to take a completely uncritical attitude towards our ordinary practices, an attitude that we do not want to take.

Response. This is simply untrue. Austin's very description of our ordinary practice of knowledge attribution highlights the extent to which making a claim to knowledge obliges the claimant to be able to meet legitimate criticism. It is entirely compatible with our ordinary practice (and, in fact, true of the history of that practice) that commonly accepted standards for proving that one knows a certain sort of claim be abandoned in the light of criticism; that challenges once thought illegitimate become recognized as legitimate, in the light of criticism.

To be sure: we don't want to take an uncritical attitude towards our practices. But there is nothing in Austin that asks, or requires, us to do so.

Objection. The responses to the two objections are themselves unsatisfying. To follow Austin, as I have construed his doctrine, is to admit that our standards of knowledge allow us to make knowledge claims even when it is possible (if only humanly possible) that we are mistaken. Such an admission itself undermines our practice's claim to propriety. For what it reveals is that there is available a much higher standard for knowledge than those we ordinarily employ, a standard on which knowledge is incompatible with even the human possibility of error. And it reveals that our ordinary standards serve as very poor substitutes for that higher standard, indeed, that, our ordinary standards don't really deserve to be regarded as standards for knowledge at all. That is to say: Austin's response to the argument from illusion manages, in the end, to issue the very concession that this argument was meant to elicit.

Response. Here an example due to Paul Edwards (1949: 145–6) will be helpful. I embellish it after my own fashion. A man comes into the room in an obvious state of outrage and tells you that: there is a village in Africa in which there has been an outbreak of a deadly hemorrhagic fever; that it has been over a week that this outbreak has been known of; that, nonetheless, there is not a single doctor within two hundred miles of the outbreak's center. Just as you are pulling out your check book, ready to make out a check to Doctors Without Borders, and looking for someplace where you can phone them and demand action, he continues, 'Imagine that! Not a single doctor, not a single person capable of diagnosing and curing any disease in under thirty minutes.' At that point your alarm disappears, your checkbook goes back in your bag. You realize that the man's news, alarming on the assumption that he meant by 'doctor' what you do, what we all do, is not alarming at all. It is completely compatible with his report that the unfortunate village is receiving the best medical care in the world.

As I have made it out, Austin's response to the argument from illusion is to point out that the argument generates its alarm by exploiting exactly the same device as this man in my story does, and that the alarm is every bit as much a false alarm. Just as the man in my story generates alarm by using 'doctor' in a peculiar way that is very much at odds with how we use it, so the argument from illusion generates the alarm it manages to generate by using 'I could be wrong' in a peculiar way very much at odds with the way we use it when thinking about what we do and do not know.

In both cases, the alarmist (the outraged man in one case, the purveyor of the argument from illusion in the other) forces us to confront, even as we come to recognize the false alarm for what it is, the fact that our use of the expressions which the alarmists have misused is in some ways deeply unhappy. Anyone who has a loved one who is seriously ill will feel very poignantly the thought of how wonderful it would be if we didn't have to settle for doctors as we use 'doctor', how wonderful it would be if we had, for our loved one, someone who could diagnose and cure his/her ailment in under thirty minutes. Likewise, we can all feel how wonderful it would be if we could know, in a sense of 'know' that is incompatible with human fallibility, the answers to some of the important questions which keep us up at night.

Yet the realization that we could reserve the term 'doctor' for someone able to diagnose and cure any disease in under a half an hour—the realization of how inadequate what we call 'doctors' are in comparison to a person who meets this more stringent qualification—in no way makes us feel that our ordinary use of 'doctor' is deficient. Even less does it make us feel that, when we are ill, we should settle for no care less accomplished than that supplied by someone who meets the more stringent qualifications.

I cannot see why we are supposed to react any differently when it is a peculiar use of 'know' or 'I could be wrong' that is responsible for the false alarm. Yes, the argument from illusion may cause us to reflect (if we hadn't had occasion to do so before) on the fact that we could reserve the word 'know' for something incompatible with human fallibility. Yes, the argument may cause us to reflect on how second-rate what we ordinarily call knowledge is in comparison to something that meets this higher standard. But I don't see why this should make us feel that our ordinary uses of 'know' and 'I might be wrong' are deficient. Still less, do I see why it should make us feel that we should abandon our ordinary practice of knowledge attribution, why, for example, I should tell a person in apparent need that I don't know where the nearest hospital is, when, by our standards, I know it perfectly well.

Objection. This response, and indeed Austin's whole approach to the argument from illusion as portrayed here, makes a fundamental mistake. Let's grant that, in ordinary life, we use 'know' and 'I might be wrong' exactly as Austin has said we do. Let's grant that it is entirely appropriate that we use these expressions this way in ordinary life, that our commitment to the practice of knowledge attribution Austin describes is eminently proper. It is entirely compatible with all we have thus granted that we *still* know much less than we ordinarily credit ourselves with knowing, and for precisely the reason given by the argument from illusion and its stable mates. This is because it is one thing to describe the conditions under which it is *appropriate in ordinary life* to say that a person knows that P. It is another to describe the conditions under which it is *true* to say that a person knows that P. That is to say, it is entirely compatible with Austin's account of when it is in ordinary life appropriate to say that a person knows that P that the truth conditions for knowledge attributions are rather different, and, indeed, more stringent.

In fact, it is quite explicable why there should be such a divergence between what it is appropriate to say, and what it is true to say, in these matters. Our ordinary practice of knowledge attribution, as some of the very examples to which I have adverted illustrate, is shaped by practical exigency. After all, suppose that we didn't have to worry about the health of the person on whose behalf (we can suppose) I am being asked whether I know where the nearest hospital is. Would my imagined response—I say I don't know, thinking that my human fallibility

makes that the only correct response—seem anywhere near so outrageous? Surely
not. But this suggests that it is, at least partly, a concern about the prudential consequences of behaving as we imagine I do, not simply about whether or not I
would be speaking truly in so behaving, that is weighing with us as we decide what
it is appropriate for me to say in the case.

If we are concerned, which as philosophers we must be, with what it is *true* to
say in the case—if we are concerned with what it is true to say about the extent and
nature of our knowledge—we must set aside the exigencies of ordinary life that so
influence what it is appropriate to say. We must consider the matter from a
detached perspective. But when one appreciates that this is the nature of our
charge as philosophers of knowledge, it is hard to see how Austin's characterizations of ordinary practice, and my defense of their propriety, can have any probat-
ive weight. What is at issue here is not what it is ordinarily appropriate for me to
say as I look out the window onto my Venetian garden. The purveyor of the argument from illusion is happy to grant that I have done nothing inappropriate in
saying that I know there is a rosebush in the garden. He is happy to concede that
the fact that I am humanly fallible in no way renders inappropriate my using
'know' in this way. What is at issue is whether, in saying that I know there is a rosebush in my garden, I have said something *true*. And the point of the argument
from illusion is to show that, however appropriate it is for me to say that I know
there is a rosebush in the garden in the ordinary circumstances we have been
imagining obtain, what I thereby say is *not* true, and it is not true precisely because
I am humanly fallible and so I could be wrong.[9]

Response. This much must surely be granted: the distinction between what it is
appropriate in ordinary circumstances to say, and what it is true to say, is a real
one. Sometimes (for example) kindness or politeness render it appropriate to say
things that are false, and that we know to be false as we are saying them. This
includes cases of knowledge attribution, as when we say to a friend who does not
know (as we do) that she is in the final stage of a terminal illness, 'Oh I know that
you will be up and about before long!' But then it is part of ordinary practice to
recognize these cases for what they are.

What the purveyors of the argument from illusion mean to be getting us to
recognize (on the construal of their intention described in the foregoing objection)
is that there are a great many more cases that are of the same type, cases that
ordinary practice does not so recognize. The argument is meant to get us to recognize that ordinary cases in which we make and credit claims to know—such as the
case in which I claim to know that there is a rosebush in the garden—are really of
a kind with cases in which, out of politeness or kindness, we say things we recognize to be false. The argument is meant to get us to see that it is entirely appropriate
to say what we do. To say such things in such circumstances is to do what is done.

⁹ For an expression of this sort of objection, see Stroud (1984: ch. 2). I discuss Stroud's critique of
Austin at length in Kaplan (2000).

But, for all that, what we therein say is false, and we are in a position (with the help of the argument) to see that it is false.

The trouble is that it is hard to see how, on this line of thought, the argument from illusion is supposed to get us into a position to see that, say, my claim to know that there is a rosebush in the garden is false. After all, the argument is a bad one. It maintains that, so long as I admit that I am humanly fallible with respect to propositions I claim to know via perceptual knowledge, I must admit that I might be wrong that there is a rosebush in the garden and, so, can't properly claim to know one is there. But (as Austin points out) this rests on a mistake: the mistake of thinking that, in agreeing (as we do) that, if I concede I might be wrong that P, then I cannot legitimately claim to know that P, we mean by 'I might be wrong' something whose truth can be established simply by noting that I am humanly fallible with respect to P. If (as is the case according to the line of thought under discussion) the purveyor of the argument from illusion does not dispute any of this, how can he hope to convince us that, all the same, the argument carries conviction? How can he hope to convince us that, contrary to how things look, my human fallibility with respect to propositions I claim to know via perception really *is* sufficient to establish that I might be wrong that there is a rosebush in the garden?

It will not do simply to say that things look as they do to us partly as a cons-equence of the practical exigencies that underwrite what it is ordinarily appropriate to say on matters having to do with knowledge attribution. Even if we grant that our ordinary standards for appropriate knowledge attribution are less stringent for the fact that they are sensitive to practical exigencies,[10] this point does the pur-veyor of the argument from illusion no good until it has been shown that sensitivity to these exigencies does anything to lead our ordinary practice of knowledge attribution into error. After all, one hypothesis about how things work with knowledge (call it the *Austinian hypothesis*) is that it is *in the nature of knowledge* to be sensitive in certain ways to practical exigency. If he is to convince us of the contrary, the purveyor of the argument from illusion needs to do more than say how this hypothesis *could* be false. He has to offer us some reason to suppose it *is*, con-trary to the appearances, false. He has to offer us some evidence that most of what it is ordinarily appropriate to say by way of knowledge attribution is, in fact, false.

The conceit behind the line of criticism under consideration is, of course, that this evidence becomes apparent once one takes the detached perspective a philosopher is supposed to take toward knowledge attribution. But, again, it is hard to see how this can be so.

It certainly cannot be so if taking a detached view simply means opting to ignore the role practical exigency plays in our practice of knowledge attribution. For then, insofar as it is true that our ordinary practice of knowledge attribution is influ-enced by practical exigency, taking a detached view would amount to deliberately

---

[10] It is not obvious to me that we should.

blinding ourselves to the possibility that it may be in the nature of veridical knowledge attribution that it is sensitive in some way or other to practical exigency. Far from revealing evidence that the Austinian hypothesis is false, taking a detached perspective would simply be to dismiss the Austinian hypothesis out of hand.

Suppose, then, that adopting a detached perspective amounts to simply refusing to take for granted the veridicality of our ordinary practice of knowledge attribution. Suppose it simply amounts to adopting a commitment to choose amongst rival theories of knowledge from a perspective that does not presuppose that our ordinary knowledge attributions are true. To adopt this perspective is not to bias the case against the Austinian hypothesis. It is simply to refuse to take it to be the burden of an account of true knowledge attribution that it faithfully capture, i.e., render largely veridical, the knowledge attributions that are appropriate in everyday life.

But, if that is *not* the burden of a theory of true knowledge attribution, what *is* supposed to constrain such a theory? To what does it have to be true? The answer, presumably, is that we have a concept of knowledge and it is fidelity to that concept to which a proper theory of knowledge aspires. But what is supposed to convince us that a given theory really is faithful to our concept of knowledge? We cannot examine the way the theory tallies with what we are ordinarily inclined to say using the word 'know'. For we would then be testing the theory as if it meant simply to codify appropriate ordinary usage, just the sort of test that (according to the line of thought under discussion) is entirely inappropriate to apply to a proper theory of knowledge. We have to look beyond what it is ordinarily appropriate to say.

But where are we supposed to look? The only source of pre-theoretic judgements concerning knowledge any of us *has* is reflection upon what she ordinarily says and does when she engages in inquiry, argument, and criticism. Our practice of inquiry, in contexts both ordinary and disciplinary, is all we have to look to in order to arrive at, and test, our respective conceptions of knowledge. Once we turn our back on the guidance offered us by our ordinary canons of inquiry and criticism, we have no source of pre-theoretic judgement at all.

To be sure, we can direct our attention to *aspects* of our ordinary practice that will offer support for a theory. Indeed, the argument from illusion does just that. We do ordinarily think that one cannot legitimately claim to know that P once one has conceded that one could be wrong. And how could we deny, even in ordinary life, that there is a straightforward reading of 'could be wrong' in which the fact that I am humanly fallible makes it the case that my claim to know that there is a rosebush in the garden could be wrong? It is from these two elements of our ordinary practice that the argument from illusion gets its apparent power to force upon us the conclusion that I really don't know that there is a rosebush in the garden after all.

The trouble is that it is an elementary rule of sound inquiry that one must evaluate the adequacy of a theory, not just on such evidence as one can find in its favor, but on *all* the available evidence. And, as Austin reminds us, when one looks at all the evidence, when, instead of picking just those aspects of our ordinary practice that lend support to the skeptical conclusion, one looks at our ordinary practice in its entirety, one sees that the evidence does not support the skeptical theory that the argument from illusion would have us adopt. One sees that, in agreeing that one cannot legitimately claim to know that P once one has conceded that one might be wrong that P, we cannot plausibly be thought to mean by 'one might be wrong' something whose truth can be established simply by noting that we are humanly fallible. For, if that were what we meant, we would never find the task of determining whether one might have been wrong as exciting as we some-times find it; if that were what we meant, we would never make, and credit, claims to know the world around us that we do make and do credit.

Is it open to the purveyor of the argument from illusion to maintain that these additional bits of evidence, to which Austin draws our attention, are less salient to evaluating the propriety of a theory of knowledge than the ones upon which the argument from illusion rests? One would hope not. For once we grant the pur-veyor of the argument from illusion the freedom to pick and choose what aspects of our ordinary practice are to be considered salient to assessing the propriety of his argument, we have to grant the same freedom to everyone else, including the philosophers who take as salient some of the aspects of our ordinary practice (for example, the aspects to which Austin draws our attention) over which the argu-ment runs roughshod. But then, with everyone free to pick and choose in this way, the enterprise of determining, from a philosopher's detached viewpoint, what we know and by virtue of what we know it, degenerates into a game in which almost every move is legal and each participant plays according to her own fancy.

As his writings make clear, Austin felt that this sort of degeneration is inevitable once epistemology abandons fidelity to what it is appropriate to say and do (cases in which we are speaking out of politeness and such aside) in ordinary life. He recognized that what it is appropriate to say and do in ordinary life is the only thing available for an epistemology to be true to, and he recognized that an epistemological theory (like any other) must be held accountable to *all* the evidence, i.e., to the story of our practice, of what it is appropriate to say and when, in all its richness. This explains why he devoted (why he was *right* to devote) so much effort to describing our ordinary practice and why he attached (and was *right* to attach) such philosophical importance to the result.

Yet, for all that, Austin never claimed that our ordinary practices, the things we ordinarily say and do, constitute the last word on all matters. In 'A Plea for Excuses' (Austin 1979: 173–204), Austin conceded that the way ordinary language arranges matters 'is likely enough to be not the best way of arranging things if our interests are more extensive or intellectual than the ordinary.' (185) His view, he wrote, was that 'ordinary language is *not* the last word: in principle it can everywhere be supplemented and improved upon and superseded. Only remember, it *is* the *first* word.' (185) That is to say that Austin was (rightly) open to the possibility that sophisticated reflection on matters, even sophisticated *philosophical* reflection on matters, might lead us to the conclusion that our ordinary practices needed changing. What he was *not* open to—and hence his admonition that we remember that ordinary language *is* the *first* word—is the idea that our epistemology needn't take on our ordinary practices. What he was not open to is the idea, expressed so clearly in the line of thought under discussion, that our epistemological research might proceed with indifference to how its results tally with ordinary practice.

Austin's requirement that epistemology be faithful to what it is appropriate to say and do in ordinary life, a requirement that, as I have just argued, we can violate only at the cost of undermining the integrity of epistemology, is thus more subtle than one might have thought. It does *not* demand that epistemology bend slavishly to the contours of ordinary practice. What it requires, rather, is that our philosophical assessment of our epistemic condition reflect our ordinary assessment of that condition. Thus, when we find our epistemological inquiries leading us to views at odds with our ordinary practices, we have only two choices. We can either reconsider the path on which those inquiries have led us or change our ordinary practices to conform to our epistemological views. The position favored by the advocates of the line of thought under discussion, a line of thought which would allow us to leave our ordinary practices as they are yet conclude that they are nonetheless unsatisfactory from a philosophical point of view, is unavailable.

Objection. What is clear in the foregoing response is that it offers a very bleak assessment of the prospects for producing a successful skeptical argument, for it will be the very nature of such an argument to urge upon us an account of knowledge on which much of what we ordinarily say, by way of knowledge attribution, is false. And this fact will itself speak in an overwhelming fashion against the propriety of the argument. What is not clear is how one can explain, given this, why anyone has ever taken the classic skeptical arguments to have any power. Yet many have. Indeed, it is predictable that there are readers of this essay who will continue to feel the power of skeptical arguments such as the argument from illusion. Doesn't this suggest that there is something to such arguments, something true in the conception of knowledge that animates them, that the Austinian hypothesis is overlooking?

Response. I think not. It seems to me that there are two things jointly responsible for the sway skeptical argument continues to exert on those who think about philosophical matters. One is the attraction of the conception of knowledge that Descartes so eloquently elaborated in his work. As I have already conceded above, the conception of knowledge at work in ordinary life looks positively second-rate in comparison to the infallibilist one of which Descartes wrote, variations of which skeptical arguments exploit. The second thing is the conviction (a conviction I have just been at pains to dispel) that we might arrive, via respectable investigative means, at the conclusion that something like Descartes's conception of knowledge is actually correct. This conviction rests on the mistaken thought that we can usefully pursue a theory of knowledge that is detached from ordinary practice, a theory of knowledge whose results are not to be evaluated according to what they would have us say and do in ordinary life, because they don't imply anything about what it is appropriate to say and do in ordinary life.

But for all this last thought's being mistaken, it is not *obviously* mistaken. It is the fact that it is not obviously mistaken that is, I think, responsible for the unhappy reception Austin's work in epistemology received in most quarters when it was published and (insofar as it is read anymore) receives to this day.[11] Austin, for all his preoccupation with detailing what is said when, did little to explain why facts about our ordinary language should carry the weight he clearly thought they carried in philosophical theorizing about knowledge. Here is one place where I have done a little filling in.

Of course, the foregoing does not explain why so many are prone to feel the tug of skeptical arguments such as the argument from illusion, in particular, why we do not spot its mistake right off and see through it (as we see through misuse of 'doctor' in the case I described above). To those who want explanations of these phenomena I have nothing to offer here, though, it seems to me, there is nothing in what Austin (or I in his defense) have said that precludes such explanations from being offered.

This much, however, is clear. There is nothing, in the fact that we are (to some degree or other) disoriented by the argument from illusion, that provides any evidence whatsoever that the conception of knowledge that animates them is (Austin and I to the contrary) correct. After all, if cognitive psychologists have taught us anything, it is this: that, by posing just the right sort of problems expressed in just the right sort of way, we can be made to commit all manner of statistical, logical, and arithmetical fallacies.[12] But we are not in the least tempted to see this as a sign that a deviant statistics, logic, or arithmetic is actually correct. We have no more reason to infer, from the mere fact that we are briefly (or even not so briefly) disoriented by the argument from illusion and its stable mates, that there is really something right about the infallibilist conception of knowledge on which the argument depends.

Is it unduly dismissive of the long philosophical career of the argument from illusion to suggest that the way it works its wiles is more appropriately explained by psychologists rather than by philosophers? I don't think so. After all, there is no suggestion here that the argument from illusion be dismissed as a mere parlor trick. On the contrary, I have argued that reflection on the argument leads us to a deeper understanding of the nature of knowledge (in particular, the relation between knowledge and fallibility), and of the constraints under which we must operate as we investigate the nature of knowledge.

And the fact is: to dwell only on the extent to which we feel the tug of the premises in a skeptical argument, to dwell only on the difficulty we may have in

---

[11] See, e.g., Chisholm (1969: 101), Cavell (1979: 57), Stroud (1984: ch. 2), McGinn (1989: 62), and Williams (1991: 147–8).   [12] See, e.g., Kahnemann, Slovic, and Tversky (1982).

putting our fingers on what is going wrong with some of those arguments, is to miss the most important part of the story about how we react to these arguments. It is to miss the fact that we are never actually *taken in* by these arguments. We never actually decide that we don't know anything about the world around us (and change our behavior to suit). Whatever the tug the arguments' premises may have, it is decisively overmatched by the repulsion we feel for the arguments' conclusions. Mightn't it be time to recognize that it is in this fact about our reaction to skeptical arguments, rather than in the disorientation we experience in the face of their clever tropes, that we should be looking to find insight into the nature of knowledge?[13]

REFERENCES

Austin, J. L. (1979). *Philosophical Papers* (3rd edn.), (eds.) J. O. Urmson and G. J. Warnock. Oxford: Oxford University Press.

Cavell, S. (1979). *The Claim of Reason: Wittgenstein, Skepticism, Morality, and Tragedy.* Oxford: Oxford University Press.

Chisholm, R. M. (1969). 'Austin's *Philosophical Papers*', in K. T. Fann (ed.), *Symposium on J. L. Austin.* London: Routledge & Kegan Paul, 101–26.

Edwards, P. (1949). 'Bertrand Russell's Doubts about Induction'. *Mind*, 58: 141–63.

Kahnemann, D., Slovic, P., and Tversky, A. (eds.) (1982). *Judgement under Uncertainty: Heuristics and Biases.* Cambridge: Cambridge University Press.

Kaplan, M. (2000). 'To What Must an Epistemology Be True?' *Philosophy and Phenomenological Research*, 61: 279–304.

—— (2006). 'Deciding What You Know', in E. J. Olsson (ed.), *Knowledge and Inquiry: Essays on the Pragmatism of Isaac Levi.* Cambridge: Cambridge University Press, 225–40.

McGinn, M. (1989). *Sense and Certainty: A Dissolution of Scepticism.* Oxford: Blackwell.

McDowell, J. (1994). *Mind and World.* Cambridge, Mass.: Harvard University Press.

Nozick, R. (1981). *Philosophical Explanations.* Cambridge, Mass.: Harvard University Press.

Snowdon, P. (2005). 'The Formulation of Disjunctivism: A Response to Fish'. *Proceedings of the Aristotelian Society*, 105: 129–41.

Stroud, B. (1984). *The Significance of Philosophical Scepticism.* Oxford: Clarendon Press.

Travis, C. (2004). 'The Twilight of Empiricism'. *Proceedings of the Aristotelian Society*, 104: 245–70.

Williams, M. (1991). *Unnatural Doubts: Epistemological Realism and the Basis of Scepticism.* Oxford: Blackwell.

---

[13] I am indebted to Adam Leite for urging me to make this last point.

12

From Knowledge to Understanding

Catherine Z. Elgin

Science, Spencer (1940: 77) contends, is organized knowledge. No doubt science is organized. Nevertheless, epistemologists speaking *ex cathedra* should deny that it is knowledge. 'Knowledge' is a factive. An opinion is not knowledge if it is not true. But even the best scientific theories are not true. Although science may produce some justified or reliable true beliefs as byproducts, if the best contemporary science is good science, the main deliverances of good science are not knowledge.

The analysis of 'knowledge' that yields this untoward verdict accords with our intuitions about the proper use of the term. We do not consider false beliefs knowledge, no matter how well grounded they may be. Once we discover that a belief is false, we retract the claim to know it. So we ought to deny that our best scientific theories are expressions of knowledge. Nevertheless, good science affords some sort of worthwhile take on nature. Epistemology should explain what makes good science cognitively good. It should explain why it is correct to say that we learn science in school rather than just that we change our minds about scientific matters. Its current focus on knowledge, being too narrow, stands in the way.

My goal in this paper is to show how epistemology's emphasis on knowledge constricts and distorts its purview, and to begin to sketch an epistemology capable of accounting for the cognitive contributions of science. Although I concentrate on science, the epistemological factors I foreground figure in other disciplines as well. My focus on science is mainly strategic. Science is undeniably a major cognitive achievement. It would be implausible in the extreme to contend that science's claim to epistemic standing is suspect. Moreover, science is methodologically self-reflective. So epistemically significant factors may be easier to recognize in science than in other disciplines. The epistemology of science then can serve as an entering wedge for a broader reconsideration of the nature and scope of human cognitive achievements.

Good science, as I use the term, is science that affords epistemic access to its subject matter. A good theory is a theory underwritten by good science. A central ambition of this paper is to begin to characterize that mode of epistemic access. For now, all that is necessary is to concede that some science is cognitively good, and that scientists often can tell what science is good. Although I will offer a sketch of how I think epistemology should approach the issue, my main purpose is to make a convincing case that it should, that something of major significance is omitted if our understanding of our epistemic condition does not account for the contributions of science.

Knowledge, as epistemology standardly conceives of it, comes in discrete bits. The objects of knowledge are individual facts, expressed in true propositions and/or stated in true declarative sentences. Judy knows (the fact) that the bus stops at the corner. Suzy knows (the fact) that ripe strawberries are red. These discrete bits are supposed to be what is justified or what is generated and sustained by reliable mechanisms. We can readily identify the evidence that supports Judy's belief, and the perceptual mechanisms that sustain Suzy's, and we can explain how they secure the beliefs in question. What emerges is a granular conception of knowledge. A subject's knowledge consists of discrete grains, each separately secured. She amasses more knowledge by accumulating more grains. Goldman (1999) labels such truth-centered epistemology *veritism*. Whether or not veritism is plausible for mundane knowledge, I contend, it is clearly inadequate for science.

Science is holistic. It is not an aggregation of separate, independently secured statements of fact, but an integrated, systematically organized account of a domain. Let us call such an account a theory.[1] There is no prospect of sentence by sentence verification of the claims that comprise a theory, for most of them lack separately testable consequences. In Quine's (1961: 41) words, they 'face the tribunal of sense experience not individually but only as a corporate body'. Independent of a theory of heat transfer, nothing could count as evidence for or against the claim that a process is adiabatic. Independent of an evolutionary theory, nothing could count as evidence for or against the claim that a behavior manifests reciprocal altruism. Together the sentences of a theory have testable implications; separately they do not. Indeed, it is not even clear that all scientific statements have truth values in isolation. If the individuation of the items they purport to refer to—a species, or a retrovirus, for example—is provided by a theory, there may be no fact of the matter as to whether they are true independent of the theory.

Such holism might seem epistemologically innocuous. One way to accommodate it would be to take the bulk of a theory as 'background knowledge' and then ask whether, together with the empirical evidence, it affords sufficient grounds to underwrite a particular claim. Given the theory and the empirical evidence, does this food sharing manifest reciprocal altruism? Although this reveals whether a theory supports a claim, it plainly does not solve our problem. For the assumption that the 'background knowledge' is genuine knowledge cannot be sustained. There is no viable non-holistic explanation of how the individual sentences of the theory serving as background could have obtained the support they require

---

[1] For simplicity of presentation, I call the unit of science 'a theory'. On this account, models are theories or are parts of theories rather than being independent of them.

to qualify as knowledge. Scientific theories are not granular in the way that epistemology takes knowledge to be.

Another, perhaps more promising, strategy is to take holism at its word. The simple sentences that comprise a theory cannot be separately justified. Evidence always bears on a theory as a whole. So evidence for the claim that a given process is adiabatic is evidence for an entire theory of heat transfer, which is tested along with the claim. This is in principle epistemologically unproblematic. The contention that knowledge is propositional says nothing about the length of the propositions that constitute knowledge. We can accommodate scientific holism by treating a theory as a conjunction of its component propositions and saying that the evidence bears on the truth or falsity of that long conjunction. If the conjunction is true, is believed, and is justified or reliably produced, it is known.

This may be as good a schema for scientific *knowledge* as we are likely to get. But it sheds little light on the cognitive value of science, for its requirements are rarely met. In particular, the truth requirement is rarely satisfied. As will emerge, theories contain sentences that do not even purport to be true. For now, however, this complication will be ignored. Still there is a problem. For even the best scientific theories confront anomalies. They imply consequences that the evidence does not bear out. Since a conjunction is false if any of its conjuncts is, if a scientific theory is a conjunction, an anomaly, being a falsifying instance, tells decisively against the theory that generates it. Since a theory that generates an anomaly is false, its cognitive deliverance is not knowledge.

Perhaps we can evade this predicament. The characterization of a theory as a conjunction might seem to offer some hope of isolating anomalies and screening off their effects.[2] All we need to do is identify and expunge the troublesome conjuncts. Consider the following conjunction:

(1) (a) Sally is in Chicago & (b) Sam is in New York.

If Sally is in fact in Detroit, (1) is false, even though Sam is in New York. If we lack adequate evidence that Sally is in Chicago, (1) is unjustified, even though we have ample evidence that Sam is in New York. If our source of information about Sally's whereabouts is suspect, (1) is the product of an unreliable belief-forming mechanism, even though our source of information about Sam's location is impeccable. (1) then is not something we are in a position to know. Still, we can rescind (a), leaving

(b) Sam is in New York,

which is true, justified, and attested to by a reliable informant. Since neither (a) nor the evidence for (a) lends any support to (b), (b)'s tenability is not undermined by the repudiation of (a). On standard accounts of knowledge, we are in a position to know that (b). If the components of a scientific theory were related to one another as loosely as (a) and (b) are related in (1), we could simply rescind the anomalous

---

[2] This maneuver is modeled on the 'corrected doxastic system' in Lehrer's (1974) epistemology.

sentences and be left with justified true beliefs which derive from reliable sources, things that could be known.

But the components of a theory lack the requisite independence. A theory is a tightly interwoven tapestry of mutually supportive commitments. Simply excising anomalous sentences would leave a moth-eaten tapestry that would not hang together. Before Einstein, physicists devised a variety of increasingly drastic revisions in their theories to accommodate the perturbation in Mercury's orbit. But even at their most desperate, they did not suggest simply inserting an exception into the theory. Although 'All planets except Mercury have elliptical orbits' is apparently true, justified, reliably generated, and believed, it pulls so strongly against the ideal of systematicity that scientists never considered incorporating it into astronomy. Temporarily bracketing anomalies may be a good tactic in theory development, but simply discounting them as exceptions is not. The reason is not merely aesthetic. An anomaly might be just a pesky irritation that stems from undetected but ultimately insignificant interference, but it might also, like the perturbation in Mercury's orbit, be symptomatic of a subtle but significant misunderstanding of the phenomena. Science would lose potentially valuable information if it simply dismissed its anomalies as exceptions that it need not explain. There is then no hope of simply extracting anomalous sentences without undermining the epistemic support for the rest of the theory. The theory rather than the individual sentence is the unit we need to focus on.

These points are familiar and uncontroversial, but their epistemological consequences are worth noting. A theory can be construed as a conjunction of the sentences that appear in it. But science does not yield knowledge expressed by such conjunctions. For the conjunction of the sentences that constitute a good scientific theory is apt to be false. The unavailability of sentence by sentence verification discredits the idea that science delivers knowledge of each component sentence. The hopelessness of selectively deleting falsehoods in and false implications of a theory undermines the plausibility of claiming that scientific knowledge is what remains when a theory's falsehoods have been expunged. Knowledge requires truth. And there seems to be no feasible way to get good scientific theories to come out true. So knowledge is not the cognitive condition that good science standardly engenders. We seem forced to admit that scientific accounts that contain falsehoods nonetheless constitute cognitive achievements. If so, to understand the cognitive contribution of science, knowledge is not the epistemic magnitude we should focus on.

Much good science falls short of satisfying the requirements for knowledge. But the problem is not just a shortfall, it is a mismatch. For mere knowledge does not satisfy the requirements of good science either. Science seeks, and often provides, a unified, integrated, evidence-based understanding of a range of phenomena. A list, even an extensive list, of justified or reliably generated true beliefs about those phenomena would not constitute a scientific understanding of them. Veritism, in concentrating on truth, ignores a host of factors that are integral to science. These factors cannot be dismissed as just instrumentally or practically valuable. They are vital to the cognitive contributions that science makes. Science distances itself from what occurs naturally. It selects, contrives, and manipulates both its data and its representations of its data in order to achieve the systematic understanding it seeks. Its relation to the phenomena is more indirect and complicated than laymen are apt to think. In assessing a theory, we should not ask, 'Does it express knowledge?' Rather, we should ask, 'Does it convey an understanding of the phenomena? Is it a good way to represent or think about a domain if our goal is to understand what is going on in that domain?'

Representation depends on categorization, the division of a domain into individuals and kinds. The members of any collection, however miscellaneous, are alike (and unlike) one another in infinitely many ways. So in seeking to devise a taxonomy, we cannot hope to appeal to overall likeness. Nor is it always wise to group items together on the basis of prescientifically salient similarities. Different diseases, such as viral and bacterial meningitis, often display the same symptoms, and a single disease, such as tuberculosis, can manifest itself in different clusters of symptoms. A science requires a taxonomy or category scheme that classifies the items in its domain in a way that furthers its cognitive interests—discovery of causal mechanisms, functional units, widespread patterns, overarching or underlying regularities, and so on. Science regularly reveals that things that are superficially alike are deeply different and things that are superficially different are deeply alike. Without an adequate system of categories, significant likenesses and differences would be missed.

Scale is critical. As Nancy Cartwright's discussion of Simpson's paradox shows, factors that are salient or important at one level of generality can be unimportant at another.

The graduate school at Berkeley was accused of discriminating against women.... The accusation appeared to be borne out in the probabilities: The probability of acceptance was much higher for men than for women. Bickel, Hammel, and O'Connell looked at the data more carefully, however, and discovered that this was no longer so if they partitioned by department. In a majority of the eighty-five departments, the probability of admission for women was just about the same as for men, and in some even higher for women than for men.... [W]omen tended to apply to departments with high rejection rates, so that department by department women were admitted in about the same ratios as men but across the whole university considerably fewer women, by proportion, were admitted.[3]

Admissions rates calculated department by department show one pattern; overall rates show another. The point is general. At different scales, the same data display different patterns. It is not unusual in biology for subpopulations to display one pattern and the larger population to show another. Each pattern is really instantiated. But to understand what is occurring in the domain requires knowing which pattern is significant.

[3] Cartwright (1983: 37). She cites Peter J. Bickel, Eugene A. Hammel, and J. William O'Connell (1977).

Both categorization and scale involve selection. The issue is what factors to focus on. The problem is that there are too many epistemically accessible facts about a domain. To obtain any sort of systematic understanding requires filtering. Science has to select, organize, and regiment the facts to generate such an understanding. It needs criteria for selection, organization, and regimentation. Veritism does not supply them.

Such criteria are far from arbitrary. It is possible to make mistakes about them. If we choose the wrong scale, we miss important patterns. We wrongly decide that Berkeley is, or that it is not, discriminating. We wrongly conclude that a genetic trait is, or that it is not, widespread in a species. If we draw the wrong lines, we miss important similarities and differences. We wrongly conclude that rabbits and hares are, or that they are not, the same sort of thing. In such cases, we fail to understand the phenomena, even if our account consists entirely of justified true beliefs.

Science places a premium on clarity. It favors sharply differentiated categories whose members are readily distinguished. One reason is that science is a collaborative enterprise grounded in shared commitments. Because current investigations build on previous findings, it is imperative that scientists agree about what has been established and how firmly it has been established. Clarity and definiteness foster intersubjective agreement and repeatable results. Repeatability requires determinacy. Unless it is possible to tell what the result of a given investigation is, it is impossible to tell whether a second investigation yields the same result or a different one; whether it yields a cotenable result or a noncotenable one. Vagueness is undesirable then, since within the penumbra of vagueness there may be irresolvable disagreements about what situation obtains.

The requisite clarity and determinacy can sometimes be achieved by fiat. We eliminate vagueness by stipulating where sharp lines will be drawn. But even if lines are sharp, instances may prove irksome. The sharp criteria for distinguishing mammals from birds may leave us bewildered or dissatisfied about the classification of the platypus. Sometimes, regimenting familiar categories does not yield a partition of the domain that suits scientific purposes. Either the lines seem arbitrary or they do not group items in ways that disclose the regularities or patterns the science seeks. 'Weight', for example, is a familiar and easily regimented category. It is of relatively limited scientific interest, though, since it is a function of gravity, which varies. 'Mass', although less familiar, is a more useful category, for it remains constant across variations in gravity. Where gravity is constant, weight may be a fine magnitude to use. Where differences in gravity matter, science does better to measure in terms of mass. To the extent that systematicity is of value, this is a reason to favor mass over weight across the board. A critical question then is what modes of representation foster the realization of scientific objectives. Phenomena do not dictate their own descriptions. We need to decide in what units they should be measured and in what terms they should be described.

Rather than characterizing familiar items in familiar terms, science often construes its phenomena as complexes of identifiable, even if unfamiliar, factors. Frequently the factors are not assigned equal significance. Some are deemed focal, others peripheral. The liquids that fall from the skies, that flow through the streams, that lie in the lakes contain a variety of chemicals, minerals, and organic material. Nonetheless, we call all these liquids 'water', acknowledging only when necessary, that there are chemical, mineral, and biological ingredients as well. Tellingly, we call such ingredients 'impurities'. H_2O then is taken as the focus, and the other components are treated as peripheral. Most of the liquid we call 'water' does not consist wholly of H_2O. To obtain pure samples of the focal substance requires filtering out impurities. The justification for calling the liquids 'water' and identifying water with H_2O is not fidelity, but fruitfulness. Our scientific purposes are served by this characterization. Sometimes, the effects of the impurities are negligible, so we can treat the naturally occurring liquid as if it were H_2O. In other cases they are non-negligible. Even then, though, H_2O serves as a least common denominator. We compare divergent samples in terms of how and how far they differ from 'pure water', that is, H_2O. There is nothing dishonest about using a description that focuses on H_2O. But it would be equally accurate to simply describe the liquid in the rain barrel, the lake, and the river more fully. Instead of characterizing them as impure water, we could simply supply the chemical, biological, and mineral profile of the liquid in Walden Pond, the liquid in the Charles River, and the liquid that fell in today's storm. Although the latter descriptions would be accurate, they would mask the common core. Treating the three samples as instances of a single substance differing only in impurities highlights features they share. And by seeing what they share we can begin to investigate their differences. Why are the impurities in one sample, for example, the water from Walden Pond, so different from the impurities in another, the water from the Charles River?

This pattern is widespread. Astronomers describe the motions of the planets in terms of regular geometric orbits with perturbations. Linguists describe verbal behavior as rule-based competence overlaid with performance errors. Engineers describe the output of a sensor as a combination of signal and noise. In all such cases the focal concept serves as a point of reference. What occurs in the domain is understood by reference to, and in terms of deviations from, the focus.

Although these examples exhibit the same conceptual configuration, the differences between them are significant. Where it is a matter of signal and noise, only the focal element, the signal, is important. It is often both possible and desirable to sharpen the signal and eliminate or dampen the effects of the noise. We fine tune our measuring devices or statistical techniques to eliminate static and highlight focal features. In cases where noise is ineliminable, it is simply ignored. What counts as signal and what counts as noise varies with interests. Ordinarily, when someone answers questions, the content of the answers is the signal. But in some psychology experiments, content is mere noise. The signal is reaction time.

Psychologists want to ascertain not what a subject answers, but how long it takes her to answer, for reaction time affords evidence about psychological and neurological processes. The choice of a focus is thus purpose-relative.

We cannot always ignore complications. If we want to understand language acquisition, we cannot simply overlook performance errors. We need to see how or whether they affect what is learned. If we want to send a probe to Mars, we cannot simply ignore the planet's deviation from a perfect elliptical orbit. We must accommodate it in our calculations. In such cases, we employ a schema and correction model. We start with the focal concept and introduce elaborations to achieve the type and level of accuracy we require.

All these cases involve streamlining the focus and sidelining or downplaying complexities. Sometimes, as in the model of signal and noise, the complexities are permanently sidelined. As much as possible, we sharpen the signal and eliminate static. We have no reason to reintroduce the static we have removed. In other cases, when the model of schema and correction is appropriate, complexities may be set aside only temporarily. They may need to be reintroduced at a later stage.

Focal points are readily defined. The choice among them turns on utility, not just accuracy. Three points described by Dennett illustrate this: The center of gravity is 'the point at which the whole weight of a body may be considered to act, if the body is situated in a uniform gravitational field' (*Oxford Dictionary of Science* 1999: 141). The center of population of the United States is 'the mathematical point at the intersection of the two lines such that there are as many inhabitants north as south of the latitude and as many inhabitants east as west of the longitude' (Dennett 1991: 28). Dennett's lost sock center is (ibid.) 'the center of the smallest sphere that can be inscribed around all the socks' that Dennett has ever lost. All three points are well defined. Each is as real as any of the others. If points are real, all three exist; if points are unreal, none of the three exists. If points are constructed through stipulative definition, all three points are equally constructs. Whatever their ontological status, all are devices of representation. We represent portions of reality in terms of them. Still, they are hardly on a par.

Gravity is a fundamental force whose effects are uniform, law governed, and ubiquitous. It is often simpler, both conceptually and computationally, to represent an extended body as a point mass located at the body's center of gravity, and to calculate, predict, and explain gravitational effects of and on the body as though it were a point mass located at the center of gravity. The center of gravity is a manifestly useful device of representation.

Dennett's lost sock center is inconsequential. It does not engage with any significant questions, even if one happens to care about Dennett's propensity for losing socks. Conceivably a biographer or psychologist might take an interest in the distribution of his lost socks. But exactly where the midpoint lies makes no difference. Dennett's lost sock center is a well-defined, utterly trivial point.

The center of population of the United States is an intermediate case. It changes over time, and its changes display both short-term fluctuations and long-term trends. It shifts, day by day, even minute by minute, as people move about, some of them crossing the crucial lines, now this way, now that. The fluctuations are insignificant. But through the fluctuations we can discern a trend. If we look at the change in the population center, not by day but by decade, we see that US population has moved westward. This is a significant demographic change. It engages with other sociological information and figures in a broader understanding of American society. So the center of population is not, like Dennett's lost sock center, a useless point. But it is not, perhaps, as useful as it might be. To discern the demographic trend, we need to see past the noise generated by the small-scale fluctuations. We might do better to devise a different device of representation. Rather than an instantaneous measure, perhaps we should concentrate on longer periods of time. The representation might still take the form of a point, but it would not represent a position at an instant. A better focus could readily be devised.

It is critical that the focus need not occur naturally. Laboratory processes may be required to obtain a refined, pure sample of a focal substance like H_2O. Computational processes may be required to fix the population points that best display important demographic trends. Sensor readings are subjected to statistical analyses to synthesize the information we seek. In yet other cases conceptual processing is called for. To understand grammatical errors it may be helpful to subject an utterance to a sort of conceptual factor analysis, construing it as consisting of invariable grammatical rules overlaid with idiosyncratic applications. The focus of representation may be fairly distant from the robust phenomena it bears on.

We construct devices of representation to serve certain purposes and can reconstruct them both to enable them to better serve their original purposes and to serve other purposes that we may subsequently form. We can revise the scope, scale, and content of our representations to improve their capacity to promote our evolving cognitive ends. In such matters there are feedback loops. As we come to understand more about a domain we refine our views about what kinds are significant, at what level of generality they should be investigated, in what terms they should be represented.

Ecologists sampling the water in Walden Pond ordinarily would not just extract a vial of liquid from any convenient place in the pond. They would consider where the liquid is most representative of the pond water, or is most likely to display the features they seek to study. If they seek a representative sample, they would not take it from the mouth of the stream that feeds the pond, nor from the shore right near the public beach, nor from the area abutting the highly fertilized golf course. They might draw their sample from the middle of the pond. Or they might take multiple samples from different areas and either mix them physically or generate a composite profile based on them. Their sampling would be guided by an understanding of where in the pond the features they are interested in are most likely to be found. This means though that even if the water in the sample occurs naturally, data collection is driven by an understanding of the domain, the way it is properly characterized and the way it is properly investigated. All these go into determining what makes a sample a representative sample.

A sample is not just an instance. It is a telling instance. It exemplifies, highlights, displays, or conveys the features or properties it is a sample of. No sample exemplifies all its features. Exemplification is selective. The sample drawn from Walden Pond is (a) more than 1,000 kilometers from the Parthenon, (b) taken by a left-handed graduate student, (c) obtained on the second Tuesday of the month. It also (d) contains H_2O, (e) contains E. coli bacteria; (f) has a pH of 5.8. In a suitable scientific context, it may well exemplify any or all of (d), (e), and (f). Although it instantiates (a), (b), and (c), it is unlikely in normal scientific contexts to exemplify any of them.

A sample then is a symbol that refers to some of the properties it instantiates (Goodman 1968; Elgin 1996). It thereby affords a measure of epistemic access to these properties. Epistemic access can be better or worse. One reason for careful sampling is to insure that the sample has the properties of interest; another is to obtain a sample that affords ready epistemic access to them. Some factors occur only in minute quantities in pond water, so although a liter of water drawn from the pond exemplifies them, they may still be hard to detect. Moreover, such a sample may include confounding factors, which although unexemplified and (for current purposes) irrelevant, impede epistemic access to exemplified properties. So instead of working with samples drawn directly from nature, scientists often process samples to amplify features of interest and/or remove confounding factors. In the lab, the water sample undergoes purification processes to remove unwanted material. What results is a pure sample in which the features of interest stand out. Scientists then experiment on this sample, and devise explanations and predictions based on its behavior. Although the lab specimen does not occur naturally in the form in which it is tested, the tests are not a sham. For the features the specimen exemplifies do occur naturally. The lab specimen's divergence from nature in exemplified features is neglible; its divergence in other respects is irrelevant.

Different sorts of samples are suited to different experiments. Scientists might experiment on a random sample of a substance, a purposeful sample, or a purified sample. In all such cases, the goal is to understand nature. An experiment is designed to reveal something directly about the sample, which can be projected back onto the natural phenomena it bears on. Just how to project from the lab to the world depends on the sort of sample used, and the operative assumptions about how it relates to the phenomena whose features it exemplifies. The extrapolation is not always straightforward. A good deal of interpretation may be required to effect the projection.

To determine whether a substance S is carcinogenic, investigators place genetically identical mice in otherwise identical environments, exposing half of them to massive doses of S while leaving the rest unexposed. The common genetic endowment and otherwise identical environments neutralize the vast array of genetic and environmental factors that are believed to standardly influence the incidence of cancer. By controlling for genetics and most aspects of the environment, scientists insure that these factors, although instantiated by the mice, are not exemplified. They arrange things so that exposure or non-exposure to *S* is the only environmental feature exemplified, thereby enabling the experiment to disclose the effects of *S*. The use of mice is grounded in the assumption that, in the respects that matter, mice are no different from humans. Given this assumption, the experiment is interpreted as exemplifying *the effect on mammals*, not just on mice. The mice are exposed to massive doses of *S*, on the assumption that the effect of lots of *S* on small mammals over a short period is reflective of the effect of small amounts of *S* on larger mammals over a long period. So the experiment is interpreted as exemplifying *the effect of S* rather than just the effect of high doses of *S*. To make its cognitive contribution, of course, the experiment must be properly interpreted. If we took the experimental situation to replicate life in the wild, we would be badly mistaken. But if the background assumptions are sound, then we understand the ways the experiment is and is not representative of nature, that is, we understand what aspects of the experiment symbolize and how they do so. That enables the experiment to advance understanding of the effect of *S* on mammals.

The experiment is highly artificial. Even the mice are artifacts, having been intentionally bred to exhibit a certain genetic structure. The exposure is to a vastly higher dose of *S* than would occur in nature. The environment is rigidly controlled to eliminate a huge array of factors that normally affect the health of mice. The experiment eliminates some ordinary aspects of mouse life, such as the dangers to life and limb that predators pose. It nullifies the effects of others, such as the genetic diversity of members of a wild population of mice. It exaggerates others, exposing the mice to much higher doses of *S* than they would be exposed to naturally. Rather than rendering the experiment unrepresentative, these divergences from nature enable the experiment to reveal aspects of nature that are normally overshadowed. They clear away the confounding features and highlight the significant ones so that the effects of *S* on mammals stand out.

Science distances itself even further from the phenomena when it resorts to models, idealizations, and thought experiments. Scientific models are schematic representations that highlight significant features while prescinding from irrelevant complications. They may be relatively austere, neglecting fine-grained features of the phenomena they concern. They may be caricatures, exaggerating features to bring subtle but important consequences to light (Gibbard and Varian 1978). They may be radically incomplete, representing only selected aspects of the phenomena (Nersessian 1993). Strictly and literally, they describe nothing in the world. For example, although financial transactions are complexes of rational and irrational behavior, economics devises and deploys models that screen off all factors deemed irrational, regardless of how large a role they play in actual transactions. Such models would provide nothing like accurate representations of real transactions, but would not be defective on that account. They operate on the assumption that for certain purposes irrationality can safely be ignored.

Construed literally, models may describe ideal cases that do not, perhaps cannot, occur in nature. The ideal gas is a model that represents gas molecules as perfectly elastic, dimensionless spheres that exhibit no mutual attraction. There are, indeed there could be, no such molecules. But the model captures the inter-dependence of temperature, pressure, and volume that is crucial to understanding the behavior of actual gases. Explanations that adduced the ideal gas would be epistemically unacceptable if abject fidelity to truth were required. Since helium molecules are not dimensionless, mutually indifferent, elastic spheres, an account that represents them as such is false. But, at least if the explanation concerns the behavior of helium in circumstances where divergence from the ideal gas law is negligible (roughly, where temperature is high and pressure is low) scientists are apt to find it unexceptionable. For in such circumstances, the effects of friction, attraction, and molecular size do not matter. Models of economic growth repres-ent the profit rate as constant. In fact, it is not. Non-economic factors such as epidemics, corruption, and political unrest interfere. But by bracketing such complications, the economic models capture features that are common to a host of seemingly disparate situations. Even though the full-blooded situations seem very different from one another, the model presents a common core and enables economists to (partially) explain seemingly disparate behaviors in terms of that core. Thus representations that are and are known to be inaccurate afford insight into the phenomena they purport to concern.

Thought experiments are imaginative representations designed to reveal what would happen if certain conditions were met. They are not actual, and often not even possible, experiments. Nonetheless, they afford an understanding of the phenomena they pertain to. By considering the experience of a person riding on an elevator with and without the presence of a gravitational field, Einstein shows the equivalence of gravitational and inertial mass. By considering how a light body tethered to a heavy body would fall, Galileo both discredits the Aristotelian theory of motion and discovers that the rate at which objects in a vacuum fall is independ-ent of their weight. In other cases, thought experiments flesh out theories by revealing what would happen in the limit. By considering how electrical currents would behave in metals cooled to absolute zero, a computer simulation yields insights into super-conductivity. The effectiveness of a thought experiment is not undermined by the fact that the imaginary conditions that set the stage never obtain.

Standardly, philosophers assume that scientific theories aim at truth, and are deficient if they are not true. Even good theories confront anomalies. But anom-alies are indications that theories are defective. So the existence of anomalies does not in itself discredit the standard view. Although idealizations, simplified models, and thought experiments neither are nor purport to be true, they are not defective. To account for the cognitive contributions of science, epistemology must accommodate their contributions. Such devices, I believe, function as fictions. So to make my case, I need to explain first how fictions advance understanding and then why it is reasonable to consider these devices fictions.

It is not unusual to emerge from an encounter with a work of fiction feeling that one has learned something. But fictions do not purport to be true. So the learning, whatever it is, cannot plausibly be construed as the acquisition of reliable information. Since fiction is indifferent to literal truth, falsity is no defect in it. A fiction need not be 'realistic'. It can transcend the limits of the possible. It can portray characters with unusual combinations of traits and situations that present unusual challenges and opportunities. It can contrive telling mismatches between characters and their situations. It can uproot characters from one environment and implant them in another. Having done such things, it plays out the consequences. If thought experiments, models, and idealizations are fictions, they do the same sorts of things. Like other fictions, they are exempt from the truth requirement. So the fact that the ideal gas law is true of nothing in the world is not a mark against it. The fact that no one ever has ridden and no one ever will ride in an elevator without a gravitational field does not discredit Einstein's thought experiment. If they are fictions, such devices are not supposed to be true. But they are not completely idle speculations either. The consequences they play out are supposed to advance understanding of the actual. The question is: If a fictional representation is not true, how can it shed light on the way the world actually is?

I suggest that it does so by exemplifying features that diverge (at most) negligibly from the phenomena it concerns.[4] To take a pedestrian sample, a commercial paint sample is a chip of a precise color. Surprisingly, it is a fiction. The color patch on the card is not a patch of paint, but of ink or dye of the same color as the paint it represents. The fiction, that it is a patch of paint, affords epistemic access to a fact— the color of paint the patch represents. Not all the paint that counts as matching it is exactly the same shade. Any color within a certain range counts as a match. The paint sample thus affords access to that narrow range of colors, colors that diverge at most negligibly from the color on the card. The ideal gas law is expressed in a formula relating temperature, pressure, and volume. The model gas is a fiction in which the formula is exactly satisfied. Real gases do not exactly satisfy the formula. Still the model affords epistemic access to the real gases that fall within a certain range of the ideal gas in the relations of temperature, pressure, and volume that they display. Both exemplars afford epistemic access to features that they do not possess, but that diverge negligibly from features that they do possess. Obviously, whether a divergence is negligible depends on a host of contextual factors. A divergence that is negligible in one context may be nonnegligible in another. Since we know how to accommodate the contextual factors, we are in a position to interpret the exemplars correctly.

A fiction exemplifies certain features, thereby affording epistemic access to them. It enables us to discern and distinguish those features, study different aspects of them, consider their causes and consequences. It is apt to be purposely contrived to bring to the fore factors that are ordinarily imperspicuous. By

---

[4] See my (1996: 180–204) and (2004).

highlighting features in a setting contrived to render them salient, it equips us with resources for recognizing them and their ilk elsewhere. Othello exemplifies a cluster of virtues and flaws that makes him vulnerable to Iago's machinations. That cluster of traits is perhaps not unusual. But the resulting vulnerability is far from obvious. To make it manifest, Shakespeare shows how Othello's character shatters under the pressure Iago exerts. The play thus exemplifies the vulnerability of a cluster of traits by devising a situation where they break down. It considers what would happen in an extreme case, to point up a vulnerability that obtains in ordinary cases. In effect, it tests the cluster of traits to destruction. Just as the medical experiment is carefully contrived to exemplify the carcinogenicity of S by subjecting the mice to massive doses of S, the play is carefully contrived to exemplify the vulnerability inherent in a cluster of seemingly admirable traits by subjecting Othello to massive evil.

Of course there are differences. A play like *Othello* is a rich, textured work that admits of a vast number of divergent interpretations. The experiment is designed so that its interpretation is univocal. This is a crucial difference between art and science, but not, I think, a difference between fiction and fact. It is the density and repleteness of the literary symbols, not their fictiveness, that makes the crucial difference. Thought experiments combine the freedom of fiction with the austere requirements of science. Like other scientific symbols, their interpretation should be univocal, determinate, and readily ascertained. It should be clear what background assumptions are operative and how they bear on the thought experiment's design and interpretation.

Einstein contrives a thought experiment to investigate what a person riding on a light wave would see. It teases out less than obvious implications of the finitude of the speed of light. It prescinds from such inconveniences as the fact that a person is too big to ride on a light wave, the fact that anyone travelling at light speed would acquire infinite mass, and the fact that such a person would be unable to see since her retina would be smaller than a photon, and so on. Since such physiological impediments are irrelevant to the thought experiment, they play no role. In effect the thought experiment instructs us to pretend that someone could ride on a light wave without ill effect and to consider what he would observe. Suspension of disbelief is required to adopt the requisite imaginative stance, but what aspects of our situation we should retain and what aspects we should abandon are clear.

A thought experiment affords insight into phenomena only if the driving assumptions about what can be fruitfully set aside are correct. Otherwise, it misleads. But this is so for all experiments. Experiments using a purified sample yield insights into their natural counterparts only if we haven't filtered out significant factors. Studying the properties of a random sample yields insight into the material sampled only if the randomly taken sample is in fact suitably representative. If we randomly select an unrepresentative sample, we will project the wrong features onto the domain. All scientific reasoning takes place against background assumptions. That is the source of both its power and its vulnerability.

To construe a model as a fiction is to treat it as a symbolic construct that exemplifies features it shares with the phenomena it models but diverges from those phenomena in other, unexemplified, respects. A tinker-toy model of a protein exemplifies structural relations it shares with the protein. It does not exemplify its color, size, or material. So its failure to replicate the color, size, and material of the protein it models is not a defect. Indeed, it is an asset. Being larger, color-coded, and durable, it is able to make the features it exemplifies manifest so that they can be discerned more easily than they are when we observe proteins directly.

The explanation of the cognitive contribution of fictions in science is that in recognizable and significant respects their divergence from the phenomena they bear on is negligible. I suggest that the same thing accounts for the cognitive contributions of otherwise good theories that contain anomalies. We say that they are right 'up to a point'. That point, I suggest, is where the divergence becomes non-negligible. Just as an ensemble of gas molecules nearly satisfies the ideal gas law, the motion of a slowly moving nearby object nearly satisfies Newton's laws. In both cases, the laws provide an orientation for investigating where, how, why, and with what consequences divergences occur. 'Negligible' is an elastic term. Sometimes we are, and should be, prepared to overlook a lot. In the early stages of theory development, very rough approximations and very incomplete models afford a modest understanding of the domain. With the advancement of science we raise our standards, refine our models, and often require a better fit with the facts. That is one way we improve our understanding of what is going on. A closer fit does not always afford a better understanding. Sometimes a stark, streamlined model that cuts through irrelevant complications is more revealing. When a point mass at the center of gravity is an effective way to conceptualize and compute the effects of gravity, a more realistic representation that specifies the actual dimensions of the planets would not obviously be preferable. The fact that in certain respects it is as if the planets were point masses is an interesting and important fact about gravitational attraction. In effect, what I am suggesting is that a theory that is known to be inadequate is consigned to the realm of fiction. It is treated as if it were an idealization. But fictions in science are cognitively significant, so to construe even our best theories as fictions is not to devalue them.

A worry remains: If the acceptability of scientific theories does not turn on their truth, the distinction between science and pseudoscience threatens to vanish. If not on the basis of truth, on what grounds are we to consider astronomy cognitively reputable and astrology bunk? The answer harks back to the previously cited passage from Quine. Although the sentences of science face the tribunal of experience only as a corporate body, they do face the tribunal of experience. Theories as a whole are answerable to empirical evidence and are discredited if they are not borne out by the evidence. Theories containing idealizations, approximations, simplified models, and thought experiments do not directly mirror reality. But because they have testable implications they are empirically defeasible. That is, there are determinate, epistemically accessible situations which, if found to obtain, would discredit the theories. If we discovered, as we could, that friction plays a major role in collisions between gas molecules, that discovery would discredit the ideal gas law and the theories that incorporate it. Pseudoscientific accounts are indefeasible. No evidence could discredit them. They cannot claim to reveal the way the world is, since they would, by their own lights, hold regardless of how the world turns out to be. This is a critical difference and shows that scientific theories that incorporate fictive devices are nonetheless empirical.

I have urged that science is riddled with symbols that neither do nor purport to directly mirror the phenomena they concern. Purified, contrived lab specimens, extreme experimental situations, simplified models, and highly counterfactual thought experiments contribute to a scientific understanding of the way the world is. I suggested that science's reliance on such devices shows that veritism is inadequate to the epistemology of science. But, one might argue, such devices play only a causal role. They enable scientists to discover the way things are. And perhaps it is significant that non-truths can do that. Nevertheless, epistemology is not primarily concerned with the causes of our beliefs, so the use of such devices does not discredit veritism. The crucial question is whether the conclusions that emerge from the deployment of these devices are true. If so, veritism is vindicated, for the role played by the untruths is causal but not constitutive of scientific cognition.

This strikes me as wrong. The devices do not just cause an understanding of the phenomena they concern, they embody that understanding. Their design and deployment is enmeshed with an understanding of the phenomena they bear on and the proper ways to investigate it. Without that understanding the laboratory experiments, models, thought experiments, and samples would not only be unmotivated, they would be unintelligible. We would have no idea what to make of them. Without some constraints on the imaginative exercise, we would have no idea what to imagine when invited to imagine what a person riding on a light wave would see. Moreover, we do not just use the devices as vehicles to generate conclusions, we think of the domain in terms of them. We represent the contents of lakes as water with impurities, the interaction of gas molecules as comporting with the ideal gas law, the orbits of the planets as perturbed ellipses. Because we do so, we are in a position to draw inferences that both test and extend our understanding.

There is a further worry: The only constraint on acceptability I have mentioned is that a theory must answer to the evidence. But a theory that included 'All planets except Mercury have elliptical orbits' would do that. Among the theories that answer to the same body of evidence, some are better than others. What makes the difference? Unfortunately, the question cannot be settled by appeal to obvious, a priori criteria. Apart from consistency, there are none. With the advancement of understanding, we revise our views about what makes a theory good, and thus our criteria of acceptability. Elsewhere (1996: 101–43) I have argued that epistemic acceptability is a matter of reflective equilibrium: The components of an acceptable theory, statements of fact, fictions, categories, methods, etc., must be reasonable in light of one another, and the theory as a whole must be at least as reasonable as any available alternative in light of our relevant antecedent commitments. This is not the place to review that argument. My point here is that because such an epistemology does not privilege literal, factual truths, it can accommodate the complex symbolization that mature science exhibits.

To understand a theory is to properly interpret its symbols. This requires distinguishing factual from fictional sentences, accommodating tacit presuppositions, accurately interpreting the scope and selectivity of exemplars, and so forth. To understand a domain in terms of a theory is to be in a position to recognize, reason about, anticipate, explain, and act on what occurs in the domain on the basis of the resources the theory supplies. Understanding thus is a matter of degree. A slight understanding equips us to recognize gross features, to give rough explanations, to reason in general terms, to form crude expectations. With the advancement of understanding our recognition, reasoning, representations, and explanations become better focused and more refined.

REFERENCES

Bickel, P. J., Hammel, E. A., and O'Connell, J. W. (1977). 'Sex Bias in Graduate Admissions: Data from Berkeley', in W. B. Fairley and F. Mosteller, *Statistics and Public Policy*. Reading, Mass.: Addison-Wesley, 113–30.

Cartwright, N. (1983). *How the Laws of Physics Lie*. Oxford: Clarendon Press.

Dennett, D. (1991). 'Real Patterns'. *Journal of Philosophy*, 88: 27–51.

Elgin, C. Z. (1996). *Considered Judgment*. Princeton: Princeton University Press.

—— (2004). 'True Enough'. *Philosophical Issues*, 14: 113–31.

Gibbard, A., and Varian, H. R. (1978). 'Economic Models'. *Journal of Philosophy*, 75: 664–77.

Goldman, A. (1999). *Knowledge in a Social World*. Oxford: Clarendon Press.

Goodman, N. (1968). *Languages of Art*. Indianapolis: Hackett.

Lehrer, K. (1974). *Knowledge*. Oxford: Clarendon Press.

Nersessian, N. (1993). 'In the Theoretician's Laboratory: Thought Experimenting as Mental Modeling'. *PSA 1992*, 2: 291–301.

Oxford Dictionary of Science (1999). Oxford: Oxford University Press.

Quine, W. V. (1961). 'Two Dogmas of Empiricism', in *From a Logical Point of View*. New York: Harper, 20–46.

Spencer, H. (1940). *Education*. London: Williams & Norgate.

13

Epistemological Puzzles about Disagreement

Richard Feldman

Disagreements among intelligent and informed people pose challenging epistemological issues. One issue concerns the reasonableness of maintaining one's beliefs in the light of such disagreement. Another concerns the possibility of there being cases in which both parties to a disagreement are reasonable in maintaining their beliefs.

Attitudes toward disagreement are diverse. At one extreme are people who regard those with whom they disagree as enemies to be discredited, humiliated, and defeated. These people view disagreement as a kind of combat in which 'victory' is the measure of success. This attitude is especially prominent in some political exchanges. At another extreme are those who find disagreement unpleasant and preach a kind tolerance. This is especially prominent in religious disagreements. One commentator has recently written that

Criticizing a person's faith is currently taboo in every corner of our culture. On this subject, liberals and conservatives have reached a rare consensus: religious beliefs are simply beyond the scope of rational discourse. Criticizing a person's ideas about God and the afterlife is thought to be impolitic in a way that criticizing his ideas about physics or history is not. (Harris 2004)

Although the ban on criticism of religious views is surely not as extensive as this author suggests, there is no doubt that the tolerant attitude is widespread. And while criticizing another person's views on history or physics is often seen as more acceptable than criticizing religious views, there is a common tendency to think that reasonable people can disagree about these topics, that more than one point of view may withstand rational scrutiny. Thus, toleration extends to these other areas as well.

Regardless of how people actually do respond to disagreement, there are perplexing questions about what the reasonable responses can be. In this paper I will describe some of these questions and I will examine a range of potential responses to those questions. I am far more confident that there are intriguing questions here than I am of anything I say about any particular answers. My primary goal is make it clear that there are puzzling questions that deserve careful examination.

The conclusion I will reach is, in a sense, skeptical. But it is unlike familiar skeptical conclusions frequently addressed by epistemologists. Traditionally, when philosophers have addressed skepticism they have worried about whether it is possible for us to know about the existence and nature of things in the external world, or whether we can know about the future, or whether we can know about the past. In this essay, I address a rather different kind of skepticism. It is less sweeping than these more familiar kinds of skepticism. It is also, in a way, less remote from real world concerns than the more traditional kinds of skepticism. It is a familiar fact that there is widespread and robust disagreement about many of the most prominent issues in our intellectual lives. This is quite obviously true in epistemology itself, as well as in philosophy more generally. There is similar disagreement about religious matters, many scientific topics, and many issues of public policy. In all these areas, informed and intelligent people disagree with one another. To make it more personal, on many of these issues about which you have a belief, informed and intelligent people disagree with you. The question I will raise concerns the reasonableness of maintaining your point of view in the light of such disagreements. My conclusion will be that, more often than we might have thought, suspension of judgement is the epistemically proper attitude. It follows that in such cases we lack reasonable belief and so, at least on standard conceptions, knowledge. This is a kind of contingent real-world skepticism that has not received the attention it deserves. I hope that this paper will help to bring this issue to life.

I. EXAMPLES OF DISAGREEMENTS

There are some disagreements in which any unbiased observer would dismiss one side as simply muddled, pig-headed, or willfully ignoring the evidence. I want to set such cases aside. My interest is in seemingly reasonable disagreements. These are cases in which intelligent people with access to the relevant available information come to incompatible conclusions. At least superficially, both parties to the disagreement seem to be reasonable in their beliefs. Cases of seemingly reasonable disagreements are all around us. I will briefly describe a few of them here.

A. Law and Science

Gideon Rosen (2001: 71–2) writes:

It should be obvious that reasonable people can disagree, even when confronted with a single body of evidence. When a jury or a court is divided in a difficult case, the mere fact of disagreement does not mean that someone is being unreasonable. Paleontologists disagree about what killed the dinosaurs. And while it is possible that most of the parties to this dispute are irrational, this need not be the case. To the contrary, it would appear to be a fact of epistemic life that a careful review of the evidence does not guarantee consensus, even among thoughtful and otherwise rational investigators.

It is easy to provide additional examples along the same lines. A seemingly limitless supply comes from medical research, where experts seem to differ about the causes and cures of various diseases.

B. Politics

As Peter van Inwagen (1996: 142) has written, 'Everyone who is intellectually honest will admit...that there are interminable political debates with highly intelligent and well-informed people on both sides.' There can be little doubt that van Inwagen is right about this. In thinking about this, it may be best to focus, at least at first, on some issue about which you are not especially passionate. Think instead about issues on which you are apt to say that 'reasonable people can disagree.' For me, issues about the legalization of drugs provide a good example. Intelligent, well-informed, well-meaning, seemingly reasonable people have markedly different views on this topic. Of course, the same is true with respect to many other issues, including those that are more volatile.

C. Philosophy

van Inwagen (1996: 138) describes a perfect example of the sort of philosophical disagreement I have in mind, as well as a question that will help to bring out the philosophical issues I want to address. He writes:

How can I believe (as I do) that free will is incompatible with determinism or that unrealized possibilities are not physical objects or that human beings are not four-dimensional things extended in time as well as in space, when David Lewis—a philosopher of truly formidable intelligence and insight and ability—rejects these things I believe and is already aware of and understands perfectly every argument that I could produce in their defense?

Of course, the philosophical puzzles van Inwagen mentions are mere examples. Many other philosophical disputes are similar in that intelligent, informed, and thoughtful philosophers come to different conclusions after examining the same arguments and evidence.

D. Religion

This is the topic that originally forced this issue into the forefront of my consciousness. I taught a class in which many of the students took a pleasantly tolerant attitude toward the religious views of other students. They recognized that there was considerable disagreement about religious matters among the students in the class, but they seemed to think that all the various beliefs were reasonable ones. There are, of course, many people who do not share this attitude. Some theists see all atheists as irrational forces for evil in the world.[1] And some, unfortunately, seem to think the same of all who fail to share their faith. However, toleration is surely a common attitude.

It would not be difficult to add to this list, but these examples will suffice for present purposes. What the cases seem to share is that they involve intelligent, serious, and thoughtful people with access to the same information who come to different and incompatible conclusions. There is at least a temptation to say that people on both sides are reasonable, and thus that they are cases in which reasonable people can disagree.

I will assume throughout this essay that the cases of apparently reasonable disagreement are cases of genuine disagreement. That is, I am assuming that the people really do disagree, that one person affirms a proposition that the other denies. There are, of course, cases of apparent disagreement that are not cases of genuine disagreement. These are cases in which people seem to disagree, but an unnoticed ambiguity or the presence of a contextually shifting term makes the disagreement merely apparent. It is entirely possible that some disagreements in the categories I mentioned above are merely apparent. For example, some people may use the sentence 'God exists' in such a watered-down way that what they intend to assert by the sentence (and what they believe) is indistinguishable from what is believed by others who deny the existence of God but accept the proposition that the Universe is vast, complex, and beyond our complete understanding. However, even if some of the disagreements are merely apparent, others are genuine.

II. SOME QUESTIONS

It is possible to pose the main questions I want to examine by reflecting on the general structure of disagreements. Assume that two individuals, Pro and Con, hold different attitudes toward some proposition, P. They have reviewed the relevant evidence, considered matters carefully, and come to different conclusions. Pro believes P and Con denies P. Pro and Con thus have a disagreement of the sort illustrated by the cases in Section I.

It will be useful to distinguish two stages at which their disagreement may be considered. One stage I will refer to as 'isolation'. In this stage, Pro and Con have examined similar bodies of evidence and, after careful and serious thought, Pro comes to the conclusion that P is true and Con comes to the conclusion that P is not true. To each person, the conclusion arrived at seems plainly true. We may add to the story that each is an intelligent person who has not found

---

[1] An example is Cal Thomas, a widely syndicated columnist.

himself or herself to be wrong very often when arriving at conclusions in this way.

The other stage I will refer to as 'full disclosure'. In this stage, Pro and Con have thoroughly discussed the issues. They know each other's reasons and arguments, and that the other person has come to a competing conclusion after examining the same information.[2] There are, of course, intermediate situations in which the various pieces of evidence and the arguments are partially shared. Indeed, almost any realistic disagreement is somewhere between isolation and full disclosure. Nevertheless, it will be useful to think about the extreme situations.

There are at least three distinct sets of questions one might ask about Pro and Con. The first set of questions concerns the reasonable attitudes that Pro and Con can have in isolation. Could it be that after examining the same body of evidence, they are both reasonable in holding their views? If so, then I will say that there can be 'reasonable disagreements in isolation'.

A second set of questions concerns the reasonable attitudes they can have in situations of full disclosure. At this point, their disagreement comes to light and they are forced to confront the fact that the other person takes the same evidence to support a different conclusion. That other person is known to be intelligent and sensible. Can it be reasonable to maintain one's beliefs in the light of disagreements of this sort? Can both Pro and Con reasonably maintain their beliefs when confronted with the other's position? If so, then I will say that there can be 'reasonable disagreements after full disclosure'.

A third set of questions involves what a party to such a disagreement can sensibly think about the other's beliefs. Suppose that the second set of questions gets affirmative answers. Can Pro and Con both reasonably think that his or her own belief is reasonable and that the other's belief is reasonable as well? If so, then Pro and Con can have what I will call a 'disagreement mutually recognized as reasonable' or a 'mutually recognized reasonable disagreement'. Thus, the third question asks whether there can be disagreements of this final kind. The fully tolerant attitude I described earlier requires that there can be reasonable disagreements of this final kind.

To clarify these questions, it will be useful to say more about how I am using the word 'reasonable'.[3] First, on one reading of the term, a reasonable person is one who has a general tendency to have reasonable beliefs. Just as an honest person might tell an infrequent lie, a reasonable person might have an occasional unreasonable belief. When he has such a belief, the reasonable person would disagree with another reasonable person who has similar evidence but is not suffering from this lapse of rationality. This shows that generally reasonable people can disagree in a situation in which one of them is being unreasonable. This is not relevant to the intended questions. They are about whether both points of view are reasonable under the circumstances.

---

[2] Whether the information they examine can be exactly the same will come up for discussion later.
[3] I will sometimes substitute the words 'rational' or 'justified'.

Second, I intend to ask questions about the current epistemic status of the beliefs, not questions about their prudential or moral value or their long-term benefits. The prudential value of a belief can make it seem 'reasonable' for a person to hold the belief even though the belief is not reasonable for another person having the same evidence. For example, a hostage and a neutral reporter on the scene may have the same evidence about the prospects for the hostage's release. The hostage, unlike the reporter, may have a motive for believing that he will be released. We might say that the hostage, but not the reporter, is reasonable in so believing, given this motive. But this is not an epistemic evaluation, and not my concern here. Somewhat similarly, having an unreasonable faith in your favorite theory now may enable you to believe many important truths later on. This shows there can be a kind of long-run *epistemic* benefit to an unjustified belief. This, too, is not my concern here. The questions I want to raise concern current epistemic evaluations, not questions about the practical rationality of belief or its long-term benefits.

In summary, my questions are about the immediate epistemic status of beliefs, not about their long-term consequences, their practical value, or the general rationality of believers.

III. EXTREME STANDARDS FOR REASONABLE BELIEF

Philosophers who hold extremely weak or extremely demanding standards for reasonable belief may think that it is rather easy to answer our questions. I will briefly consider those views in this section.

People sometimes use 'reasonable' as a near synonym for 'not crazy'. By that standard, it is easy to see that there can be mutually recognized reasonable disagreements. Pro can readily agree that Con need not be crazy in believing differently than she does. But Pro might also think that Con is mistaken, and more importantly, that Con is misconstruing the evidence in some way and is therefore not reasonable in his belief. This judgement appeals to a higher standard for reasonable belief than the absurdly low 'not crazy' standard. My questions are about a higher standard than that. At least a modest level of positive epistemic status is required.

At the other extreme, an infallibilist about the evidence needed for reasonable belief will argue that there cannot be reasonable disagreements of any sort. An infallibilist is likely to be unmoved by the examples with which I began. In all those cases, an infallibilist would say that the parties to the disagreement fail to have good enough evidence for their beliefs, whether or not they have information about the fact that others disagree. Infallibilism implies that there should not be any disagreements because no one can reasonably believe anything about controversial matters in the first place.[4] In fact, one need not insist that evidential

[4] Suppose that Pro and Con do maintain their beliefs after full disclosure. I assume that they do not have conclusive evidence about whether or not their beliefs are reasonable ones, or even about what the other person believes. So, presumably, infallibilism implies that they cannot reasonably believe that they are having a reasonable disagreement.

standards rise all the way to infallibilist standards to diminish greatly the impact of the questions I have raised. One can just hold that reasonable belief requires very strong evidence, stronger evidence than we ever get on issues such as those mentioned in the examples of disagreements described earlier. Like infallibilism, this view implies that there are no reasonable disagreements in the relevant cases because there are no reasonable beliefs at all about the issues about which we disagree.

I believe that this response simply dodges the issues by setting the standards for reasonable belief far too high. Surely we can have reasonable beliefs (but perhaps not knowledge) about some political, scientific, philosophical, or religious matters, even if disagreement sometimes undermines our justification for those beliefs. I will not attempt to defend this view here.

IV. IN SUPPORT OF REASONABLE DISAGREEMENTS

There is a variety of ways in which one might attempt to defend the view that there can be reasonable disagreements. Some imply only that there can be reasonable disagreements in isolation, some imply that there can be reasonable disagreements after full disclosure, and some suggest that there can be mutually recognized reasonable disagreements. In this section I will discuss the most prominent of these possibilities.

A. Private Evidence

One of the assumptions that makes the puzzle cases puzzling is the assumption that the parties to the disagreement have the same evidence. Depending upon exactly how we understand what evidence is, this assumption may be unrealistic or, worse, impossible to realize. If evidence includes private sensory experiences, then two people will never have exactly the same evidence, even if the differences may be only minimal. Perhaps there is also what we might call 'intellectual evidence' resulting from the strong impression that the observable evidence supports one's conclusion. This is what others have called 'intuitions'. If there is this sort of intellectual evidence, then it is clear that in our example Pro and Con do not have the same evidence. In addition to whatever it is that is common to their experiences, each has an intuition that differs markedly from the other person's intuition. So they do not have the same evidence.

An idea along these lines emerges in Gideon Rosen's (2001) discussion of disagreement in ethics. He talks of the sense of 'obviousness' of the proposition under discussion. He writes (88):

[I]f the obviousness of the contested claim survives the encounter with . . . [another person] . . . then one still has some reason to hold it: the reason provided by the seeming. If, after reflecting on the rational tenability of an ethos that prizes cruelty, cruelty continues to strike me as self-evidently reprehensible, then my conviction that it is reprehensible has a powerful and cogent ground, despite my recognition that others who lack this ground may be fully justified in thinking otherwise.

The idea, then, is that the seeming obviousness, or the intuitive correctness, of one's position counts as evidence. After full disclosure, Pro and Con have somewhat different bodies of evidence, and they are justified in retaining their original beliefs. Pro's evidence, including the intuition that the shared evidence supports P, does support P. Con's evidence, including the intuition that the shared evidence supports not-P, supports not-P. Both are reasonable in their beliefs. Furthermore, as the final sentence of the quoted passage indicates, each is justified in attributing reasonable belief to the other. If this is right, then there can be mutually recognized reasonable disagreements.

Suppose we grant the assumption that intuitions or 'seemings' count as evidence. Suppose we grant the further, perhaps dubious, assumption that they can tip the balance in their favor in these cases. This implies that there can be disagreements in isolation; each party to a disagreement can be reasonable. However, things are different when we turn to cases of full disclosure. To see why, compare a more straightforward case of regular sight, rather than insight or intuition. Suppose that you and I are standing by the window looking out on the quad. We think we have comparable vision and we know each other to be honest. I seem to see what looks to me like a person in a blue coat in the middle of the quad. (Assume that this is not something odd.) I believe that a person with a blue coat is standing on the quad. Meanwhile, you seem to see nothing of the kind there. You think that no one is standing in the middle of the quad. We disagree. In isolation—before we talk to each other—each of us believes reasonably. But suppose we talk about what we see and we reach full disclosure. At that point, we each know that something weird is going on, but we have no idea which of us has the problem. Either I am 'seeing things' or you are missing something. I would not be reasonable in thinking that the problem is in your head, nor would you be reasonable in thinking that the problem is in mine.

Consider Pro and Con once again. Each may have his or her own special insight or sense of obviousness. But once there has been full disclosure, each knows about the other's insight. These insights may have evidential force. But then there is no basis for either Pro or Con retaining his or her own belief simply because the one insight happens to occur inside of him or her. A point about evidence that plays a role here is this: evidence of evidence is evidence. More carefully, evidence that there is evidence for P is evidence for P. Knowing that the other has an insight provides each of them with evidence.

In each case, one has one's own evidence supporting a proposition, knows that another person has comparable evidence supporting a competing proposition, and has no reason to think that one's own reason is the non-defective one. To think otherwise requires thinking something like this: 'You have an insight according to which ~P is true. I have one according to which P is true. It's reasonable for me to believe P in light of all this because *my* insight supports P.' This is tenacious and stubborn, but not reasonable.

Thus, the private evidence—the insights or intuitions—does not support the view that there can be mutually recognized reasonable disagreements, or even that there can be reasonable disagreements after full disclosure. If the insights count as evidence, once one reaches a position of full disclosure, one knows that there are insights on both sides. It is difficult to see why this evidence better supports one's own view rather than the competing view, and just as difficult to see how it supports an attribution of reasonableness to the other person. The competing insights cancel each other out.

Those who would appeal to private evidence do have a straw to grasp at. They can insist that one's evidence that another person has a competing insight is always weaker than one's evidence that one has an insight oneself. And this, it can be argued, justifies retaining one's belief. If correct, this would show that there can be reasonable disagreements after full disclosure. It makes it less clear that there can be mutually recognized reasonable disagreements. The reason for this is that if one person, say Pro, is not justified in believing that Con really does have an insight, then Pro is also not justified in believing that Con's belief is justified. One might resort to the view that Pro is justified in believing that Con does have an insight, but not as well justified in this belief as in his belief that he himself has an insight. Perhaps a defense of reasonable disagreements along these lines can be worked out. However, I think that the prospects are really quite bleak. This is because, in fact, the doubts about the existence of the (apparent) insights or intuitions of the conversational partner are really extremely minimal, far too weak to make one's overall evidence have the desired characteristics.

B. Frameworks and Starting Points

Another possible response to our problem relies on the idea that people can come to disagreements with different 'starting points'. The idea is not that people begin life with different beliefs that somehow shape their subsequent beliefs. The 'starting points' are not to be thought of temporally. Instead, I have in mind the idea that people have some more global outlook on the world, a general view that shapes much of what they believe. One might also characterize these starting points in terms of 'frameworks' or 'epistemic principles'. Perhaps some would say that a religious outlook counts as a starting point. Perhaps others would say that a specifically Christian outlook counts as a starting point. And perhaps others would say that only far more general guiding ideas count as starting points, such as the idea that reasonable belief always requires supporting evidence, or the idea that reasonable belief in some domains can be a matter of faith without evidence.

Although sophisticated philosophical discussions about frameworks and starting points could be used to illustrate the idea, a simpler political example may serve just as well. It seems clear that people have widely different views about the ability of governmental action to solve social problems. The columnist David Brooks (2004) illustrates the idea this way:

We're used to this in the realm of domestic politics. Politicians from the more sparsely populated South and West are more likely, at least in the political and economic realms, to champion the Goldwateresque virtues: freedom, self-sufficiency, individualism. Politicians from the cities are likely to champion the Ted Kennedyesque virtues: social justice, tolerance, interdependence.

Politicians from sparsely populated areas are more likely to say they want government off people's backs so they can run their own lives. Politicians from denser areas are more likely to want government to play at least a refereeing role, to keep people from bumping into one another too abusively.

Brooks's point seems to be that these framework views shape discussions of specific issues. He concludes that 'This debate could go on for a while since both sides represent legitimate points of view, and since both sides have concrete reasons to take the positions they do'.

As Brooks suggests, the different starting points can easily lead thinkers to different conclusions. To get to the conclusion that both parties to a disagreement can be reasonable, we must supplement this descriptive account of how people arrive at their different conclusions with an evaluative claim about rationality. Brooks's final sentence hints at such a claim. It can be interpreted in two slightly different ways. One is that each person is justified in accepting his or her preferred starting point. The rationality of these starting points, in effect, comes for free. Another possibility, perhaps only verbally different from the first, is that these starting points are not amenable to rational evaluation and that rationality consists only in properly drawing out the consequences of one's starting points in the light of the information one has acquired. Either way, people faced with the same external evidence can reasonably come to different conclusions.

Some prominent philosophers have advocated the idea that there are differing starting points or fundamental principles or framework principles. It would be naïve to think that a brief discussion here will deal with such views adequately. Nevertheless, I think that it is possible to raise some questions about the possibility of this approach yielding a satisfactory response to puzzles about disagreement.

It is difficult to accept the claim that the starting points are beyond rational scrutiny. Consider again the example from David Brooks. Perhaps it is somewhat plausible to think that in situations of isolation each side to the dispute might be reasonable in its beliefs. Perhaps the propositions that constitute starting points have a kind of intuitive appeal that renders them justified. This may make the present proposal similar in some respects to the private evidence view just considered. However, in situations of full disclosure, it is very difficult to see why that intuitive appeal retains its justifying power. The fact that one's own starting point has, let us grant, some justification in isolation hardly suffices to defend the view that it retains that justification once one realizes that other people, otherwise as capable as oneself, have a different starting point with as much 'objective' initial credibility as one's own. This makes it difficult to see how the different starting points can be used to support the idea that there can be reasonable disagreements after full disclosure.

The point is especially telling when applied to the question of mutually recognized reasonable disagreements. Suppose a participant in a disagreement, say Pro, thinks that his own starting point and the competing starting point are equally good or viable. He must think this if he is to get the result that both his own and Con's resulting beliefs are justified. But if both alternatives are reasonable, and he lacks a reason to prefer his own alternative, then accepting that alternative rather than the other is arbitrary. It is difficult to see why anything 'downstream' from this arbitrarily selected alternative counts as justified. It is therefore implausible to think that he can regard the disagreement as a mutually reasonable one.

Perhaps, then, Pro and Con should not view the other alternative as an equally acceptable starting point. On this alternative, they are both reasonable in maintaining their views after full disclosure, but also reasonable in rejecting the other's starting point. There can be reasonable disagreements after full disclosure, but they cannot be recognized as such. This is an odd result, implying that one cannot recognize the truth of one's situation. Moreover, there is little to recommend the discriminatory attitude it endorses. Apart from the fact that it conflicts with one's own starting point, by hypothesis neither person has a reason not to view the other starting point as equally acceptable. The problem is that once these starting points are brought out into the open, they are every bit as open to rational scrutiny as anything else is. Once one sees that there are alternatives to a starting point one has previously preferred, either one has a reason to continue with that preference or one does not. If one does, then that reason can be voiced and its merits assessed. And the result of that assessment will be that one side in a disagreement withstands scrutiny or that suspension of judgement is called for.

Just as in the case of private evidence, one can try to make something out of the fact that one is more familiar with one's own situation than with another person's. Thus, one might have a clearer idea of one's own starting point than of someone else's. And perhaps this fact can be used to defend the existence of reasonable disagreements of some sort. However, again, I do not see much hope along these lines.

C. Self-trust

An idea that has played a significant role in the thinking of some epistemologists is 'self-trust'. For example, in discussing skeptical issues Roderick Chisholm (1989: 5) writes that 'epistemologists presuppose that they are *rational* beings.' A similar theme has played a central role in Keith Lehrer's (1997) philosophical work. Michael DePaul has suggested to me that this idea can help deal with the problems of disagreement.[5] It is another way to defend the view that there can be reasonable disagreements.

Suppose that Pro and Con engage in their discussion and wind up in a situation as close to full disclosure as people are capable of getting. After their discussion, it still seems to Pro that P is true and it still seems to Con that P is false. Each thinks that the shared evidence supports his or her view. At this point, Pro and Con have slightly different total bodies of evidence. Pro's evidence is whatever is in the shared evidence plus the fact that it seems true to Pro that P is true. Con's evidence is whatever is shared plus the fact that it seems true to Con that P is false. Finally, as I have noted earlier, Pro's evidence includes information supporting the fact that it seems to Con that P is false and Con's evidence includes information supporting the fact that it seems to Pro that P is true. DePaul claims that if Pro were to suspend judgement under these circumstances, it would be 'a violation of [her] epistemic authority'. It would, in effect, be submitting to the authority of another person rather than going with one's own judgement. Of course, comparable remarks apply to Con as well. Suitable trust in oneself leads to maintaining belief in the light of disagreement, even after full disclosure. And, perhaps, it is even reasonable for each to believe that the other is reasonable in maintaining belief. This seems to allow for the possibility of mutually recognized reasonable disagreements.

Although this response to the puzzles has some attractiveness, I do not think that it is successful. There are general questions about whether self-trust is really an epistemic merit rather than idle hope. I will not pursue this issue here. I do want to examine the application of the self-trust principle to the current situation. I believe that it does not have the desired implications.

The more general use to which self-trust is put in the philosophical literature is in response to skeptical worries. The issues are easiest to state in the first person. If skeptical arguments get me worried about whether I know anything about the world through perception or by means of reasoning, I can wonder how I can ever do anything to alleviate those worries. I will be relying on my own powers of reasoning when I try to think my way out of them. Any such exercise seems to some to be illegitimate.[6] The view that self-trust is appropriate may provide some relief from this predicament.

However meritorious self-trust may be in dealing with skeptical puzzles, it does not yield helpful results in the context of disagreement. In situations of full disclosure, one has identified another person whom one regards as generally trustworthy. One has a reason, based on how things seem to that person, that counterbalances the reason based on how things seem to oneself. One's own perspective on things supports the view that this other person's views have intellectual merit. In other words, one's general allegedly legitimate self-trusting stance does not dictate that one should resolve the disagreement in one's favor. One is not

---

[5] In his comments on a version of this paper presented at the SOFIA conference in Puerto Alegre, Brazil in May 2004.   [6] For an anti-skeptical response, see Earl Conee (2004).

sacrificing one's autonomy by giving evidential weight to sources that one believes one in general ought to trust. Self-trust cuts both ways, in cases of disagreement with peers.

Throughout this discussion I have made use of a concept of reasonable belief that is used in the evaluation of beliefs rather than in the evaluation of changes in belief. Some philosophers pay greater attention to this latter concept. It may be thought that a variant of the self-trust principle, when applied to it, explains how mutually recognized reasonable disagreements are possible. The view I have in mind holds that it is reasonable to change one's beliefs only when one's evidence better supports some rival belief.[7] In effect, maintaining one's belief is, by default, reasonable until something better comes along. Applied to Con's situation, then, it is reasonable for her to maintain her belief in ~P, since the evidence emerging from the discussion with Pro does not yield *better* evidence for P. Analogous considerations apply to Pro. And, since each can recognize that this is in fact their situation, they can have a mutually recognized disagreement.

In my view, this defense of reasonable disagreements fares no better than the previously discussed appeal to self-trust. This is because something better than maintaining their attitudes *has* come along for both Pro and Con. That better alternative is suspending judgement. The idea that it is reasonable to maintain a belief until better evidence for some rival comes along is ludicrous, at least in some situations. Suppose I read the baseball scores in two equally reliable newspapers each morning. The list of scores in the paper I look at first shows my favorite team winning, 4–3. I believe that my team won. Then I look at the other paper and it shows that my team lost by that same score. It is not credible that it is reasonable to maintain my belief in this situation. Nor is it credible to think that I could have a mutually recognized reasonable disagreement about the outcome with my wife, who read the papers in the opposite order.

Even if our topic is reasonable belief change, rather than just reasonable belief, sometimes changing to suspension of judgement is the reasonable thing to do. This approach does not provide a better defense of reasonable disagreements.

D. Divided Evidence and Multiple Choices

A final way to argue for the existence of reasonable disagreements relies on the idea that in cases in which one has evidence that equally supports either of two views one can justifiably believe either of those views. Suppose you have two friends, George and Gracie, who each own a particular model and color of car. You see a car of that kind arrive at your house but cannot see the driver. You have a good reason to think that George has just arrived, since George has a car of that kind. However, you have an equally good reason to think that Gracie has just arrived. Suppose (unrealistically) that you are certain that no one else with that

---

[7] This idea was suggested to me by an anonymous referee.

kind of car would arrive at your house. One might argue that in cases such as this, it is reasonable for you to believe that George has just arrived, but equally reasonable for you to believe that Gracie has just arrived. In effect, you get to choose. Of course, it would not be reasonable for you to believe that both George and Gracie have arrived. And if you do believe that it is George who has arrived and your spouse believes that it is Gracie, you can grant that both beliefs are reasonable, even after full disclosure. Thus, you can have a mutually recognized reasonable disagreement.

One can supplement this view by adding factors that appear to make this result more palatable. For example, you can add that a great deal rides on your choice. The end result is a view something like one seemingly defended by William James (1911): when a decision is live, forced, and momentous, then making a choice is reasonable even if there is no intellectual basis for that choice.

I will not attempt to discuss in detail this Jamesian view about the ethics of belief. I will make a few brief comments. First, suspending judgement is in fact always an option. The choice between believing that George has arrived (rather than Gracie) and that Gracie has arrived (rather than George) is not forced, since one can suspend judgement. Even if a great deal turns on who is there, suspending judgement is a possibility. Second, I think that suspending judgement is intellectually demanded in the case at hand. This does not change when the stakes rise. Finally, it is a mistake to think that the case can be altered by reframing the options as believing that George has arrived (or that God exists) and not believing that George has arrived (or that God exists). Not-believing includes both disbelieving and suspending judgement. And the choice between believing and not-believing can be intellectually decided. It is decided in favor of not-believing. It may be that there is some practical benefit to forming a belief. These practical benefits can be enormous.

Compare this case with an example in which one must choose between two behavioral options for which the evidence is divided. Suppose that we are traveling together and we come to a fork in the road. The map shows no fork and we have no way to get more information about which way to go. We have to choose. You choose the left path and I choose the right path. Each of us may be entirely reasonable in choosing as we did. Of course, we would have been reasonable in choosing otherwise. We can each endorse the other's choice as a reasonable one. This is a useful case to consider, since it brings out a crucial difference between belief and action. As you go left and I go right, neither of us can reasonably believe that we've chosen the correct path. We should suspend judgement about which path is best, yet pick one since, we may assume, not taking either path would be the worst choice of all. In this case, there is no good behavioral analogue to suspending judgement. And this undermines the view that important choices like this provide the basis for a defense of reasonable disagreements.

In this section I have discussed several lines of thought according to which there can be reasonable disagreements. I have agreed that it is possible that there can be reasonable disagreements in isolation. Perhaps private evidence and different starting points can help to explain why. Possibly even self-trust provides some help with this as well, though I am less confident of that. None of the views considered provides a good basis for the view that there can be reasonable disagreements after full disclosure or that there can be mutually recognized reasonable disagreements.

V. ONE-WAY RATIONALITY

If there cannot be reasonable disagreements after full disclosure, then a question arises about what the rational attitude toward disagreements should be. If it is not reasonable for both sides to maintain their beliefs after full disclosure, then either it is reasonable for one side but not the other to maintain belief or it is not reasonable for either side to maintain belief. I will discuss the former view in this section and the latter view in the final section.

In some disagreements, one side is simply unreasonable. Consider the dispute about the merits of astrology. It is possible, perhaps, to take this to be a case in which two groups of people look at the same information, try to be reasonable, and come to different conclusions. van Inwagen (1996: 141) says that 'It is clear, for example, that someone who believes in astrology believes in something that is simply indefensible.' His point, I think, is that those who believe in astrology are believing something that simply is not supported by their evidence. Perhaps their views are not justified even in isolation. And surely they are not justified after full disclosure. Of course, the challenging cases are not like the astrology example. The challenging cases exhibit at least a kind of superficial symmetry. People on both sides have at least approximately the same evidence and they seem to be capable of dealing with that information in a reasonable way. No one can sensibly just dismiss the views of either party to the disagreement. In the philosophical example described earlier, it may be that van Inwagen judges Lewis to be wrong. Perhaps, in the end, he will judge him to be unreasonable. But Lewis's position seems comparable. It may be, however, that the challenging cases are more like the astrology example than this suggests. Perhaps one side is unreasonable, at least after full disclosure. This is the view that I will discuss in this section.

A. Objective Evidential Support

The reasonable thing to believe on the basis of a particular body of evidence may not always be entirely obvious. In such cases, one can be sincere and conscientious in one's efforts to get at the truth, yet come to a conclusion that is not supported by one's evidence. This may be what is happening in (some) cases of apparently reasonable disagreement: one side is simply assessing the evidence incorrectly and coming to an unreasonable conclusion. In effect, this defense of a one-way rationality view appeals to non-obvious asymmetries. The cases are really like the astrology example, but the unreasonable side is not so obviously unreasonable.

The current view assumes that an evidential support relation is an 'objective' matter that is independent of what a believer thinks about it. It can be present even when a believer fails to see it. There is room for disagreement about the connection between the evidential support relation and the logical and probabilistic relations that can hold between a body of evidence and a potential conclusion. Whatever the details about this are, what the current view insists on is that in cases of disagreement the evidence supports (at most) one side of the dispute and the party to the disagreement with the belief that is objectively supported by the evidence is justified and the other person is not. Furthermore, and this is a key point, full disclosure does not change things. So there cannot be reasonable disagreements after full disclosure.

This idea can be applied to the case of Pro and Con. According to this view, the evidence supports one side of the issue. Let us assume that it is Pro's side. So Pro's belief that P is reasonable and Con's belief that ~P is not reasonable. However, since this fact about evidential support is not obvious, an intelligent, conscientious, serious, fair-minded, and unbiased person such as Con can come to the unjustified conclusion. Despite these virtues, he has failed to believe what his evidence supports. Of course, there can also be cases in which the evidence is in fact equally good on both sides. That, however, may well be the unusual case. Presumably, in the political, philosophical, scientific, and religious disagreements with which we began, the evidence does typically support some view. The people who hold that view are reasonable in their beliefs, whereas the others are not. They are less extreme versions of astrologers.

I have considerable sympathy for the view that some of the disagreements are best understood in this way. However, I do not believe that this does justice to the apparent symmetry of the central cases once there has been full disclosure. Consider, then, Pro and Con once they have reached a situation in which there has been full disclosure. Pro believes that P is true. We are assuming, provisionally, that the evidence supports P and thus that in isolation this belief is justified. Con believes not-P, and we are assuming, at least provisionally, that in isolation this belief is not justified. But we are also assuming that it is not obvious to Pro and Con which belief the evidence really does support. Presumably, Pro will think that the evidence supports P and Con will think that evidences supports ~P. Notice that the mere fact that the evidence does support P does not automatically make Pro justified in believing that the evidence supports P. Perhaps in isolation it seemed to her that it did support P. Perhaps, in isolation, she was justified in this belief as well. However, the discussion about this with Con seems to lead to a standoff. I find it very hard to see how the situation differs in any significant way from the situation in the example about the people who differ about whether there is a person on the quad. Pro knows that either she or Con is not properly evaluating the evidence. But I do not see what justifies her in thinking that the error is Con's and not her own, while making it the case that Con is not justified in thinking that he is assessing the evidence properly.[8] And if, after disclosure, Pro is not justified in believing that her evidence supports P, then I do not see how she can be justified in believing P.

The point here, I want to emphasize, is not that a justified believer must always know (or be justified in believing) that one's evidence is good evidence. Perhaps the evidential support relation can hold in the absence of a believer's realization that it obtains. But once one thinks explicitly about the topic, it becomes harder to see how it can remain reasonable to maintain belief once one realizes that one has no good reason to think one's evidence supports that belief. In effect, this realization serves as a defeater of whatever support the original evidence provided. The underlying idea is that it is harder to reasonably maintain belief once one reflects on one's epistemic situation in the way that disagreements with full disclosure demand. It is not that the standards are higher in reflective situations. Rather, it is that reflection can, and in these cases does, make it evident that one does not have a good reason to think that one's belief is well supported, and this in turn undermines the support one initially had for that belief.

My argument here has two steps that should be made fully explicit. Neither step is clearly true, though both strike me as quite plausible. In disagreements where there is full disclosure, a person is forced to confront a question about the merits of his case in favor of his initial belief. This involves a kind of reflection that may not occur in ordinary beliefs in isolation. In the examples in question, this reflection must be made with the knowledge that another person, as generally competent as oneself, assesses the evidence differently. It is difficult to see why such a person would be justified in believing that his own assessment of the evidence is in fact the correct one. Consider, for example, the dispute between Lewis and van Inwagen about freedom and determinism. I fail to see the basis for the judgement that one of them, say van Inwagen, is justified in believing that the evidence supports his own view while Lewis is not. Even if it is true that the evidence does in fact support van Inwagen's view, this clearly is not enough to make him justified in believing that the evidence supports his view. The first step of my argument concludes it is not the case that just one side of the dispute is justified in his belief about the merits of the evidence.

The second step of my argument concerns what follows from the first. Suppose that Pro's original evidence, E, does in fact objectively support P. After full disclosure, Pro's evidence has changed. If the first step of my argument is right, then this expanded evidence does not support the view that E supports P. It makes suspending judgement on this matter the reasonable attitude. But then it is hard to see how the expanded body of evidence can still support P. For if it still does support P, then it supports Pro reasonably having a complex attitude that she could express as follows: I believe P, but I suspend judgement on whether my evidence supports P. Perhaps there are some circumstances in which some such attitude can be reasonable.

---

[8] If Con is justified in thinking that he is assessing the evidence properly, then he has a good argument for ~P: the evidence supports ~P, so ~P. This returns us to views such as those discussed in the previous section.

But it is surely very odd. Yet this is what a defender of the current view must accept in order to maintain the view that the person who in fact had the right view about the evidence originally remains justified in his beliefs after full disclosure.

B. Externalism

Throughout this essay I have taken for granted an evidentialist view about justification and rationality. I have assumed that questions about the justified responses to disagreement depended upon the evidence of the believers and what that evidence supported. That view about justification is not universally accepted. It is possible that abandoning evidentialism will help to resolve the puzzles. I will discuss this possibility briefly in this section, using one non-evidentialist theory as a model. I will not discuss other theories, but I believe similar remarks apply to them.

One non-evidentialist view about justification (Plantinga 1993) holds that a belief is justified when it results from a properly functioning cognitive system.[9] I will ignore all the details of developed versions of this view. And while I am dubious about the merits of the view, I will not address its general adequacy here. (See Kvanvig 1996 for discussion.) Suppose that some such view is correct. What does it imply about disagreements?

Suppose for the sake of argument that in the disagreement between Pro and Con, one of them is suffering from some sort of malfunction. One is failing to see a truth that a properly functioning human mind would see. Assume that Con is the one suffering this lapse. Given this, proper functionalism implies that, in isolation, Pro is reasonable and Con is not. Perhaps that view is correct. In this respect, an externalist view is similar to the objective evidence views just considered.

Once they reach the stage of full disclosure, both Pro and Con will be in a position to realize that (at least) one of them is suffering from some such lapse. If they both maintain their beliefs, each may think that it is the other who is suffering the lapse. But this fact about what they are likely to do does not tell us what the proper function theory implies about the epistemic status of these meta-level beliefs. Nor does it tell us what implications this will have for the object-level beliefs.

One possibility is that the proper function theory will respect the seeming symmetry of the situation and say that it is proper function for each of them to think that the external lapse has occurred in the other. But this has a plainly implausible implication: Con is reasonably thinking that he is functioning properly when he believes $\sim P$ and that Pro is malfunctioning when she believes P, but he is not reasonable in believing $\sim P$. Surely, however, a properly functioning system will include $\sim P$ among its beliefs when it properly includes the first two beliefs about proper function. Proper function cannot plausibly require the near incoherence just described.

---

[9] Strictly speaking, Plantinga's view is about 'warrant' rather than 'justification'. It is probably best to take the present discussion to be about the plausibility of applying a view like Plantinga's to the present issues.

Another possibility is that the proper function theory will hold that Pro functions properly when she thinks that Con is malfunctioning, but Con is not functioning properly when he thinks that Pro is malfunctioning. This strikes me as quite implausible. The symmetry of the situation still obtains. It surely must be part of any sensible proper functionalist account of reasonable belief that one aspect of proper function is to treat like case alike. Suppose Pro and Con each had a thermometer and used it to determine the temperature. Suppose the thermometers reported different temperatures. Suppose further that background information about the thermometers provides no reason to think that one is more accurate than the other. It would be plainly contrary to proper function for Pro to insist that his own thermometer is correct, even if in fact it is correct. It is equally improper for Pro to think that his own cognitive system rather than Con's is the one that is working correctly. Even if externalist theories have something useful to say about why spontaneous non-reflective beliefs are justified, they cannot plausibly say that stubbornly insisting that the malfunction occurs in the other person in seemingly symmetrical situations of full disclosure constitutes proper function.

Another possibility is that proper function theory rules that both Pro and Con are functioning properly when they acknowledge that they have no idea which of them is malfunctioning. Still, it might be said, Pro in fact is functioning properly in believing P. Thus, Pro is reasonable in continuing to believe P, even in situations of full disclosure, just as he was in isolated situations. What he has learned along the way—about Con—makes no difference. This, too, strikes me as highly implausible, even if there is something sensible about externalist views more generally. The problem is that an externalist view such as proper functionalism must have something plausible to say about proper function in reflective situations such as those under consideration here. And what the current proposal attributes to Pro strikes me as plainly not sensible. For it says that Pro would be functioning properly, and thus be reasonable, if he were to think 'P, but I have no idea whether I am believing properly when I believe P.' While this is not paradoxical in the way 'P but I do not believe P' may be, it is extremely puzzling. A properly functioning system must take into account information it has about itself. Once it properly comes to the view that it has no judgement about the merits of its belief that P, the next proper step will be to abandon the belief that P.

The arguments of this section are, I admit, less than conclusive. In part, I think that externalist accounts of reasonable belief are not plausible, and I find it difficult to assess their application to the present circumstances without addressing their more general inadequacies. Still, I think that the problem with externalist solutions to the puzzles about disagreement can be stated in a loose but informative way. Even if it is true that externalist theories provide some suitable account of ordinary beliefs about the world, it is difficult to see how anything other than an evidentialist approach can correctly account for the justification of beliefs in the more reflective circumstances demanded by situations of full disclosure. Even if, in ordinary non-reflective situations, our beliefs about the world are justified when they result from proper function of the cognitive system, there is little reason to think that this externalist account can legitimize either party to a disagreement to respond to seemingly symmetrical disagreements by insisting that it is the other person who has the external epistemic defect. And if they know that at least one party to the disagreement has an external defect, and no reason to think that it is the other person, then it is hard to see how maintaining belief can be justified even by externalist lights.

VI. A SKEPTICAL CONCLUSION

The remaining response to the puzzles about disagreement is that in situations of full disclosure, where there are not evident asymmetries, the parties to the disagreement would be reasonable in suspending judgement about the matter at hand. There are, in other words, no reasonable disagreements after full disclosure, and thus no mutually recognized reasonable disagreements. The cases that seem to be cases of reasonable disagreement are cases in which the reasonable attitude is really suspension of judgement.

I am inclined to think that this is in fact the truth about many of the disagreements with which I began. Consider those cases in which a person is justifiably inclined to think that he is in a reasonable disagreement. That is, consider those cases in which the reasonable thing to think is that another person, every bit as sensible, serious, and careful as oneself, has reviewed the same information as oneself and has come to a contrary conclusion to one's own. And, further, one finds oneself puzzled about how that person could come to that conclusion. An honest description of the situation acknowledges its symmetry. I think that this is the situation both van Inwagen and Lewis find themselves confronting in the example about free will. The same may be true of some of the other examples with which I began. These are cases in which one is tempted to say that 'reasonable people can disagree' about the matter under discussion. In those cases, I think, the skeptical conclusion is the reasonable one: it is not the case that both points of view are reasonable, and it is not the case that one's own point of view is somehow privileged. Rather, suspension of judgement is called for. And this is true even if suspending judgement in such cases might be extremely difficult to do.

There are, of course, cases that are asymmetric. I used the astrology example to illustrate this earlier. Perhaps some of the examples with which I began are more like that. It would be good to have a clearer understanding of what differentiates that example from the more puzzling examples that have been my focus in this paper. Developing such an understanding, as well as exploring in more detail the various views I have discussed earlier in this paper, is work that remains to be done.[10]

[10] Parts of this paper borrow from Feldman (forthcoming). In working on this paper I have benefited a great deal from many discussions with many people including John Bennett, Thomas Kelly, Allen Orr, Jim Pryor, and Ed Wierenga. This paper is a heavily revised version of talks given at Ohio State University, Washington University, the University of Miami, the University of Michigan, the Inland Northwest Philosophy Conference, and the Sociedad Filosofica Ibero-American. I am grateful to the audiences and commentators on all those occasions.

REFERENCES

Brooks, D. (2004). 'Not Just a Personality Clash, a Conflict of Visions'. *New York Times*, 12 October 2004.

Chisholm, R. (1989). *Theory of Knowledge* (3rd edn.). Englewood Cliffs, NJ: Prentice Hall.

Conee, E. (2004). 'First Things First', in E. Conee and R. Feldman, *Evidentialism: Essays in Epistemology*. Oxford: Clarendon Press, 11–36.

Feldman, R. (forthcoming). 'Reasonable Religious Disagreements', in L. Antony (ed.), *Philosophers Without God*. Oxford: Oxford University Press.

Harris, S. (2004). *The End of Faith: Religion, Terror, and the Future of Reason*. New York: W. W. Norton.

James, W. (1911). *The Will to Believe and Other Essays in Popular Philosophy*. New York: David McKay.

Kvanvig, J. (ed.) (1996). *Warrant in Contemporary Epistemology: Essays in Honor of Plantinga's Theory of Knowledge*. Lanham, MD: Rowman & Littlefield.

Lehrer, K. (1997). *Self-Trust: A Study of Reason, Knowledge, and Autonomy*. Oxford: Clarendon Press.

Plantinga, A. (1993). *Warrant and Proper Function*. New York: Oxford University Press.

Rosen, G. (2001). 'Nominalism, Naturalism, Philosophical Relativism'. *Philosophical Perspectives*, 15: 69–91.

van Inwagen, P. (1996). 'It Is Wrong Everywhere, Always, and for Anyone to Believe Anything on Insufficient Evidence', in J. Jordan and D. Howard-Snyder (eds.), *Faith, Freedom, and Rationality: Philosophy of Religion Today*. Lanham, MD: Rowman & Littlefield, 137–53.

Index

238 *Index*